Collins

easy
German

D0067925

HarperCollins Publishers
Westerhill Rd, Bishopbriggs, Glasgow, G64 2QT

www.harpercollins.co.uk

First published 2001
This edition published 2006

© HarperCollins Publishers 2006

Reprint 10 9 8 7 6 5 4 3 2

ISBN-13 978-0-00-720839-5
ISBN-10 0-00-720839-1

A catalogue reference for this book is available from
The British Library

Photography: Miroslav Imbrisevic/Brighteve Productions
With additional photography/material from:
Christine Bahr, Marianne Davidson & Gordon Noble,
Hertie (Mainz), Hotel Dorint (Mainz), Open-Bad (Wiesbaden)
Artville (pp. 96, 97, 98, 99, 100, 102, 104, 105, 107, 108)
Anthony Blake (pp. 79, 95, 99[tr], 101, 102[tl], 103, 105[tr],
106, 107[tr], 109[b]
Wine material: Andrea Gillies
Food Map: Heather Moore
Layout & Origination: The Printer's Devil and
Davidson Pre-Press Graphics Ltd, Glasgow

Other titles in the Collins Easy Photo Phrase Book series:
French (0 00 720840 5)
Greek (0 00 720837 5)
Italian (0 00 720836 7)
Portuguese (0 00 720835 9)
Spanish (0 00 720833 2)
These titles are also published in a CD pack containing
a 60-minute CD and Easy Photo Phrase Book.

Printed in China by Imago

Contents

Useful Websites	4
Introduction	5
Speaking German	6
Everyday Talk	7
Addressing People	7
Asking for Things	8
Key Phrases	9
Keywords	10
Meeting People	11
Problems	12
Complaints	13
Everyday Germany	14
Asking the Way	18
Banks & Money	20
When is...?	22
Timetables	24
Tickets	26
Public Transport	28
Bus, Tram	29
U-Bahn, S-Bahn	30
Train	32
Taxi	34
Car Hire	35
Driving & Maps	36
Map of Germany	36
Signs	38
Motorway	40
Parking	41
Petrol	43
Problems	44
Berlin District	45
Berlin City	46
Frankfurt District	47
Vienna District	48
Shopping	49
Supermarket	50
Quantities	51
Labels	52
Everyday Foods	53
Fruit & Vegetables	54
Department Stores	55
Clothes & Shoes	56
Stamps, Post Office, Film	57
Phones	59
E-mail, Internet, Fax	61
Out & About	63
Art Galleries & Museums	64
Sport & Leisure	65
Accommodation	67
Finding a Room	68
Self-catering	69
Youth Hostels	70
Camping	71
Launderette	72
Special Needs	73
With Kids	74
Health	75
Pharmacy	75
Doctor & Dentist	76
Hospital	77
Emergency	78
Food & Drink	79
German Food	80
Places to Eat	81
Snacks	82
Meals	84
Reading the Menu	86
Beer	88
Wine	90
Flavours of Germany	92
Special Diets	94
Menu Reader	95
Dictionary	111
How German Works	187

Useful Websites

Currency converters
www.xe.com
www.oanda.com

UK Passport Office
www.passport.gov.uk

Foreign Office travel advice
www.fco.gov.uk

Health advice
www.traveldoctor.co.uk
www.dh.gov.uk/PolicyAndGuidance/
  HealthAdviceForTravellers/fs/en/

Pet advice
www.defra.gov.uk/animalh/
  quarantine/index.htm

Facts and figures
www.cia.gov/cia/publications/
  factbook/

Weather
www.bbc.co.uk/weather

Internet cafes
www.cybercafes.com

Hotels
www.hrs.com

Hostels
www.hostels.com
europeanhostels.com
www.djh.de

Private guest rooms
www.bed-and-breakfast.de

Planning your trip
www.willgoto.com

Rail fares and tickets
www.raileurope.co.uk

Railways
www.bahn.de

Driving abroad
www.drivingabroad.co.uk

Airlines
www.lufthansa.co.uk
www.germanwings.com

Ferries
www.dfsseaways.co.uk

Tourist info
www.germany-info.org
www.germany-tourism.de

Farm tourism
www.landtourismus.de

Christmas markets
www.germany-christmas-
  market.org.uk

Eating out
www.gastroscout.com

Wine
www.germanwine.de

Munich beer festival
www.oktoberfest.de

Skiing
www.goski.com

Rhine riverboats
www.k-d.com

**UNESCO world heritage sites
 in Germany**
www.unesco-welterbe.de

Berlin
www.berlin-tourist-information.com

Hamburg
www.hamburg-tourism.de

Cologne
www.koeln.de

Munich
www.muenchen.de

Bavaria
www.bayern.by

Austria
www.austria-tourism.at

Switzerland
www.myswitzerland.com

Introduction

In the age of the euro, the internet and cash machines that offer a choice of languages, foreign travel might seem less of an adventure than it once was. But English is not the universal language yet, and there is much more to communication than knowing the right words for things. Once out of the airport you will not get far without some idea of the language, and also the way things are done in an unfamiliar culture. Things you might assume are the same everywhere, such as road signs and colour-coding, can turn out not to be. Red for trunk roads and skimmed milk, blue for motorways and full cream? Not everywhere! You may know the word for 'coffee' but what sort of coffee will you get? Will they understand what you mean when you say you're a vegetarian? What times do the shops open, and which ticket gives you the best deal? *Collins Easy Photo Phrase Books* keep you up to speed with handy tips for each topic, and a wealth of pictures of signs and everyday objects to help you understand what you see around you. Even if your knowledge of the language is excellent, you may still find yourself on the back foot when trying to understand what's on offer in a restaurant, so the food and drink section features a comprehensive menu reader to make sure eating out is a pleasure.

The unique combination of practical information, photos and phrases found in this book provides the key to hassle-free travel. The colour-coding below shows how information is presented and how to access it as quickly as possible.

 General, practical information which will provide useful tips on getting the best out of your trip.

< keywords

rechts
rekhts
right

links
links
left

these are words that are useful to know both when you see them written down or when you hear them spoken

key talk >

short, simple phrases that you can change and adapt to suit your own situation

excuse me!   **can you help me?**
entschuldigen Sie!   können Sie mir helfen?
skoo-zee   *kur'-nen zee meer hel-fen*

do you know where…?
wissen Sie, wo…?
vis-sen zee voh…

The **Food Section** allows you to choose more easily from what is on offer, both for snacks and at restaurants.

The practical **Dictionary** means that you will never be stuck for words.

Speaking German

We've tried to make the pronunciation under the phrases as clear as possible. We've split up words to make them easy to read, but don't pause too long between the syllables. German is not all that hard to pronounce and once you get the hang of unfamiliar letters or letter combinations, you should find yourself reading straight from the German phrases.

You'll notice some differences in the way the language is written. The most obvious is that all nouns begin with capital letters, eg table becomes **Tisch**. There is also a letter which doesn't exist in English – ß – as for instance in **Fuß** which is like **ss**.

Most letters are pronounced in much the same way as their English equivalents. However, when they appear at the end of a word **b** is pronounced like **p** (**halb** *halp*), **d** like **t** (**Hand** *hant*), and **g** like **k** (**Betrag** *be-***trahk**); and in general **v** is pronounced like **f** (**Vogel** *foh-gel*), except in words of non-German origin, where **v** is pronounced like **v** in English (**Vase** *vah-ze*).

The German **w** is also pronounced like **v** in English (**Wasser** *vasser*). **S** is pronounced like **sh** in **shock** before **p** (**Spiel** *shpeel*) and **t** (**Stein** *shtine*) when they are at the beginning of a word, and when it is combined with **ch** (**Schule** *shoo-le*).

The umlaut ¨ often appears over German vowels, namely a (**Gaststätte** *gast-shte-te*), o (**Löffel** *lur'-fel*) and u (**süß** *zoos*), and makes a difference to the pronunciation. The two sounds, **ö** and **ü**, are rather different from anything in English. We show **ö** as **ur'** because the nearest sound to it is in English words like hurt, but don't roll the **r**! The sound of **ü** can be made if you purse your lips and try to say **ee**. We give this sound as **oo** in the pronunciation.

A final **e** is always pronounced, and sounds like a in sof**a** or e in Porsch**e**. So German **bitte** sounds like English bitter.

The syllable to be stressed is the one in *heavy type*.

Here are a few other rules to be aware of:

german	sounds like	example	pronunciation
au	*ow*	**Auto**	*ow-to*
äu	*oy*	**Säule**	*zoy-le*
ch	*kh*	**ich**	*ikh*
ei	*eye*	**ein**	*ine*
ie	*ee*	**sie**	*zee*
eu	*oy*	**neun**	*noyn*

Everyday Talk

*There are two forms of address in German, formal (**Sie**) and informal (**du**). You should always stick with the formal until you are invited to use the informal. For the purposes of this book, we will use the formal.*

yes
ja
ya

no
nein
nine

ok/that's fine
okay
okay

please
bitte
bi-te

thank you
danke
dang-ke

thanks very much
danke vielmals
dang-ke feel-mals

don't mention it
bitte
bi-te

that's very kind
das ist sehr freundlich
das ist zehr froynt-likh

hello
guten Tag
gooten tahk

goodbye
auf Wiedersehen
owf vee-der-zayn

good evening
guten Abend
gooten ahbent

good night
gute Nacht
goo-te nakht

see you later
bis später
bis shpayter

excuse me!
entschuldigen Sie!
entshool-di-gen zee

sorry!
Entschuldigung!
entshool-di-goong

I am sorry
das tut mir Leid
das toot meer lite

I don't understand
ich verstehe nicht
ikh fer-shtay-e nikht

I don't know
ich weiß nicht
ikh vice nikht

Addressing people

When Germans meet they generally shake hands. The words for Mr and Mrs are **Herr** and **Frau**. Note that **Fräulein** is no longer used for Miss as it sounds rather patronising. Between young people, you will almost immediately be addressed in the informal form. As a rule, note how people address you and mirror their approach. You could, for instance, be addressed by your first name but still in the formal form. Here are some informal phrases.

hi, Michael
hallo, Michael
hal-loh mikha-el

bye, Christine
tschüss, Christine
tshoos kris-tee-ne

see you later
bis später
bis shpayter

how's life?
wie geht's?
vee gayts

what's up?
was gibt's?
vas gipts

(i) *The simplest way to ask for something in a shop or bar is by naming what you want and adding **bitte**.*

1	**eins**	*ines*
2	**zwei**	*tsvy*
3	**drei**	*dry*
4	**vier**	*feer*
5	**fünf**	*foonf*
6	**sechs**	*zekhs*
7	**sieben**	*zeeben*
8	**acht**	*akht*
9	**neun**	*noyn*
10	**zehn**	*tsayn*

keywords keywords keywords

a ... please
einen/eine/ein ... bitte
ine-en/ine-e/ine ... bi-te

a coffee please
einen Kaffee bitte
ine-en kafay bi-te

a phonecard please
eine Telefonkarte bitte
ine-e taylay-fon-kar-te bi-te

a beer please
ein Bier bitte
ine beer bi-te

a lemonade and 2 beers please
eine Limonade und zwei Bier bitte
ine-e leemo-nah-de oont tsvy beer bi-te

the ... please
den/die/das ... bitte
den/dee/das ... bi-te

my ...
meinen/meine/mein...
mine-en/mine-e/mine...

the menu please
die Speisekarte bitte
dee shpy-ze-kar-te bi-te

the bill please
zahlen bitte
tsah-len bi-te

another/more ...
noch/mehr ...
nokh/mehr ...

more money
mehr Geld
mehr gelt

another beer
noch ein Bier
nokh ine beer

another tea
noch einen Tee
nokh ine-en tay

2 more beers
noch zwei Bier
nokh tsvy beer

2 more coffees
noch zwei Kaffee
nokh tsvy kafay

2 bus tickets
zwei Fahrkarten
tsvy fahr-kar-ten

6 stamps
sechs Briefmarken
zechs breef-marken

To catch someone's attention

In a shop or bar you would attract the attention of the assistant or waiter with **bitte**. If you want to attract someone's attention in the street, for example, to ask directions, you would say *entschuldigen Sie!* When you ask the way to somewhere you use either *zum* (with *der/das* nouns), *zur* (with *die* nouns) or *nach* (with place names).

excuse me!
entschuldigen Sie!
entshool-di-gen zee

can you help me?
können Sie mir helfen?
kur'-nen zee meer hel-fen

do you know where ... is?
wissen Sie, wo ... ist?
vis-sen zee voh ... ist

do you know how I get to... ?
wissen Sie, wie ich zum/zur/nach ... komme?
vis-sen zee vee ikh tsoom/tsoor/nakh ... komme

By combining key words and phrases you can build up your language and adapt the phrases to suit your own situation.

haben Sie...? **do you have...?**	**do you have a map?** haben Sie eine Karte? *hah-ben zee ine-e **kar**-te*	**do you have a room?** haben Sie ein Zimmer? ***hah**-ben zee ine **tsimmer***
was kostet es? **how much is it?**	**how much is the ticket?** was kostet das Ticket? *vas **kos**tet das **ti**cket*	**how much is the film?** was kostet der Film? *vas **kos**tet der film*
ich möchte... **I'd like...**	**I'd like a red wine** ich möchte einen Rotwein *ikh **mur'kh**-te ine-en **roht**vine*	**I'd like an icecream** ich möchte ein Eis *ikh **mur'kh**-te ine ice*
ich brauche... **I need...**	**I need a taxi** ich brauche ein Taxi *ikh **brow**-khe ine **ta**xi*	**I need a receipt** ich brauche eine Quittung *ikh **brow**-khe ine-e **kvi**-toong*
wann? **when?**	**when does it open?** wann macht es auf? *van makht es owf*	**when does it close?** wann macht es zu? *van makht es tsoo*
	when does it leave? wann fährt es ab? *van fayrt es ap*	**when does it arrive?** wann kommt es an? *van komt es an*
wo? **where?**	**where is the bank?** wo ist die Bank? *voh ist dee bank*	**where is the hotel?** wo ist das Hotel? *voh ist das ho-**tel***
gibt es...? **is there...?**	**is there a market?** gibt es einen Markt? *gipt es ine-en markt*	**where is there a market?** wo gibt es einen Markt? *voh gipt es ine-en markt*
es gibt kein... **there is no...**	**there is no bread** es gibt kein Brot *es gipt kine broht*	**is there no train?** gibt es keinen Zug? *gipt es **kine**-en tsook*
kann ich...? **can I...?**	**can I smoke?** kann ich rauchen? *kan ikh **row**-khen*	**can I go by train?** kann ich mit dem Zug fahren? *kan ikh mit dem tsook **fah**-ren*
	where can I buy milk? wo kann ich Milch kaufen? *voh kan ikh milkh **kow**fen*	**where can I hire...?** wo kann ich ... mieten? *voh kan ikh ... **mee**ten?*
ist es...? **is it...?**	**is it near?** ist es nah? *ist es nah*	**is it far?** ist es weit? *ist es vite*
ich mag... **I like...**	**I like red wine** ich mag Rotwein *ikh mahk **roht**vine*	**I don't like cheese** ich mag keinen Käse *ikh mahk **kine**-en **kay**-ze*

These are a selection of small but very useful words.

keywords keywords keywords keywords keywords keywords keywords

groß
grohs
large

klein
kline
small

ein bisschen
ine bis-khen
a little

genug
genook
enough

nächste
naykh-ste
nearest

weit
vite
far

zu teuer
tsoo toy-er
too expensive

und
oont
and

mit/ohne
mit/oh-ne
with/without

für
foor
for

mein
mine
my

das hier/das dort
das heer/das dort
this one/that one

sofort
zo-fort
straightaway

später
shpayter
later

a large car
ein großes Auto
ine groh-ses owto

a small portion
eine kleine Portion
ine kline-e port-syon

a little please
ein bisschen bitte
ine bis-khen bi-te

that's enough thanks
das ist genug danke
das ist genook dang-ke

where is the nearest chemist?
wo ist die nächste Apotheke?
voh ist die naykh-ste apo-teh-ke

it is too expensive
es ist zu teuer
es ist tsoo toy-er

it is too small
es ist zu klein
es ist tsoo kline

is it full?
ist es voll?
ist es foll

is it free?
ist es frei?
ist es fray

a tea and a coffee
einen Tee und einen Kaffee
ine-en tay oont ine-en kafay

with sugar
mit Zucker
mit tsoo-ker

with cream
mit Sahne
mit zah-ne

without sugar
ohne Zucker
oh-ne tsoo-ker

without cream
ohne Sahne
oh-ne zah-ne

for me
für mich
foor mikh

for her/for him
für sie/für ihn
foor zee/foor een

my passport
mein Pass
mine pass

my keys
meine Schlüssel
mine-e shloo-sel

I'd like this one
ich möchte das hier
ikh mur'kh-te das heer

I'd like that one
ich möchte das dort
ikh mu'rkh-te das dort

I need a taxi straightaway
ich brauche sofort ein Taxi
ikh brow-khe zo-fort ine taxi

I'll call you later
ich rufe Sie später an
ikh roo-fe zee shpayter an

It is always good to be able to say a few words about yourself to break the ice, even if you won't be able to tell your life story.

my name is...
mein Name ist...
*mine **nah**-me ist...*

I am from...
ich komme aus...
*ikh **komme** ows...*

I am on holiday
ich bin im Urlaub
*ikh bin im **oor**-lowp*

I am on business
ich bin geschäftlich hier
*ikh bin ge-**sheft**-likh heer*

I am single
ich bin alleinstehend
*ikh bin al-**line**-shteh-ent*

I am married
ich bin verheiratet
*ikh bin fer-**hey**-ra-tet*

I have a partner *(male)*
ich habe einen Lebenspartner
*ikh **hah**-be ine-en **lay**-bens-partner*

I have a partner *(female)*
ich habe eine Lebenspartnerin
*ikh **hah**-be ine-e **lay**-bens-partnerin*

I am a widow
ich bin Witwe
*ikh bin **veet**-ve*

I am a widower
ich bin Witwer
*ikh bin **veet**-ver*

I am divorced
ich bin geschieden
*ikh bin ge-**shee**-den*

I am separated
ich lebe getrennt
*ikh **lay**-be ge-**trennt***

I have a child
ich habe ein Kind
*ikh **hah**-be ine kint*

I have ... children
ich habe ... Kinder
*ikh **hah**-be ... **kin**-der*

I work
ich arbeite
*ikh **ar**-by-te*

I am retired
ich bin im Ruhestand
*ikh bin im **roo**-he-shtant*

I am a student
ich bin Student
*ikh bin shtoo**dent***

this is a beautiful country
dieses Land ist sehr schön
***dee**-zes lant ist zehr shur'n*

I love your food
ich mag das Essen hier
*ikh makh das **es**-sen heer*

people are very kind
die Menschen sind sehr freundlich
*dee **men**-shen zint zehr **froynt**-likh*

I look forward to coming back
ich werde gern wieder kommen
*ikh **ver**-de gern **vee**-der **kom**men*

thank you very much for your kindness
vielen Dank, Sie waren sehr freundlich
***fee**-len dank zee **vah**-ren zehr **froynt**-likh*

I have enjoyed myself very much
es hat mir sehr gut gefallen
*es hat meer zehr goot ge-**fal**-len*

we will be back
wir werden wieder kommen
*veer **ver**-den **vee**-der **kom**men*

please keep in touch
bitte melden Sie sich mal
*bi-te **mel**-den zee zikh mal*

can I have your address?
kann ich Ihre Adresse haben?
*kan ikh **ee**-re a-**dress**-e **hah**-ben*

Although problems are not something anyone wants, you might come across the odd difficulty, and it is best to be armed with a few phrases to cope with the situation.

excuse me!
entschuldigen Sie!
entshool-di-gen zee

can you help me?
können Sie mir helfen?
kur'-nen zee meer hel-fen

I don't speak...
ich spreche kein...
ikh shpre-khe kine...

I am sorry, I did not know
Entschuldigung, das wusste ich nicht
entshool-di-goong das voos-te ikh nikht

I am lost (in car)
ich habe mich verfahren
ikh hah-be mikh fer-fahren

we are lost (on foot)
wir haben uns verlaufen
veer hah-ben oons fer-lowfen

I have lost...
ich habe ... verloren
ikh hah-be ... fer-lohren

my money
mein Geld
mine gelt

my tickets
meine Tickets
mine-e tickets

my passport
meinen Pass
mine-en pass

I have left...
ich habe ... vergessen
ikh hah-be ... fer-gessen

in the restaurant
im Restaurant
im restoh-rong

on the train
im Zug
im tsook

I have missed...
ich habe ... verpasst
ikh hah-be ... fer-past

my flight
meinen Flug
mine-en flook

the train
den Zug
den tsook

the coach
den Bus
den boos

I need to get to...
ich muss nach...
ikh moos nakh...

how can I get there today?
wie komme ich heute noch dorthin?
vee komme ikh hoy-te nokh dort-hin

my luggage hasn't arrived
mein Gepäck ist nicht angekommen
mine ge-pek ist nikht an-ge-kommen

my case has been damaged
mein Koffer ist beschädigt worden
mine kof-fer ist be-shay-dikht vorden

my bag...
meine Handtasche...
mine-e hant-ta-she...

my purse...
mein Portemonnaie...
mine port-moh-nay...

my wallet...
meine Brieftasche...
mine-e breef-ta-she...

...has been stolen
...ist gestohlen worden
...ist ge-shtoh-len vorden

please send my case to this address
bitte schicken Sie meinen Koffer an diese Adresse
bi-te shi-ken zee mine-en kof-fer an dee-ze adres-se

I need to go to hospital
ich muss ins Krankenhaus
ikh moos ins kranken-hows

I have no money
ich habe kein Geld
ikh hah-be kine gelt

I can't find my child
ich kann mein Kind nicht finden
ikh kan mine kint nikht fin-den

go away!
hau ab!
how ap

that man is following me
dieser Mann folgt mir
dee-zer man folgt meer

Germans expect to receive good service and quality. They will complain when things are not to their liking.

there is no...
es gibt kein/keine...
es gipt kine/kine-e...

there is no soap
es gibt keine Seife
es gipt kine-e zay-fe

it is dirty
es ist schmutzig
es ist shmootsik

they are dirty
sie sind schmutzig
zee zint shmootsik

it is broken
es ist kaputt
es ist ka-putt

they are broken
sie sind kaputt
zee zint ka-putt

the ... does not work
der/die/das ... funktioniert nicht
der/dee/das ... foonk-tsyo-neert nikht

the ... do not work
die ... funktionieren nicht
dee ... foonk-tsyo-neeren nikht

the window doesn't open
das Fenster lässt sich nicht öffnen
das fens-ter lesst sikh nikht ur'f-nen

the window doesn't close
das Fenster lässt sich nicht schließen
das fens-ter lesst sikh nikht shlee-sen

the room is noisy
das Zimmer ist laut
das tsimmer ist lowt

the room is too small
das Zimmer ist zu klein
das tsimmer ist tsoo kline

the room is too hot
das Zimmer ist zu warm
das tsimmer ist tsoo varm

the room is too cold
das Zimmer ist zu kalt
das tsimmer ist tsoo kalt

it is too expensive
es ist zu teuer
es ist tsoo toy-er

you are charging too much
Sie verlangen zu viel
zee fer-langen tsoo veel

I want to complain
ich möchte mich beschweren
ikh mur'kh-te mikh be-shveh-ren

where is the manager?
wo ist der Manager?
voh ist der manager

we want to order
wir möchten bestellen
veer mur'kh-ten be-shtellen

the service is very bad
der Service ist sehr schlecht
der service ist zehr shlekht

this food is cold
das Essen ist kalt
das es-sen ist kalt

this coffee is cold
dieser Kaffee ist kalt
dee-zer kafay ist kalt

this isn't what I ordered
das habe ich nicht bestellt
das hah-be ikh nikht be-shtelt

please take it off the bill
bitte nehmen Sie das von der Rechnung
bi-te nay-men zee das fon der rekh-noong

there is a mistake
hier liegt ein Fehler vor
heer ligt ine fay-ler for

please check the bill
bitte überprüfen Sie die Rechnung
bi-te oober-proofen zee dee rekh-noong

Everyday Germany

 The next four pages should give you an idea of the type of things you will come across in Germany.

open

opening hours

Geschäftszeiten:		
Montag:	9.00 – 12.30	Uhr
Dienstag:	9.00 – 12.30	Uhr
Mittwoch:		Uhr
Donnerstag:	8.30–12.30	14.30–18.00 Uhr
Freitag:	8.30–12.30	14.30–18.00 Uhr
Samstag:	8.30–12.30	Uhr

Shops are open generally from 9am–8pm Monday–Friday and until 4pm on Saturday. Shops are shut on Sunday except for tourist areas where they may open to sell holiday items. In smaller towns shops will close at 6pm on weekdays and at 2pm on Saturday.

Geschlossen
von 13.00 bis 14.30 Uhr

closed

Drücken

FALSCHGELD · KEINE ...

push

Ziehen

pull

snack bar

IMBISS

Germans are fond of snacks and there are numerous roadside stalls. There should be no worries over trying the food, as there are hygiene laws governing the operation of stalls.

Information hier drücken

press here for information

Kasse→

cash desk/pay here

lottery ticket

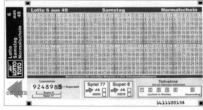

There is one lottery draw on Saturday night and two on Wednesday night. You have to mark 6 numbers out of 49. You can buy tickets where you see the sign *Lotto*.

do you have...?	**stamps**	**phonecards**
haben Sie...?	Briefmarken	Telefonkarten
hah-ben zee...	*breef-marken*	*taylay-fon-kar-ten*
where can I get...?	**a ticket**	**a map**
wo kann ich ... bekommen?	Fahrscheine	eine Karte
voh kan ikh ... be-kommen	*fahr-shy-ne*	*ine-e kar-te*

Train ticket machine for cash payment (and card payment).

Train ticket machine for card payments only.

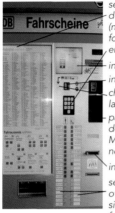

select destination (number code for town/station) enter here

instructions

insert coins

choice of language

payment with debit card (e.g. Maestro, but not credit cards)

insert bank notes

select type of ticket, e.g. single, group, family

(tickets for train journeys in the whole of Germany)

choice of language and instructions on the screen (by touching the white fields, you're led to your train ticket step by step)

ticket and receipt

insert card (maestro etc.)

enter PIN

receipt

cancel

insert coins

Quittung

cancel

C is more common for cancel than **Storno**.

Automat gibt Rückgeld

change given

EINGANG

entrance

(A vehicle entrance is marked **Einfahrt**)

Postboxes are yellow.

Ausgang

exit

(A vehicle exit is marked **Ausfahrt**)

out of service

An airmail letter or postcard will usually arrive in Britain the third day after posting.

excuse me...
entschuldigen Sie...
ent**shool**-di-gen zee...

what do I have to do?
was muss ich tun?
vas moos ikh toon

how does this work?
wie funktioniert das?
vee foonk-tsyo-**neert** das

what does this mean?
was bedeutet das?
vas be-**doy**-tet das

talking

Alle Preise inkl. Bedienungsgeld
und Mehrwertsteuer

*all prices include service
and VAT*

Tipping in Germany is not compulsory and
should be simply an appreciation of good service.
You would tend to round your bill up to about
1 or 2 Euros more than the amount asked for.

Waste separation at a train station.

At train stations and in city centres,
you often find partitioned bins for
glass, recyclable packaging
(including most plastics), paper
and normal waste.

Germans are very recycling-
conscious and you must use
the correct bin for your rubbish.

*glass   paper   packaging (with waste
recycling symbol)*

Recycling stations in
residential areas do not only
include containers for glass,
paper and clothes, but also
often have a little box for
batteries. Bottles (glass and
plastic) and cans carry a
deposit (**"Pfand"**, usually
25 cents), which you get
back when you return them
to a super-
market.

*biodegradable paper   general   packaging carry-
material   waste   ing the recycling
symbol (left)*

Zutritt
verboten

entry prohibited

DER GRÜNE PUNKT

recycling symbol

1,0 l

NICHTRAUCHER-ZONE

Bitte nehmen Sie Rücksicht auf die Nichtraucher

no smoking zone

Smoking is not
allowed in public
buildings except in areas where
ashtrays are provided. In most restaurants smoking will be
allowed, only some have a dedicated non-smoking area.

can I smoke here?
kann ich hier rauchen?
*kan ikh heer **row**-khen*

I don't smoke
ich rauche nicht
*ikh **row**-khe nikht*

an ashtray please
einen Aschenbecher bitte
*ine-en **ashen-be**kher **bi**-te*

do you mind if I smoke?
stört es Sie, wenn ich rauche?
*shtur't es zee ven ikh **row**-khe*

please don't smoke
bitte rauchen Sie nicht
***bi**-te **row**-khen zee nikht*

a non-smoking table please
einen Tisch in der Nichtraucherzone bitte
*ine-en tish in der **nikht**-rowkher-tsoh-ne **bi**-te*

talking

There aren't very many public toilets around in Germany. Wherever you go, you will be expected to pay or at least leave a tip for the attendants. Check out shopping centres for toilets and some department stores will have them. In bigger cities, make for public buildings such as the railway station if you are looking for a toilet. You can also follow the city signpost system. In most petrol stations you will have to ask the attendant for the key to the toilet.

toilets

HERREN

gents

Ladies and Gents are usually shown with a pictogram.

DAMEN

ladies

hot

Trinkwasser

drinking water

Frei

free

Besetzt

occupied

cold

excuse me! where is the toilet?
entschuldigen Sie! Wo ist die Toilette?
*ent**shool**-di-gen zee voh ist dee twa-**le**-te*

do you have the key for the toilet?
haben Sie den Schlüssel für die Toilette?
***hah**-ben zee den **shloo**-sel foor dee twa-**le**-te*

is there a disabled toilet?
gibt es hier eine Toilette für Behinderte?
*gipt es heer ine-e twa-**le**-te foor be-**hin**-derte*

is there a parent and child toilet?
gibt es hier eine Toilette für Mutter und Kind?
*gipt es heer ine-e twa-**le**-te foor **moot**-ter oont kint*

talking talking talking

Asking the Way

i Newsagents, bookshops and kiosks sell **Stadtplan** – very handy street directories. You can ask for a free transport map when you buy your metro or bus tickets from stations or travel centres. Most cities will have maps of the centre displayed.

townplan of Lübeck with surrounding area

4th edition
street index
with postcodes

RECHTS
right

LINKS
left

you are here

Street signs are usually blue. They often have additional information on the person or even the event the street was named after.

excuse me!
entschuldigen Sie!
*ent**shool**-di-gen zee*

do you know where ... is?
wissen Sie, wo ... ist?
***vis**-sen zee voh ... ist*

how do I get to...?
wie komme ich zum/zur/nach...?
*vee **kom**me ikh tsoom/tsoor/nakh...*

is this the right way to...?
ist das hier richtig zum/zur/nach...?
*ist das heer **rikh**tikh tsoom/tsoor/nakh...*

do you have a map of the town?
haben Sie einen Stadtplan?
*hah-ben zee ine-en **shtat**-plan*

can you show me on the map?
können Sie mir das auf der Karte zeigen?
***kur'**-nen zee meer das owf der **kar**-te **tsy**-gen*

we're looking for...
wir suchen...
*veer **zoo**khen...*

where is...?
wo ist...?
voh ist...

is it far?
ist es weit?
ist es vite

a street directory
ein Straßenverzeichnis
*ine **shtra**-sen-fer-tsykh-nis*

talking talking

no entrance *(on foot)*

<table>
<tr><td>KEIN AUSGANG</td></tr>
</table>

no exit *(on foot)*

Pedestrian city signs.
Each city uses a different design
and colour, and there is no set
colour coding.

*St Stephan's with
a window
(**Fenster**) designed
by Chagall* —

old town —

cathedral —

Gutenberg museum —

boats on the Rhine —

*weekly market
Tue, Fri, Sat
7am–2pm*

On town road signs, local signs are in white and
yellow signs are for out-of-town destinations.

Ribnitz-Damgarten 14 km	— *out-of-town destination*
Rathaus	— *town hall*
Polizei	— *police*
Seebrücke	— *pier*
Jugendherberge	— *youth hostel*

nach rechts
nakh rekhts
to the right

nach links
nakh links
to the left

geradeaus
grah-de-ows
straight ahead

gehen Sie
gay-en zee
go

biegen Sie ab
bee-gen zee ap
turn

Straße
shtra-se
road

Platz
plats
square

Ampel
am-pel
traffic lights

Kirche
kir-khe
church

erste
ers-te
first

zweite
tsvy-te
second

weit
vite
far

in der Nähe
in der nay-e
near

neben
ne-ben
next to

gegenüber
gay-gen-oober
opposite

bis
bis
until

keywords keywords keywords keywords keywords keywords

Banks & Money

i Germany is in the eurozone. The euro has now replaced the Dèutschmark (**DM**) – the former currency of Germany. If your bank card supports Maestro or Cirrus services, you will be able to use it in German cash dispensers, selecting English to carry out the transaction. Otherwise most cash dispensers also accept credit cards. Credit cards are now becoming widely accepted and most purchases can be paid with them.

Öffnungszeiten

opening times

Banks are usually open Monday–Friday 8.30am–1pm and from 2pm–4pm (sometimes longer on Thursdays). They are closed on Saturday and Sunday.

Most banks can be identified by the word **Bank** or **Sparkasse**. Among the big banks in Germany are **Sparkasse**, **Deutsche Bank** and **Dresdner Bank**.

cash dispenser

Abbruch **cancel**

Korrektur **correct/error**

Bestätigung **enter**

Geldwechsel and *Reise Bank* are both **Bureau de Change**

Germany is in the eurozone. This is the symbol for the euro.

Germany's currency is the euro, which breaks down into 100 euro cents. Euro notes are the same across Europe. The reverse of the coins carry different designs in each European member country.

Notes: 5, 10, 20, 50, 100, 200, 500

Coins: 2 euro, 1 euro, 50 cent, 20 cent, 10 cent, 5 cent, 2 cent, 1 cent

keywords keywords keywords keywords keywords

Kreditkarte
kre-deet-kar-te
credit card

Geldautomat
gelt-owto-maht
cash dispenser

PIN-Nummer
pin-noomer
pin number

Kleingeld
kline-gelt
change

einwerfen
ine-verfen
insert

Betrag eingeben
be-trahk ine-gay-ben
press amount

Banknoten
bank-no-ten
notes

Bargeld
bar-gelt
cash

Münze
moon-tse
coin

talking talking

where is there...?
wo gibt es...?
voh gipt es...

a bank
eine Bank
ine-e bank

a bureau de change
eine Wechselstube
ine-e veksel-shtoo-be

where can I change money?
wo kann ich hier Geld wechseln?
voh kan ikh heer gelt vek-seln

I would like small notes
ich möchte kleine Scheine
ikh mur'kh-te kline-e shy-ne

where is the nearest cash dispenser?
wo ist der nächste Geldautomat?
voh ist der naykh-ste gelt-owto-maht

I want to change these travellers' cheques
ich möchte diese Reiseschecks einlösen
ikh mur'kh-te dee-ze ry-ze-sheks ine-lur'zen

the cash dispenser has swallowed my card
der Geldautomat hat meine Karte geschluckt
der gelt-owto-maht hat mine-e kar-te ge-shlookt

When is...?

 *The 24-hour clock is used in timetables. With the 24-hour clock, the words half (**halb**) and quarter (**Viertel**) are not used.*

keywords keywords keywords

Morgen
morgen
morning

Nachmittag
nakh-mitahk
afternoon

heute Abend
hoy-te ahbent
this evening

heute
hoy-te
today

morgen
morgen
tomorrow

gestern
gestern
yesterday

später
shpayter
later

sofort
zo-fort
straightaway

jetzt
yetst
now

13:00	
14:00	
15:00	
16:00	
17:00	
18:00	
19:00	
20:00	
21:00	
22:00	
23:00	
24:00	

at...

um dreizehn Uhr
oom dry-tsayn oor

um vierzehn Uhr
oom feer-tsayn oor

um fünfzehn Uhr
oom foonf-tsayn oor

um sechzehn Uhr
oom zekh-tsayn oor

um siebzehn Uhr
oom zeep-tsayn oor

um achtzehn Uhr
oom akh-tsayn oor

um neunzehn Uhr
oom noyn-tsayn oor

um zwanzig Uhr
oom tsvan-tsikh oor

um einundzwanzig Uhr
oom ine-oont-tsvan-tsikh oor

um zweiundzwanzig Uhr
oom tsvy-oont-tsvan-tsikh oor

um dreiundzwanzig Uhr
oom dry-oont-tsvan-tsikh oor

um null Uhr
oom nool oor

talking

When is...? wann fährt...? *van fayrt...*	**the next train** der nächste Zug der **naykh**-ste tsook	**the next bus** der nächste Bus der **naykh**-ste boos	**the next boat** das nächste Schiff das **naykh**-ste shiff
When is...? wann ist...? *van ist...*	**breakfast** Frühstück *froo-shtook*	**lunch** Mittagessen *mitahk-es-sen*	**dinner** Abendessen *ahbent-es-sen*

When does it leave?
wann ist die Abfahrt?
*van ist dee **ap**-fahrt*

When does it arrive?
wann ist die Ankunft?
*van ist dee **an**-koonft*

When does it open?
wann wird geöffnet?
*van virt ge-**ur'f**net*

When does it close?
wann wird geschlossen?
*van virt ge-**shlos**-sen*

Note that with **halb** Germans refer to the full hour to come not the past hour! For instance, **halb acht** actually means 7.30.

at...

um zwölf
oom tsvur'lf

um elf
oom elf

um eins
oom ines

um zehn
oom tsayn

um zwei
oom tsvy

um neun
oom noyn

um drei
oom dry

um acht
oom akht

um vier
oom feer

um sieben
*oom **zee**ben*

um fünf
oom foonf

um sechs
oom zekhs

um achtzehn Uhr fünfundvierzig
*oom akh-tsayn oor foonf-oont-**feer**-tsikh*
at 18.45

um Viertel vor...
*oom **feer**tel for...*
at quarter to...

um Mitternacht
*oom **mit**-ter-nakht*
at midnight

um Viertel vor...
*oom **feer**tel for...*
at quarter to...

um zwanzig vor...
*oom **tsvan**-tsikh for...*
at twenty to...

um halb...
oom halp...
at half past...

excuse me!
entschuldigen Sie!
*ent**shool**-di-gen zee*

what time is it please?
wie spät ist es bitte?
*vee shpeht ist es **bi**-te*

what is the date?
der Wievielte ist heute?
*der vee-**feel**-te ist **hoy**-te*

it is the 8th May
heute ist der achte Mai
***hoy**-te ist der **akh**-te my*

16th September 2006
der sechzehnte September zweitausendsechs
*der **zekh**-tsayn-te sep-**tem**-ber **tsvy**-towzent-**zekhs***

which day?
welcher Tag?
***vel**-kher tahk*

which month?
welcher Monat?
***vel**-kher **moh**-nat*

Timetables

 Timetables use the 24-hour clock. Bus and train timetables usually change once a year in May. The German for timetable is **Fahrplan**.

Montag
mohn-tahk
Monday

Dienstag
deens-tahk
Tuesday

Mittwoch
mit-vokh
Wednesday

Donnerstag
donners-tahk
Thursday

Freitag
fry-tahk
Friday

Samstag
zams-tahk
Saturday

Sonntag
zon-tahk
Sunday

timetables
Make sure you are looking at the timetable for the right station, e.g. Frankfurt **Hbf** not Frankfurt **Flughafen** (airport – they are often shown next to each other). Yellow timetables are departures, white are arrivals.

Abfahrt Departure
Chemnitz Hbf

Ankunft Arrival
Chemnitz Hbf

boat timetable

departure —

arrival —

	Termine & Preise:		— times & prices
Abfahrt	19.30	Mainz-Fischtor	
	20.00	WI-Biebrich	
Ankunft	23.00	WI-Biebrich	
	23.30	Mainz	
	Mi. 05. Juli, Mi 19. Juli,		
	Mi. 09. August und Mi. 30. August		— €40 incl. 4-course meal
	€40, - inkl. 4-Gänge-Menü		

München Hbf
→ **Chemnitz Hbf**
Fahrplanauszug – Angaben ohne Gewähr – Gültig von 28.05.2005 bis 09.06.2006

not a complete timetable (does not list all the trains on this route)

valid from   until

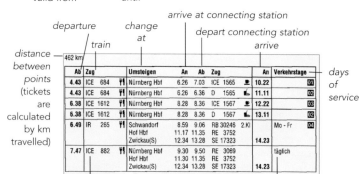

distance between points (tickets are calculated by km travelled)

departure   change at   arrive at connecting station   depart connecting station   arrive   days of service

train   type of train   daily

462 km

Ab	Zug		Umsteigen	An	Ab	Zug		An	Verkehrstage
4.43	ICE	684	Nürnberg Hbf	6.26	7.03	ICE	1565	10.22	01
4.43	ICE	684	Nürnberg Hbf	6.26	6.36	D	1565	11.11	02
6.38	ICE	1612	Nürnberg Hbf	8.28	8.36	ICE	1567	12.22	03
6.38	ICE	1612	Nürnberg Hbf	8.28	8.36	D	1567	13.11	02
6.49	IR	265	Schwandorf	8.59	9.06	RB	30246 2.Kl		Mo - Fr 04
			Hof Hbf	11.17	11.35	RE	3752		
			Zwickau(S)	12.34	13.28	SE	17323	14.23	
7.47	ICE	882	Nürnberg Hbf	9.30	9.50	RE	3069		täglich
			Hof Hbf	11.30	11.35	RE	3752		
			Zwickau(S)	12.34	13.28	SE	17323	14.23	

bus overhead-board

Abfahrt in Minuten
departure in minutes

line direction

Linie	Richtung	Abfahrt in Minuten
16	ESWE-FREIZEITBAD	4
21	FAHRPLANAUSZUG :	17:00 17:21 17:41
22	FAHRPLANAUSZUG :	17:18 18:08 18:48
28	FAHRPLANAUSZUG :	16:52 17:23 17:52
46	WIESBADEN PL. D. DT. EINHEIT	11
48	WIESBADEN PL. D. DT. EINHEIT	2
806	FAHRPLANAUSZUG :	16:53 17:23 17:53

next services

Rostock, Dierkower Kreuz
Tarifzone: 1   gültig ab: 28.05.2005

Detailed, minute-by-minute timetables like this are usually found at bus stops.

keywords

Fahrplan
fahr-plan
timetable

Ab (Abfahrt)
ap-fahrt
departure

An (Ankunft)
an-koonft
arrival

umsteigen
oom-shtygen
change at

täglich
tehkh-likh
daily

nicht
nikht
no service

bis
bis
until

auch
owkh
also

gültig von
gooltikh fon
valid from

Jan Jan
Feb Feb
März March
Apr April
Mai May
Jun June
Jul July
Aug Aug
Sep Sep
Okt Oct
Nov Nov
Dez Dec

do you have a timetable?
haben Sie einen Fahrplan?
hah-ben zee ine-en fahr-plan

can you explain the timetable?
können Sie mir den Fahrplan erklären?
kur'-nen zee meer den fahr-plan er-kleh-ren

talk

Tickets

 Tickets for transport (bus, tram and train) are **Fahrkarten**. For entertainment or museum entry, etc, use simply **Karten** or **Tickets**.

choose your ticket type

2. Wählen Sie bitte Ihre Fahrkarte

Einzelfahrt ——— single ticket *(for immediate travel)*

Zuschlag ——— supplement *(per person) in addition to ticket*

Tageskarte day ticket
(valid from purchase to end of service of same day)

Sammelkarte multiple tickets
(to validate at the start of each journey)

Single bus tickets.

3rd & 4th journey from book of tickets.
Validate one end for each journey.

train ticket from ticket machine

SH (special tariff)
day ticket   2nd class
1 person
incl. wider district of Hamburg
valid on 15.07.06
between 0100 Hamburg main station
and   6000 Lübeck
via   Bad Oldesloe
*   not valid on ICE/IC/EC!*

date   time   Price category 10
**18.80 EUR incl. VAT

tram ticket

single journey
1 Zone
validate at start of journey →
valid for 1 hour
*   1.60 EUR*

date   hour

suburban train ticket from Hamburg

single ticket 2nd class
wider district of Hamburg

(main station)
(date + hour)   **2.40 EUR

(issued by S-Bahn Hamburg GmbH)

The *Partner-Tageskarte* allows unlimited travel for a family or a group for a day.

— unlimited travel in entire zone

— valid from stamping until 6am the following morning for 5 people. Two children (6–14 years old) count as one person

Fahrkarte
fahr-kar-te
bus/metro ticket

Mehrfahrten-karte
mehrfahrten-kar-te
book of tickets

Eintrittskarte
ine-tritts-kar-te
entry ticket

Pass
pass
travel card

einfach
ine-fakh
single

hin und zurück
hin oont tsoorook
return

Erwachsener
er-vak-se-ner
adult

Kind(er)
kind(er)
child(ren)

Student
shtoodent
student

Rentner
rent-ner
OAP

Behinderter
be-hin-der-ter
disabled

Familie
famee-lee-e
family

keywords keywords keywords keywords keywords keywords

KARTEN HIER ERHÄLTLICH!

buy your tickets here!

Karten für die heutige Vorstellung

tickets for today's performance

Halber Preis für alle Senioren für Hin- und Rückfahrten bei Tages-fahrten am Montag und Mittwoch.

Red text indicates that all seniors pay half price.

Junioren: bis 5 Jahre frei, bis 15 Jahre halber Preis, in den hessischen und rheinland-pfälzischen

Red text indicates that children up to 5 go free, between 5 and 15, half-price.

Public Transport

*Most German cities operate an integrated transport system which means that all the different kinds of transport are part of one network and you can use any of them with your ticket. You buy your ticket in advance (see **Tickets**, p. 26). You validate your ticket in the validating machine when you get on board the bus or tram. With the **U-Bahn** and **S-Bahn** you validate your ticket on entering the station or platform. There are no ticket barriers. Most cities have a night service.*

bus stop
The ticket machine is located next to it. Often tickets can also be purchased from the driver.

sign at bus stop in Hamburg

name of stop/ street

departure (immediately) (... minutes)

line/number of bus   destination

Validator which you find on boarding the bus.

bus tickets for sale

bus stop
On buses, you often have to ring a bell to get off at a stop.

bus stop location and zone

you can change onto **U-** or **S-Bahn**

you can change onto long-distance rail network

N in front of a service number indicates it is a night service

Bus timetables are usually posted on the bus stop (see p. 25).

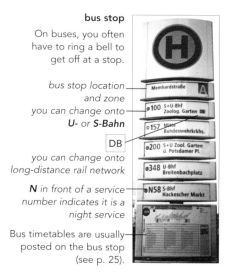

tram

indicates room for 2 bikes

push to open the doors

bus

Hauptbahnhof — *main station*

50 Hechtsheim Bürgerhaus

51 Hechtsheim Bürgerhaus

numbers of the services that leave from here

tram stop

where do I catch a bus to...?
von wo fährt der Bus nach...?
fon voh fayrt der boos nakh...

is there a bus to...?
gibt es einen Bus nach...?
gipt es ine-en boos nakh...

which number goes to...?
welche Linie fährt nach...?
vel-khe lee-nee-e fayrt nakh...

does this bus go to...?
fährt dieser Bus zum/zur/nach..?
fayrt dee-zer boos tsoom/tsoor/nakh...

must I ring the bell to get off?
muss man das Aussteigen anmelden?
moos man das ows-shtygen an-mel-den

which bus goes to the centre?
welcher Bus fährt ins Zentrum?
vel-kher boos fayrt ins tsentroom

please tell me when to get off
bitte sagen Sie mir, wann ich aussteigen muss
bi-te zahgen zee meer van ikh ows-shtygen moos

excuse me, I'm getting off!
darf ich bitte vorbei!
darf ikh bi-te for-by

what time is the next bus to...?
wann fährt der nächste Bus nach...?
van fayrt der naykh-ste boos nakh...

i *U is the sign for the metro (U-Bahn), S the sign for suburban trains (S-Bahn). Both are part of the integrated transport system of a city. Parts of the U-Bahn are overground. Lines can be identified by the U or S followed by the number.*

indicates number of line and destination

Station sign showing that both **U-Bahn** and **S-Bahn** operate from there.

Ticket validators are located at the entrance to stations.

validate here

This sign shows which lines stop at the station. The lines are colour-coded.

If you are travelling to the airport, look out for this sign meaning airport transfer service.

stand on the right, walk on the left

overhead platform board

hält in Frankfurt (M) Hbf
train stops at
Frankfurt Central Station

departure

all of the
train is
going
(the front
and rear
carriages
are not
separating)

The smaller board beside the main
destination board shows the train is going
via Mainz-Kastel and Frankfurt Airport.

*Offenbach Ost is
the final destination.*

a single
eine Einzelfahrkarte
*ine-e **ine**-tsel-fahr-kar-te*

a day ticket
eine Tageskarte
*ine-e **tah**ges-kar-te*

a group ticket
eine Gruppenkarte
*ine-e **groo**-pen-kar-te*

a book of tickets
eine Mehrfahrtenkarte
*ine-e **mehr**-fahrten-kar-te*

a weekly ticket
eine Wochenkarte
*ine-e **vo**-khen-kar-te*

a monthly ticket
eine Monatskarte
*ine-e **moh**-nats-kar-te*

have you a map of the U-Bahn?
haben Sie einen U-Bahn-Plan?
***hah**-ben zee ine-en **oo**-bahn-plan*

where is the nearest U-Bahn station?
wo ist die nächste U-Bahn-Station?
*voh ist dee **naykh**-ste oo-bahn-shtah-**tsyohn***

I want to go to...
Ich möchte zum/zur/nach...
*ikh **mur'kh**-te tsoom/tsoor/nakh...*

do I have to change?
muss ich umsteigen?
*moos ikh **oom**-shty-gen*

where?
wo?
voh

which line do I take?
welche Linie muss ich nehmen?
***vel**-khe **lee**-nee-e moos ikh **nay**-men*

in which direction?
in welche Richtung?
*in **vel**-khe **rikh**-toong*

which stop is it for...?
wo ist die Haltestelle für...?
*voh ist dee **hal**-te-shtel-le foor...*

which station is it for ...?
welche Station muss ich für ... nehmen?
***vel**-khe shta-**tsyohn** moos ikh foor ... **nay**-men*

excuse me! I want to get off
entschuldigen Sie! Ich möchte aussteigen
*ent**shool**-di-gen zee ikh **mur'kh**-te **ows**-shty-gen*

talking talking talking talking

i The Bahn offers discounted fares on long-distance travel in Germany: **Sparpreis 25** and **Sparpreis 50**, giving 25% and 50% respectively off standard return fares if passengers book in advance, restrict themselves to a particular day and train, and make a return journey to and from the same station.

For unlimited travel for a whole day within a certain region one of Deutsche Bahn's **Länder-Tickets** is the best choice.

If you are travelling on Saturday or Sunday, you can make use of the **Schönes-Wochenende-Ticket**. It is valid for up to 5 people in second class on local services (not the fast trains ICE, IC, EC or IR) and on most city transport networks. The ticket can be used on Saturday OR Sunday from midnight until 3am the following day. There are more offers for group and family travel. Children up to 6 years travel free. Children from 6–14 years pay nothing if travelling with a parent or grandparent, and just 50% of the standard fare if travelling alone. Check www.bahn.co.uk for information.

Always buy your ticket before you board the train. Check if a supplement (**ein Zuschlag**) is required (as for the InterCity Express ICE). It is always a good idea to pre-book seats on ICE trains during busy periods.

ReiseZentrum

Travel Centre for information and tickets. If you are not sure of what you want queue at the counter marked **Information**. If you know what you want go to the **Express-Schalter** where no information is given but service is faster.

train tickets	**Fahrscheine**
information	**Information**
reservations	**Reservierungen**
tickets for local transport	**RMV-Fahrkarten**

---

a single to...
einmal einfach nach...
ine-mal ine-fakh nakh...

2 singles to...
zweimal einfach nach...
tsvy-mal ine-fakh nakh...

a child's ticket
ein Kind
ine kint

first class
erste Klasse
er-ste kla-se

second class
zweite Klasse
tsvy-te kla-se

what special offers do you have?
was für Sonderangebote haben Sie?
vas foor zonder-an-ge-bo-te hah-ben zee

do I need a reservation?
muss ich eine Platzkarte kaufen?
moos ikh ine-e plats-kar-te kowfen

is there a supplement to pay?
muss man einen Zuschlag kaufen?
moos man ine-en tsoo-shlak kow-fen

do I have to change?
muss ich umsteigen?
moos ikh oom-shty-gen

I want to book...
ich möchte ... buchen
ikh mur'kh-te ... boo-khen

2 seats
zwei Sitzplätze
tsvy sits-plet-se

window seats
Fensterplätze
fenster-plet-se

talking talking

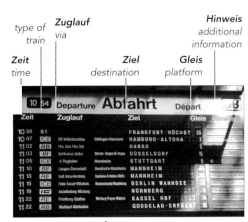

type of train — **Zuglauf** *via*
Zeit *time*
Ziel *destination*
Gleis *platform*
Hinweis *additional information*

departures

to the trains

platform number

You need a coin to operate the luggage trolley.

Richtung ——— direction

Heerstraße/Hausen

keywords keywords keywords keywords keywords

Abteil
ap-**tyl**
compartment

Hinfahrt
hin-fahrt
single

Rückfahrt
rook-fahrt
return

Reservierung
ray-zer-**vee**-roong
reservation

Zuschlag
tsoo-shlak
supplement

besonderer Fahrpreis
be-**zon**-derer
fahr-price
special rate

Ermäßigung
er-**may**-sigoong
reduction

Gang
gang
aisle

Gepäckauf-bewahrung
ge**pek**-owf-bevahroong
left-luggage

Fenster
fens-ter
window

Schienenersatz-verkehr
sheenen-er**sats**-ferkehr
bus operates

Schließfächer
shlees-fe-kher
lockers

talking

the train to...
der Zug nach...
der tsook nakh...

is this the train for...?
ist das der Zug nach...?
ist das der tsook nakh...

which platform does it leave from?
von welchem Bahnsteig fährt er ab?
fon vel-khem bahn-shtike fayrt er ap

this is my seat
das ist mein Platz
das ist mine plats

Taxi

i Most German taxis are cream with a yellow sign on the roof
(there is no light to show if the taxi is booked or not). In Germany,
to get a taxi you have to find a taxi rank (Taxistand) or call a taxi
company. German taxi drivers will usually expect a small tip.

Taxi sign in station.

Taxi sign on car roof.

German taxis are cream.

The number to call for a taxi.

talking talking

where is the nearest taxi stand?
wo ist der nächste Taxistand?
*voh ist der **naykh**-ste **t**axi-shtant*

to ... please
zum/zur/nach ... bitte
*tsoom/tsoor/nakh ... **bi**-te*

how much is it to...?
wie viel kostet es zum/zur/nach...?
*vee feel **kos**tet es tsoom/tsoor/nakh...*

please order me a taxi
bitte bestellen Sie mir ein Taxi
*bi-te be-**shtel**-len zee meer ine **t**axi*

for now
für sofort
*foor zo-**fort***

for...
für...
foor...

can I have a receipt?
kann ich eine Quittung bekommen?
*kan ikh ine-e **kvi**-toong be-**kom**men*

keep the change
der Rest ist für Sie
der rest ist foor zee

is there a special rate for the airport?
gibt es einen besonderen Tarif zum Flughafen?
*gipt es ine-en be-**zon**-deren ta**reef** tsoom **flook**-hafen*

Car Hire

Major rental companies operate internationally so that you can pre-book a car in the UK. Cars can also be booked in Germany at airports or local car hire offices (Autovermietungen).

To rent a car from most agencies in Germany, you need to be at least 21 years old and must have held your licence for at least a year.

When checking car hire prices, bear in mind that in Germany, these usually only include 3rd party insurance. Fully comprehensive insurance often comes on top of the price quoted.

I want to hire a car
ich möchte ein Auto mieten
*ikh **mur'kh**-te ine **owto meeten***

for one day
für einen Tag
foor ine-en tahk

for ... days
für ... Tage
*foor ... **tah**-ge*

I want...
ich möchte...
*ikh **mur'kh**-te...*

a small car
einen Kleinwagen
*ine-en **kline**-vahgen*

a large car
ein großes Auto
*ine **groh**-ses **owto***

a people carrier
einen Minivan
ine-en mini-van

an automatic
ein Auto mit Automatikgetriebe
*ine **owto** mit owto-**mah**-tik-ge-tree-be*

how much is it?
wie viel kostet es?
*vee feel **kos**tet es*

what petrol must I use?
was muss ich tanken?
*vas mus ikh **tang**-ken*

I am ... old
ich bin ... Jahre alt
*ikh bin ... **jah**-re alt*

here is my driving licence
hier ist mein Führerschein
*heer ist mine **fooh**-rer-shine*

what is included in the insurance?
was ist alles in der Versicherung inbegriffen?
*vas ist **al**-les in der fer-**zikh**eroong **in**-be-griffen*

how do the controls work?
wie funktionieren die Schalter?
*vee foonk-tsyo-**nee**-ren dee **shal**-ter*

where are the documents?
wo sind die Fahrzeugpapiere?
*voh zint dee fahr-tsoyk-pa**pee**-re*

what do we do if...?
was tun wir bei...?
vas toon veer by...

we breakdown
einer Panne
*ine-er **pan**-ne*

have an accident
einem Unfall
*ine-em **oon**-fall*

can we hire a child-seat?
können wir einen Kindersitz mieten?
***kur'**-nen veer ine-en **kin**der-zits **mee**ten*

how is it fitted?
wie wird er montiert?
*vee virt er mon-**teert***

talking talking talking talking talking talking talking

Driving

Seatbelts must be worn by all passengers in the car. For children under 4 years, child seats are required and children up to the age of 12 must use booster seats and are not allowed to sit in the front.

Remember to overtake on the left; passing on the right is prohibited. The blood alcohol limit is 0.5 per mille. Some driving rules are different and watch out for right of way from the right when no priority signs are displayed. Pedestrians always have the right of way, so take care when turning at traffic lights when you and the pedestrians can have a green light showing at the same time. You must carry in your car a first-aid kit, towing rope and warning triangle. Always carry your driving licence, car documents and passport when driving.

Speed restrictions

built up area	50km/h
ordinary roads	100km/h
motorway	no restriction,

but 130km/h is recommended and some sections will have speed restrictions

German number plate

D on the blue panel is for **Deutschland**. The first 2 letters indicate which district the car is registered (WI = **Wiesbaden**).

colour-coded German road signs

 motorways

Germany has an extensive network of numbered motorways.

E 36 *European routes*

Green signs with E and a number indicate European routes.

 secondary roads

Tourist and other information signs may also appear in yellow.

Rathaus *local destinations*

Where you see the sign below you must give way to the priority road. Drivers on the priority road must indicate when turning. Drivers on the top secondary road must yield to drivers on the bottom, as they are on their right.

north **Nord**

West *east* **Ost**

west

Süd *south*

detour

If no more detour signs are displayed, follow the priority road, as marked.

Restricted zone sign A 30km/h speed limit is in force. You only see the sign on entering the zone so you may be unaware that you are in a speed-restricted area. The enforcement ends at the end-of-zone sign.

priority sign

the arrow indicates you can only go in this direction

red phase 5 mins please turn off engines

You should switch off your engine if you are stopped for some time (not at regular traffic lights, but at road works or level crossings). Watch what the people around you do.

talking

we are going to...
wir sind auf dem Weg nach...
veer zint owf dem vehk nakh...

is the road good?
ist die Straße gut?
ist dee shtra-se goot

is the pass open?
ist der Pass geöffnet?
ist der pass ge-ur'fnet

which is the best route?
welche Route ist die beste?
vel-khe roo-te ist dee bes-te

can you show me on the map?
können Sie mir das auf der Karte zeigen?
kur'-nen zee meer das owf der kar-te tsy-gen

do we need snow chains?
brauchen wir Schneeketten?
brow-khen veer shneh-ket-ten

one-way street

city centre

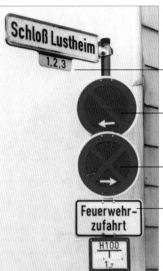

German parking signs can be complicated. If in doubt, don't park! Signs for parking restrictions only apply to the side of the road where they stand.

the house numbers you find along this street

no waiting from this point onwards, i.e. to the left of this sign

no stopping from this point onwards, i.e. to the right of this sign

fire engine access

tourist-route sign only refers to the wine areas

Yellow road signs are for out-of-town destinations.

---

is this the road to...?
ist das die Straße nach...?
*ist das dee **shtra**-se nakh...*

how do I get to...?
wie komme ich nach...?
*vee **kom**-me ikh nakh...*

I am sorry, I did not know...
Entschuldigung, ich wusste nicht, dass...
*ent-**shool**-digoong ikh **voos**-te nikht, das...*

this was a one-way street
das eine Einbahnstraße ist
*das ine-e **ine**-bahn-shtra-se ist*

this was a 30km/h zone
das eine Zone 30 ist
*das ine-e **tsoh**-ne **dry**-sikh ist*

I could not park here
ich hier nicht parken kann
*ikh heer nikht **par**-ken kan*

talking

*German motorways (**Autobahn**) are free. There is no speed restriction, but 130km/h is recommended, and some sections have lower speed limits. There are usually two lanes (except in areas of heavy traffic where there are three or more) which means you have to watch out for fast upcoming cars before pulling out to overtake.*

Sign directing to motorway 66.

Sign indicating the motorway entrance. (The exit is **Ausfahrt**.)

motorway services sign

SOS box

motorway number

motorway exit number

Unlike German motorways, Austrian and Swiss motorways are not free. This sign indicates Austrian motorway stickers are sold here.

If you break down on the motorway

If you break down on the motorway, first you should put on your warning lights and place your warning triangle about 100m behind the car. Then make your way to the emergency phone. An arrow on the distance indicator will show you which way the nearest phone is. It is never more than 1km away. The police will arrange for a recovery vehicle to come to you.

my car's broken down
ich habe eine Panne was
*ikh **hah**-be ine-e **pan**-ne*

what should I do?
soll ich tun?
vas zoll ikh toon

my children are in the car
meine Kinder sind im Auto
*mine-e kin-der zint im **ow**to*

I am on my own
ich bin allein
*ikh bin al-**line***

it is a blue Fiat
es ist ein blauer Fiat
*es ist ein **blow**-er fee**at***

registration number...
Kennzeichen...
ken-tsy-khen...

the car is...
das Auto ist...
*das **ow**to ist...*

after junction...
nach Abfahrt...
*nakh **ap**-fahrt...*

before junction...
vor Abfahrt...
*for **ap**-fahrt...*

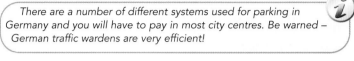
There are a number of different systems used for parking in Germany and you will have to pay in most city centres. Be warned – German traffic wardens are very efficient!

Sign indicates pay at this machine.

paying (i.e. not free)

pay & display parking

Parkschein-automat Fischtorplatz

pay & display ticket from Chemnitz

put behind windscreen, well visible from the outside

location

end of parking time

Petrol stations sell parking disks. Put the disk in sight on the dashboard. It works in 30-minute blocks: always rotate the arrow so it points to the next half hour or hour from your start time (i.e. if you arrive at 10.15, point the arrow to 10.30).

pay & display ticket

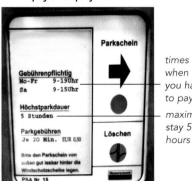

times when you have to pay

maximum stay 5 hours

The picture of the parking disk on this sign indicates you must display a parking disk. You can park for 2 hours (**2 Std.**); this restriction applies Monday–Saturday 9am–6pm.

This tells you to park on the kerb (see how the car is parked on the sign).

Parking system guiding you to car parks. *(Don't be misled by **Frei** – it means spaces, not free of charge. Full is **Belegt**.)*

Parkhaus is a multi-storey car park – note the roof over the P!

Instead of a paper ticket, you often get a **Parkchip**, a plastic token to use at the exit barrier.

exit *(note that Pedestrian Exit is **Ausgang**)*

entrance *(note that Pedestrian Entrance is **Eingang**)*

ring for assistance

---

where is there a car park?
wo ist hier ein Parkplatz?
*voh ist heer ine **park**-plats*

can I park here?
kann ich hier parken?
*kan ikh heer **par**-ken*

where can I get a parking disk?
wo kann ich eine Parkscheibe kaufen?
*voh kan ikh ine-e **park**-shy-be **kow**fen*

where is the best place to park?
wo sollte ich am besten parken?
*voh **zoll**-te ikh am **bes**-ten **par**-ken*

how long for?
für wie lange?
*foor vee **lan**-ge*

the ticket machine doesn't work
der Automat funktioniert nicht
*der owto-**maht** foonk-tsyo-**neert** nikht*

*Avoid filling at motorway service stations, unless you have to, as petrol is much more expensive. A cheaper alternative when you are on the motorway is an **Autohof** (a trucker stop) which you find just off the motorway.*

petrol pumps

Benzin
petrol

bleifrei
unleaded

Diesel
diesel

Petrol price display.

car wash

Tanken Tag und Nacht
fill up day and night

water   air

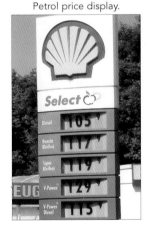

where is the nearest petrol station?
wo ist die nächste Tankstelle?
*voh ist dee **naykh**-ste **tank**-shtel-le*

...worth of unleaded petrol
für ... Bleifrei
*foor ... **bly**-fry*

a token for wash number...
einen Chip für Waschprogramm Nummer...
*ine-en chip foor **wash**-pro-gram **noo**mer...*

fill it up please
voll tanken bitte
*foll **tang**-ken **bi**-te*

pump number...
Säule Nummer...
zoy-le **noo**mer...

how much is that?
wie viel macht das?
vee feel makht das

talking

i Most repair shops are run by dealerships such as Audi, Ford, etc. However, there are some chains such as **Pit-Stop** which will do repairs while you wait.

exhaust — Auspuff
Bremsen — brakes
tyres — Reifen
Ölwechsel — oil change
shock absorbers — Stoßdämpfer

I have broken down
ich habe eine Panne
ikh hah-be ine-e pan-ne

the car won't start
das Auto springt nicht an
das owto shpringt nikht an

the battery is flat
die Batterie ist leer
dee ba-teree ist layr

I have a flat tyre
ich habe einen Platten
ikh hah-be ine-en plat-ten

I need new tyres
ich brauche neue Reifen
ikh brow-khe noy-e ry-fen

I have run out of petrol
ich habe kein Benzin mehr
ikh hah-be kayn bentseen mehr

where is the nearest garage?
wo ist die nächste Werkstatt?
voh ist dee naykh-ste verk-shtat

there is something wrong with...
es stimmt etwas nicht mit...
es shtimt et-vas nikht mit...

the ... is not working
der/die/das ... funktioniert nicht
der/dee/das ... foonk-tsyo-neert nikht

the ... are not working
die ... funktionieren nicht
dee ... foonk-tsyo-nee-ren nikht

can you repair it?
können Sie es reparieren?
kur'-nen zee es raypa-reeren

how long will it take?
wie lange wird das dauern?
vee lan-ge virt das dow-ern

when will it be ready?
wann ist es fertig?
van ist es fer-tikh

how much will it cost?
wie viel wird es kosten?
vee feel virt es kosten

can you replace the windscreen?
können Sie die Windschutzscheibe ersetzen?
kur'-nen zee dee vint-shoots-shy-be er-zetsen

please change...	**the oil**	**the water**	**the tyres**
bitte wechseln Sie...	das Öl	das Wasser	die Reifen
bi-te vek-seln zee...	*das ur'l*	*das vasser*	*dee ry-fen*

Berlin District

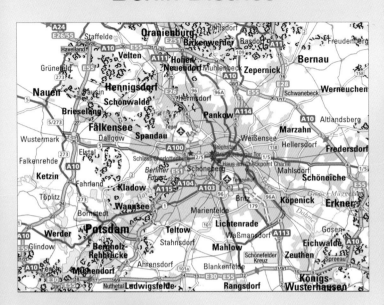

Motorway signs are blue and numbered.

end of priority road

diversion

Secondary roads signposted in yellow and local destinations in white.

E 36

A green sign with E and a number indicates that it is a European route.

Where you see this sign you must give way to the priority road. Drivers on the priority road must indicate when turning. Drivers on the top secondary road must yield to drivers on the bottom, as they are on their right. The yellow diamond indicates a priority road.

Speed restrictions

built up area	50km/h
ordinary roads	100km/h
motorway	no restriction, but 130km/h is recommended and some sections will have speed restrictions

Berlin City

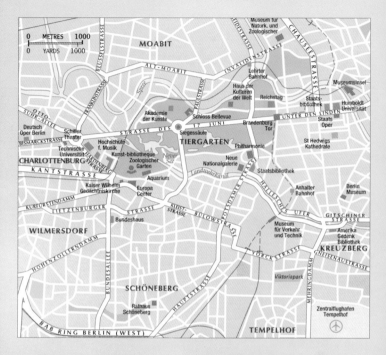

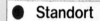

Standort

you are here

RECHTS

right

LINKS

left

town centre

Innenstadt

Rathaus — *town hall*

Polizei — *police station*

The numbers under the sign tell you the house numbers you can find.

cathedral   *old part of town*

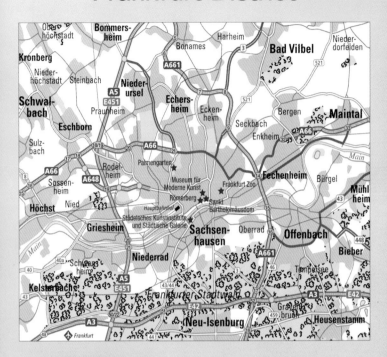

Motorway signs are in blue.
66 is the number
of the motorway.

This symbol
indicates the
exit number.

exit

Unlike German motorways, Austrian and
Swiss motorways are not free.

motorway

Autobahn

Austrian
motorway toll
sticker for sale
(valid for 10
days, 2 months
or one year).In
Switzerland you
buy a sticker
that is valid for
one year.

Vienna District

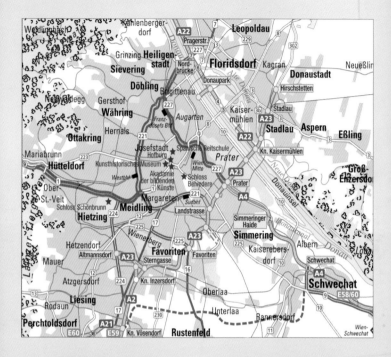

entrance (for vehicle)

exit (for vehicle)

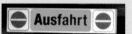

Fahrt comes from *fahren* ('to drive'), so *Einfahrt* and *Ausfahrt* are used on road signs. *Gang* comes from *gehen* ('to walk'), so you see *Eingang* and *Ausgang* on signs for pedestrians.

entrance

EINGANG

KEIN AUSGANG

no exit
Kein means 'no'

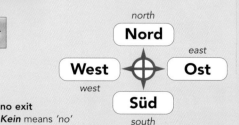

north
Nord

east

West ⊕ **Ost**

west

Süd
south

Shopping

*Shop opening hours are generally 9am or 10am to 6pm or 8pm (larger shops and department stores) Monday–Friday. On Saturday shops are usually open until 4pm. There is no Sunday opening (except in tourist areas where shops selling holiday items may be open). Petrol stations selling snacks, bread, drinks, etc, are open on Sundays. Baker's can also open on Sunday mornings. In most German towns there are weekly markets (**Wochenmarkt**), usually held on Saturday (and some-times another week day), where you can buy fresh local produce.*

butcher's

(**Metzgerei** is a southern German term
for butcher; see below)

cake shop

baker's

keywords keywords

Bäckerei
be-ke-rye
baker's

Metzgerei
mets-ge-rye
butcher's

Delikatessen
delicatessen
delicatessen

Lebensmittelladen
laybens-mittel-laden
grocer's

Konditorei
kon-dee-to-rye
cake shop

Supermarkt
sooper-markt
supermarket

Reformhaus
re-form-hows
health food

Netto is a brand of supermarket

butcher's

baker's

Lotto-Toto is a type of tobacconist's and newsagent's. They sell lottery tickets

insurance office

Tele Service Nord is a phone company

fruit & veg

Werbung & Schrift is an advertising agency

**traders' board at a
shopping centre**

(i) *Supermarkets are generally open from 8am–8pm Monday–Friday and 8am–4pm on Saturday. They are closed on Sundays. Most products are cheaper in supermarkets than in smaller shops; this includes film and tapes for camcorders. Supermarkets have a separate area for drinks and mineral waters, **Getränkemarkt**. Most bottles and carriers carry a deposit which you get back on returning them. It is not as common as in the UK to use your credit card in a supermarket. Most people pay by cash or debit card.*

You need coins to release your trolley. Watch out for kids wanting to offer you their trolley for the euro coins – they may have plastic coins inside which means you won't get your money back.

only
nur
means
only,
ab
means
from.

talking talking talking

where can I buy…?	**batteries**	**a tin-opener**
wo kann ich … kaufen?	Batterien	einen Dosenöffner
*voh kan ikh … **kow**fen*	*ba-te**ree**-en*	*ine-en **doh**zen-ur'fner*
do you have…?	**how much is that?**	
haben Sie…?	wie viel kostet das?	
hah-ben zee…	*vee feel **kos**tet das*	
I am looking for…	**a present**	**a good wine**
ich suche…	ein Geschenk	einen guten Wein
*ikh **zoo**-khe…*	*ine ge-**shenk***	*ine-en **goo**ten vine*
is there a market?	**which day?**	
gibt es hier einen Markt?	an welchem Tag?	
gipt es heer ine-en markt	*an **vel**-khem tahk*	
can I pay with this card?		
kann ich mit dieser Karte bezahlen?		
*kan ikh mit **dee**-zer **kar**-te be-**tsah**len*		

*Quantities are expressed in kilos and grams. A **Pfund** (meaning pound) is frequently used in markets and shops but it refers to half a kilo, or 500g, rather than an Imperial pound. In everyday talk, **ein Pfund** and **ein halbes Pfund** are often preferred to 500g (**fünfhundert Gramm**) and 250g (**zweihundertfünfzig Gramm**). Just keep in mind that it is slightly more than our pound and half pound, and much easier to say than the metric equivalent.*

Sausages are sold either by the piece and weighed, for instance liversausage; in slices (for sliceable sausages); or in pairs (such as frankfurters).

Cheese is sold either by the piece or by the packet.

Vegetables are sold by the kilo, individually (cauliflower) or by the bunch (radishes).

Look out for the words **biolog.** indicating organic. It is an abbreviation for **biologisch**.

aus eigenem biolog. dyn. Anbau — artichokes grown on our own organic farm

Artischocken — *frisch und zart* — fresh and tender

kg nur 3,70 — only 3,70 euro per kg

Fruit is sold by the kilo, individually (e.g. kiwi, grapefruit) or by the punnet when in season (e.g. strawberries and cherries).

 talking talking talking talking talking talking talking

a piece of that cheese
ein Stück von diesem Käse
*ine shtook fon **dee**-zem **kay**-ze*

a little more
etwas mehr
***et**-vas mehr*

a little less
etwas weniger
***et**-vas **veh**-ni-ger*

that's fine thanks
das reicht danke
*das rykht **dang**-ke*

10 slices of ham
zehn Scheiben Schinken
*tsayn **shy**-ben **shin**-ken*

thick slices
dicke Scheiben
***dee**-ke **shy**-ben*

thin slices
dünne Scheiben
***doo**-ne **shy**-ben*

a carton of milk
einen Karton Milch
*ine-en kar-**ton** milkh*

a bottle of mineral water
eine Flasche Mineralwasser
*ine-e **fla**-she mineral-vasser*

still	**fizzy**
still	sprudelnd
shtill	***shproo**delnd*

a tin of...	**a roll of...**
eine Dose...	eine Rolle...
*ine-e **doh**-ze...*	*ine-e **rol**-le...*

a jar of...	**a bottle of...**
ein Glas...	eine Flasche...
ine glahs...	*ine-e **fla**-she...*

a packet of...
ein Päckchen...
*ine-**pek**-khen...*

that is everything thanks
das ist alles danke
*das ist **al**-les **dang**-ke*

Graubrot, one of the most popular of the many types of bread.

Kann Spuren von anderen Nüssen, Erdnüssen und Weizeneiweiß enthalten.

may contain traces of nuts, peanuts and wheat protein

**Nährwertangaben:
100 ml zubereitete Sächs.
Kartoffel-suppe enthalten
durchschnittlich:**
nutritional info: 100 ml prepared product contains on average:

kjoules—	**Kilojoule (kJ)**	**111**
calories—	**Kilokalorien (kcal)**	**26**
protein—	**Eiweiß**	**0,7g**
carbohydrates—	**Kohlenhydrate**	**5,6g**
fat—	**Fett**	**0,1g**

Indicates a product is organic. Also look out for **Öko**.

gluten-free product

symbol for a vegetarian product

also micro-waveable

Here is a list of basic foodstuffs you might need.

Everyday Foods Lebensmittel *lay*bens-mittel

biscuits die Kekse *kayk*-se
bread das Brot *broht*
bread roll das Brötchen *brur't*-khen
bread (sliced) das Brot in Scheiben
  broht in *shy*-ben
butter die Butter *boo*-ter
cereal die Cornflakes *corn*-flakes
cheese der Käse *kay*-ze
chicken das Hühnchen *hoohn*-khen
coffee der Kaffee *ka*fay
cream die Sahne *zah*-ne
cream cheese der Frischkäse
  frish-kay-ze
crisps die Chips *chips*
eggs die Eier *eye*-er
fish der Fisch *fish*
flour das Mehl *mehl*
ham (cooked) der gekochte Schinken
  ge-*kokh*-te *shin*-ken
ham (cured) der rohe Schinken
  roh-e *shin*-ken
herbal tea der Kräutertee *kroy*-ter-tay
honey der Honig *hoh*-nikh
jam die Marmelade mar-me-*lah*-de

juice der Saft *zaft*
margarine die Margarine margah-*ree*-ne
marmalade die Orangenmarmelade
  oronjen-mar-me-*lah*-de
meat das Fleisch *flysh*
milk die Milch *milkh*
mustard der Senf *zenf*
oil das Öl *ur'l*
orange juice der Orangensaft
  o*ron*jen-zaft
pasta die Nudeln *noo*-deln
pepper der Pfeffer *pfef*-fer
rice der Reis *rice*
salt das Salz *zalts*
sausage die Wurst *woorst*
sugar der Zucker *tsoo*-ker
stock cubes die Brühwürfel
  broo-voor-fel
tea der Tee *tay*
tomatoes (tin) die Dosentomaten
  *doh*zen-tomah-ten
tuna der Tunfisch *toon*fish
vinegar der Essig *es*-sikh
yoghurt der Jogurt *yo*-goort

Vegetables Gemüse *ge-moo-se*

artichokes die Artischocken
  *arti-**sho**-ken*

aubergines die Auberginen
  *ohber-**jee**-nen*

asparagus der Spargel *shpar-gel*

carrots die Möhren *mur'h-ren*

cauliflower der Blumenkohl
  ***bloo**-men-kohl*

celery der Sellerie *ze-le-ree*

courgettes die Zucchini *tsoo-**ki**-ni*

cucumber die Gurke *goor-ke*

french beans die grünen Bohnen
  *groo-nen **bohnen***

garlic der Knoblauch *knohp-lowkh*

leeks der Porree *po-ray*

lettuce der Salat *za-laht*

mushrooms die Pilze *pil-tse*

onions die Zwiebeln *tswee-beln*

peas die Erbsen *erp-sen*

peppers die Paprika *pa-pri-ka*

potatoes die Kartoffeln *kar-tof-feln*

radishes die Radieschen *radees-khen*

spinach der Spinat
  *shpi-**naht***

spring onions die
  Frühlingszwiebeln
  froo-lings-tswee-beln

tomatoes die Tomaten *to-mah-ten*

turnip die Steckrübe *shtek-roo-be*

Fruit Obst *obst*

apples die Äpfel *ep-fel*

apricots die Aprikosen *apree-
  kohzen*

bananas die Bananen *ba-**nah**-nen*

cherries die Kirschen *kir-shen*

figs die Feigen *fy-gen*

grapefruit die Grapefruit *grape-fruit*

grapes die Trauben *trow-ben*

lemon die Zitrone *tsitroh-ne*

melon die Melone *me-loh-ne*

nectarines die Nektarinen
  *nekta-**ree**-nen*

oranges die Orangen *oronjen*

peaches die Pfirsiche *pfeer-zi-khe*

pears die Birnen *bir-nen*

pineapple die Ananas *ana-nas*

plums die Pflaumen *pflow-men*

raspberries die Himbeeren
  him-beh-ren

OBST / GEMÜSE
Karin Ohler

strawberries die
Erdbeeren *ert-beh-ren*

watermelon die
Wassermelone *vasser-
me-loh-ne*

There are a number of good German department stores – such as **Kaufhof**, **Karstadt** and **Hertie**. Department stores are generally open from about 9am–8pm Monday–Friday and 9am–4pm on Saturday.

changing rooms

EG *Untergeschoss* basement

UG *Erdgeschoss* ground floor

1.OG
1. Obergeschoss first floor

LEBENSMITTEL — food
BÜCHER — books
SPORT·REITEN·GOLF — sport / riding / golf

Sign indicating a reduction on men's shoes.

alterations

cash desk

keywords keywords keywords keywords

which floor is the...?
auf welcher Etage ist...?
owf vel-kher eta-zhe ist...

lingerie
die Unterwäsche
dee oonter-ve-she

food department
die Lebensmittelabteilung
dee laybens-mittel-ap-ty-loong

shoe department
die Schuhabteilung
dee shoo-ap-ty-loong

talking

Women's clothes sizes

UK/Australia	8	10	12	14	16	18	20	22
Europe	36	38	40	42	44	46	48	50
US/Canada	6	8	10	12	14	16	18	20

Men's clothes sizes (suits)

UK/US/Canada	36	38	40	42	44	46
Europe	46	48	50	52	54	56
Australia	92	97	102	107	112	117

Shoes

UK/Australia	2	3	4	5	6	7	8	9	10	11
Europe	35	36	37	38	39	41	42	43	45	46
US/Canada women	4	5	6	7	8	9	10	11	12	-
US/Canada men	3	4	5	6	7	8	9	10	11	12

Children's Shoes

UK/US/Canada	0	1	2	3	4	5	6	7	8	9	10	11
Europe	15	17	18	19	20	22	23	24	26	27	28	29

talking talking

do you have size...?
haben Sie Größe...?
*hah-ben zee **grur'**-se...*

do you have this in my size?
haben Sie das in meiner Größe?
*hah-ben zee das in **mine**-er **grur'**-se*

it is too big
es ist zu groß
es ist tsoo grohs

I need a smaller/larger size
ich brauche eine kleinere/größere Größe
*ikh **brow**-khe ine-e **kline**-e-re/**grur'**-se-re **grur'**-se*

do you have a smaller/larger size?
haben Sie eine kleinere/größere Größe?
*hah-ben zee ine-e **kline**-e-re/**grur'**-se-re **grur'**-se*

do you have this in...?
haben Sie das in...?
hah-ben zee das in...

shoe size...
Schuhgröße...
*shoo-**grur'**-se...*

I take size...
ich habe Größe...
*ikh **hah**-be **grur'**-se...*

it is too small
es ist zu klein
es ist tsoo kline

black/brown
schwarz/braun
shwarts/brown

other colours
anderen Farben
*an-deren **far**-ben*

You can buy stamps at the post office counter or from the machines that are usually found there. Post office opening hours are 8am–6pm Monday–Friday and 8am–2pm on Saturday. There is no first and second class postage in Germany. The website of the German post-office www.deutschepost.de also has information in English.

The word **Postbank** indicates there is a post office savings bank in the post office.

Postboxes are yellow. Collection times are marked. The red dot indicates a Sunday collection. The

Post Office logo

box should also list the nearest postbox (**nächster Briefkasten**) with different collection times.

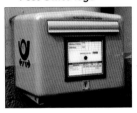

Slot for letters.

---

where is the post office?
wo ist die Post?
voh ist dee post

do you have stamps?
haben Sie Briefmarken?
hah-ben zee breef-marken

10 stamps please
zehn Briefmarken bitte
tsayn breef-marken bi-te

for postcards
für Postkarten
foor post-kar-ten

for letters
für Briefe
foor bree-fe

to Britain
nach Großbritannien
nakh grohs-bri-Tan-ee-en

to America
nach Amerika
nakh a-me-rika

to Australia
nach Australien
nakh owstra-lee-en

I want to send this registered...
ich möchte das eingeschrieben schicken...
ikh mur'kh-te das ine-ge-shreeben shi-ken...

I want to send this parcel...
ich möchte dieses Paket schicken...
ich mur'kh-te dee-zes pa-keht shi-ken...

fast mail
per Express
per eks-press

surface mail
auf dem Landweg
owf dem lant-vehk

airmail
per Luftpost
per looft-post

talking talking talking

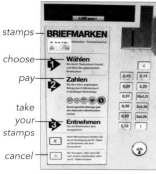

A standard letter within Europe up to 20g costs 0.55€, a postcard costs 0.45€.

stamps — **BRIEFMARKEN**

choose — **Wählen**

pay — **Zahlen**

take your stamps — **Entnehmen**

cancel

The drug-store is a cheaper place to get photos developed than a photographic shop (but may take longer).

keywords

Film
film
film

Batterie
ba-teree
battery

matt
matt
matt

Hochglanz
hokh-glants
glossy

Dias
dee-as
slides

Digitalkamera
dee-gee-tahl-kam-era
digital camera

Stamp for (standard) postcard within Europe.

Stamps for standard letter within Europe.

where can I buy film?
wo kann ich einen Film kaufen?
voh kan ikh ine-en film kowfen

a colour film
einen Farbfilm
ine-en farp-film

a slide film
ein Diafilm
ine dee-a-film

with ... pictures
mit ... Bildern
mit ... bil-dern

24
vierundzwanzig
feer-oont-tsvan-tsikh

tapes for this camcorder
Bänder für diesen Camcorder
ben-der foor dee-zen camcorder

36
sechsunddreißig
zekhs-oont-dry-sikh

can you develop this film?
können Sie diesen Film entwickeln?
kur'-nen zee dee-zen film ent-vikeln

can you take a picture of us?
können Sie ein Foto von uns machen?
kur'-nen zee ine foto fon oons makhen

when will the photos be ready?
wann sind die Fotos fertig?
van zint dee fotos fer-tikh

can we film here?
können wir hier filmen?
kur'-nen veer heer fil-men

Phones

*Coin phones are not easily found. The majority of phone boxes operate with phonecards (**Telefonkarte**) which you can buy at the post office, newsagents' and telecommunications shops. There are numerous private phone companies operating each with their own cheap rates using a system of dialling prefixes.*

card-operated
phone

card-phone symbol

Important numbers
are displayed
inside phone boxes
and emergency
calls are free.

do you have phonecards?
haben Sie Telefonkarten?
*hah-ben zee taylay-**fon**-kar-ten*

a phonecard please
eine Telefonkarte bitte
*ine-e taylay-**fon**-kar-te **bi**-te*

Mr Meier please
Herrn Meier bitte
*hayrn **mei**-er bi-te*

extension...
Apparat Nummer...
*apa-**raht** noomer...*

can I speak to Paul?
kann ich bitte Paul sprechen?
*kan ikh **bi**-te paul **shpre**-khen*

this is Caroline
hier ist Caroline
heer ist Caroline

can I have an outside line please?
kann ich bitte eine Amtsleitung bekommen?
*kan ikh **bi**-te ine-e **amts**-ly-toong be-**kom**men*

I'd like to make a reverse charge call
ich möchte ein R-Gespräch anmelden
*ikh **mur'kh**-te ine **er**-ge-shpraykh **an**-mel-den*

what is your phone number?
wie ist Ihre Telefonnummer?
*vee ist **ee**-re taylay-**fon**-noomer*

my phone number is...
meine Telefonnummer ist...
*mine-e taylay-**fon**-noomer ist...*

talking talking talking talking talking

keywords keywords keywords

Telefonkarte
*taylay-**fon**-kar-te*
phonecard

Handy
*han*dy
mobile

Vorwahl
for-vahl
code

Auskunft
ows-koonft
directory
enquiries

Telefonbuch
*taylay-**fon**-bookh*
phone book

Gelbe Seiten
gel-be **zye**-ten
yellow pages

Vermittlung
*fer-**mitt**-loong*
operator

back of a
phonecard
Like other
items in
Germany,
phonecards
are recycled.
Dispose of
used ones in
a slot below
the phone in call boxes; they are
collected and the chips reused.

Freecall is the
equivalent to the
UK's Freephone
and begins with
0800.

yellow pages

phone book

Coin-operated
phones are
becoming
increasingly
rare.

---

talking

I will call back...
ich rufe ... zurück
*ikh **roo**-fe ... tsoo**rook***

later
später
*sphay*ter

tomorrow
morgen
*mor*gen

do you have a mobile?
haben Sie ein Handy?
*hah-ben zee ine **han**dy*

which network are you on?
bei welchem Netzbetreiber sind Sie?
*by **vel**-khem **nets**-be-tryber zint zee*

what is your mobile number?
wie ist Ihre Handynummer?
*vee ist **ee**-re **han**dy-noomer*

my mobile number is...
meine Handynummer ist...
*mine-e **han**dy-noomer ist...*

E-mail, Internet, Fax

> You will be able to find an internet café in most big cities.
> The most common internet service providers are T-Online and AOL.
> German websites end in *.de* for **Deutschland**.

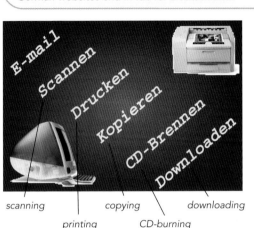

scanning

printing

copying

CD-burning

downloading

Some bookshops now have internet cafés.

what is your e-mail address?
wie ist Ihre E-Mail-Adresse?
*vee ist **ee**-re **ee**-mail-a**dres**-se*

my e-mail address is...
meine E-Mail-Adresse ist...
*mine-e **ee**-mail-a**dres**-se ist...*

caroline.smith@anycompany.co.uk
caroline.smith@anycompany.co.uk
caroline poonkt smith at anycompany poonkt tsay oh poonkt oo kah

can I send an e-mail?
kann ich eine E-Mail schicken?
*kan ikh ine-e **ee**-mail **shi**-ken*

did you get my e-mail?
haben Sie meine E-Mail bekommen?
*hah-ben zee mine-e **ee**-mail be-**kom**men*

can I send and receive e-mail here?
kann ich hier E-Mails schicken und erhalten?
*kan ikh heer **ee**-mails **shi**-ken oont er-halten*

how much does an hour of netsurfing cost?
wie viel kostet eine Stunde Internet-Surfen?
*vee feel **kos**tet ine-e **shtoon**-de internet-**surfen***

talking talking

Schreiben
shry-ben
compose

Zurück
tsoo-rook
back

Vor
for
forward

Neu laden
noy lah-den
reload

Anfang
an-fang
home

Suchen
zoo-khen
search

Lesezeichen
lay-ze-tsy-khen
bookmark

Sicherheit
zikher-hite
security

pocket-money surfing

for pupils and students

3 € per hour

National and local tourist and what's-on information can be accessed via the internet.

I want to send a fax
ich möchte ein Fax schicken
ikh mur'kh-te ine faks shi-ken

can I send a fax from here?
kann ich von hier ein Fax schicken?
kan ikh fon heer ine faks shi-ken

how much is it to send a fax?
was kostet es, ein Fax zu schicken?
vas kostet es ine faks tsoo shi-ken

what is your fax number?
wie ist Ihre Faxnummer?
vee ist ee-re faks-noomer

I am trying to send a fax
ich versuche, ein Fax zu schicken
ikh fer-zoo-khe ine faks tsoo shi-ken

do you have a fax?
haben Sie ein Fax?
hah-ben zee ine faks

can I receive a fax here?
kann ich hier ein Fax erhalten?
kan ikh heer ine faks er-hal-ten

it has ... pages
es hat ... Seiten
es hat ... zye-ten

please confirm your number
bitte bestätigen Sie Ihre Nummer
bi-te be-shtay-ti-gen zee ee-re noomer

did you get my fax?
haben Sie mein Fax bekommen?
hah-ben zee mine faks be-kommen

Out & About

*Monday is not a good day for sightseeing, as most places such as museums and art galleries are generally closed on Mondays. If you are going to a city with lots of tourist attractions, look out for tickets that allow you multiple entry. Tourist offices organise city walks (**Stadtrundgänge**) and there are also city bus tours (**Stadtrundfahrten**).*

Tourist Offices are generally open 9am–6pm Monday–Friday and Saturday mornings. In smaller places opening hours may be restricted.

Information about the city walk and bus tour.

VERKEHRSBÜRO WIESBADEN

STADTRUNDGÄNGE

April - Oktober: jeden Samstag 10.00 Uhr
November - März: jeden 1. und 3. Samstag im Monat 10.00 Uhr

Dauer: ca. 1,5 Stunden
Kosten: DM 10,00 Erwachsene
DM 6,00 Kinder bis 12 Jahre
DM 6,00 Kurgäste

STADTRUNDFAHRTEN

ganzjährig: Mittwoch 14.30 Uhr
Samstag 14.00 Uhr

Dauer: ca. 2 Stunden
Kosten: DM 20,00 Erwachsene
DM 10,00 Kinder bis 12 Jahre
DM 15,00 Kurgäste

Gerne arbeitet das Verkehrsbüro Wiesbaden auch maßgeschneiderte Programme und Tagesfahrten für Gruppen aus.

buy your tickets here

KARTEN HIER ERHÄLTLICH!

ÖFFNUNGSZEITEN

DI~So   1.4~30.9.
9⁰⁰~18⁰⁰

DI~So   1.10~31.3.
10⁰⁰~16⁰⁰

Montags geschlossen

closed on Mondays

Museum sign showing opening hours.

Sign for a listed building.

keywords keywords keywords keywords

Stadthalle
shtat-hal-le
civic hall

Ausstellung
ows-shte-loong
exhibition

Wanderweg
van-der-vehk
trek, ramble

Weinprobe
vine-proh-be
wine tasting

Kirmes
kir-mes
funfair

Kirche
kir-khe
church

Dom
dome
cathedral

Schloss
shloss
castle

Rathaus
raht-hows
town hall

city sign

Ticket for the Munich Pinakothek Art Gallery.

Kunsthalle Art Gallery

talking talking talking

excuse me, where is the tourist office?
entschuldigen Sie, wo ist die Touristeninformation?
entshool-di-gen zee voh ist dee tooristen-infor-ma-tsyohn

do you have...?
haben Sie...?
hah-ben zee...

a map of the town
einen Stadtplan
ine-en shtat-plan

leaflets in English
Broschüren in Englisch
bro-shoo-ren in eng-lish

we want to visit...
wir möchten ... besuchen
veer mur'kh-ten ... be-zookhen

how do we get there?
wie kommen wir dorthin?
vee kommen veer dort-hin

when can we visit...?
wann können wir ... besuchen?
van kur'-nen veer ... be-zoo-khen

when does it close?
wann ist es geschlossen?
van ist es ge-shlos-sen

is there a city walk?
gibt es einen Stadtrundgang?
gipt es ine-en shtat-roont-gang

is there a city bus tour?
gibt es eine Stadtrundfahrt?
gipt es ine-e shtat-roont-fahrt

i

*There are many outdoor swimming pools open in the summer. Look out for the word **Freibad**. You can also swim in the many lakes. There are tourist resorts along the Baltic and North Sea. As in other areas of German life, there are a number of rules to observe.*

a sign along the sand dunes

Textil means you must wear a costume (no nudist bathing)

no windsurfing

next crossing point this way is 16/6

this crossing point is number 4. It is suitable for wheelchairs

emergency numbers

there are no lifeguards on this section of the beach

dogs are allowed on this beach

next crossing point this way is 3a/

please keep the beach tidy!

do not walk on the dunes!

where can we...?	**play tennis**	**play golf**
wo können wir...?	Tennis spielen	Golf spielen
*voh **kur'**-nen veer...*	*tennis **shpee**-len*	*golf **shpee**-len*
how much is it...?	**to hire mountain bikes**	**to go fishing**
was kostet es...?	Mountainbikes zu mieten	zu angeln
*vas **kos**tet es...*	*moun**tain**-bikes tsoo **mee**ten*	*tsoo **ang**eln*
per hour/per day	**can we hire equipment?**	
pro Stunde/pro Tag	können wir die Ausrüstung mieten?	
*pro **shtoon**-de/pro tahk*	*kur'-nen veer dee **ows**-roostoong **mee**ten*	

is there a swimming pool?	**is it dangerous to swim here?**
gibt es hier ein Schwimmbad?	ist das Baden hier gefährlich?
*gipt es heer ine **shwim**-baht*	*ist das **bah**-den heer ge-**fayr**-likh*

where can we go...?	**windsurfing**	**waterskiing**
wo können wir...?	surfen	Wasserski fahren
*voh **kur'**-nen veer...*	*surfen*	*vasser-shee **fah**-ren*

how do we hire a beach hut?
wie können wir einen Strandkorb mieten?
*vee **kur'**-nen veer ine-en shtrant-korb **mee**-ten*

talking talking

You can hire a beach hut. You will be given a key with a number corresponding to the hut. The huts are good at keeping out a chill wind.

Sign indicating nudist bathing is allowed.

Bike route following a wine theme through a wine-growing area.

hiking-path sign

Poster advertising a football match.

Plan of a football stadium.

Haupttribüne *main stand*

Sitztribüne Nord *seating stand north*

Stehtribüne Süd *standing stand south*

Gegengerade *far stand*

Gästeblock *guest area*

we'd like to go to a football match
wir möchten ein Fußballspiel sehen
*veer **mur'kh**-ten ine **foos**ball-shpeel **zay**-en*

where can we get tickets?
wo können wir Tickets bekommen?
*voh **kur'**-nen veer **t**ickets be-**kom**men*

how do we get to the stadium?
wie kommen wir zum Stadion?
*vee **kom**men veer tsoom **shtah**-dee-ohn*

who is playing?
wer spielt?
ver shpeelt

how much are the tickets?
was kosten die Tickets?
*vas **kos**ten dee **t**ickets*

what time is the match?
wann fängt das Spiel an?
van fengt das shpeel an

Accommodation

The German Tourist Office has brochures showing all private and hotel accommodation in their area. They will be able to advise and find the particular type of accommodation you are after.

Pension
Similar to a Hotel Garni.

HOTEL
— GARNI —
☎ 06326 / 708 - 0

Hotel Garni
This is usually a smaller hotel offering bed & breakfast prices. In other hotels, breakfast is not always included in the price.

Haus Sonnblick
Gasthof Laschitz

Gasthof Löffler
Komfortzimmer

Gasthof
This is usually a pub or winebar with guestrooms. **Gasthofs** are usually a good-value option.

Booking in advance

The German Tourist Board in your country will be able to send you brochures about the area you want to visit, listing the different types of accommodation available. When you have chosen a place, you can either contact them direct or through the German Tourist Board.

I would like to book a room
ich möchte ein Zimmer buchen
ikh mur'kh-te ine tsimmer boo-khen

a single/a double
ein Einzelzimmer/Doppelzimmer
ine ine-tsel-tsimmer/dop-pel-tsimmer

for ... nights
für ... Nächte
foor ... nekh-te

from ... to...
vom ... bis...
fom ... bis...

I will fax to confirm
ich schicke ein Fax zur Bestätigung
ikh shi-ke ine faks tsoor be-shtay-tigoong

my name is...
mein Name ist...
mine nah-me ist...

my credit card number is...
meine Kreditkartennummer ist...
mine-e kre-deet-kar-ten-noomer ist...

my phone number is...
meine Telefonnummer ist...
mine-e taylay-fon-noomer ist...

Hotel Garni

Hotel rates for different types of rooms.

Preisliste — *price list*
gültig ab 01. Januar — *valid from 1 Jan*

Typ *grade*	Belegung *use of room*	€ pro Tag ohne Frühstück	€ pro Tag mit Frühstück
A I	Doppel	€ 85 -	€ 102 -
	Einzel	€ 72 -	€ 79 -
A II	Doppel	€ 77 -	€ 92 -
	Einzel	€ 62 -	€ 69 -
B	Doppel	€ 69 -	€ 84 -
	Einzel	€ 56 -	€ 64 -
C	Doppel	€ 62 -	€ 91 -
	Einzel	€ 51 -	€ 62 -

euro pro Tag — euro per day

ohne Frühstück — without breakfast

mit Frühstück — with breakfast

Typ *grade*
Belegung *use of room*
Doppel *double*
Einzel *single*

---

do you have a room for tonight?
haben Sie ein Zimmer für heute Nacht?
hah-ben zee ine tsimmer foor hoy-te nakht

a single room	**a double room**	**a family room**
ein Einzelzimmer	ein Doppelzimmer	ein Familienzimmer
ine ine-tsel-tsimmer	*ine dop-pel-tsimmer*	*ine famee-lee-en-tsimmer*

with ensuite bath
mit Bad
mit baht

with shower
mit Dusche
mit doo-she

for tonight	**for one night**	**for ... nights**
für heute Nacht	für eine Nacht	für ... Nächte
foor hoy-te nakht	*foor ine-e nakht*	*foor ... nekh-te*

how much is it?
wie viel kostet es?
vee feel kostet es

is breakfast included?
ist das Frühstück inbegriffen?
ist das froo-shtook in-be-grif-fen

how much is half board?
wie viel kostet Halbpension?
vee feel kostet halp-pensyon

how much is full board?
wie viel kostet Vollpension?
vee feel kostet foll-pensyon

can I see the room?
kann ich das Zimmer ansehen?
kan ikh das tsimmer an-zay-en

what time should we check out?
wann sollen wir auschecken?
van zol-len veer ows-tshe-ken

talking talking talking

holiday flat

The local tourist office will have a brochure listing all private and hotel accommodation in their area.

reception

Where you see a sign for holiday accommodation you can go in and ask what is available.

self-catering holiday house

vacancies

rooms

no vacancies

bed & bike

This is a scheme run by the German Bicycle Club (ADFC) which can coordinate accommodation on cycling tours.

rooms

keywords keywords keywords

Geschirrspülmittel
*ge-**shir**-shpool-mittel*
washing-up liquid

Waschmittel
vash-mit-tel
washing powder

Seife
zay-fe
soap

Dosenöffner
doh-zen-ur'fner
tin-opener

Kerzen
ker-tsen
candles

Streichhölzer
shtraykh-hur'l-tser
matches

Gasbehälter
gas-be-hel-ter
gas cylinder

Sicherungen
zikh-eroon-gen
fuses

Wäscherei
ve-she-rye
laundry service

symbol for German Youth Hostel

German youth hostels welcome everyone – you don't have to be a member, though members of the international youth hostel association pay a reduced rate.

sign to a local youth hostel

talking talking talking

there is/are no...
es gibt kein/keine...
es gipt kine/kine-e...

can you show us how this works?
bitte zeigen Sie uns, wie das funktioniert?
*bi-te **tsy**-gen zee oons vee das foonk-tsyo-**neert***

how does ... work?
wie funktioniert...?
*vee foonk-tsyo-**neert**...*

the cooker
der Herd
der hert

the dishwasher
der Geschirrspüler
*der ge-**shir**-shpoo-ler*

the washing machine
die Waschmaschine
*dee **vash**-ma-shee-ne*

the microwave
die Mikrowelle
*dee **mee**kro-vel-le*

who do I contact if there are problems?
an wen wende ich mich bei Problemen?
*an ven **ven**-de ikh mikh by pro-**bleh**-men*

when is the rubbish collected?
wann wird der Müll abgeholt?
*van virt der mooll **ap**-geholt*

where do we leave the rubbish?
wo tun wir den Müll hin?
voh toon veer den mooll hin

can you give us an extra set of keys?
können Sie uns noch einen Satz Schlüssel geben?
*kur'-nen zee oons nokh ine-en sats **shloo**-sel **gay**ben*

Campingplatz is a campsite with facilities. *Wohnmobilstellplatz* is a parking site for caravans where you can stay overnight, fill your water tanks and empty your toilet but usually don't have facilities such as showers. *Entsorgungsstation* is a dump station.

road sign for a campsite

campsite sign

is there a campsite near here?
gibt es hier in der Nähe einen Campingplatz?
gipt es heer in der nay-e ine-en kamping-plats

have you any vacancies?
haben Sie freie Plätze?
hah-ben zee fry-e plet-se

we want to stay for ... nights
wir möchten ... Nächte bleiben
veer mur'kh-ten ... nekh-te bly-ben

how much is it?
wie viel kostet es?
vee feel kostet es

per tent
pro Zelt
pro tselt

per caravan
pro Wohnwagen
pro vohn-vahgen

where are...?
wo sind...?
voh zint...

the showers
die Duschen
dee doo-shen

the toilets
die Toiletten
dee twa-le-ten

is there a restaurant on the campsite?
gibt es ein Restaurant auf dem Campingplatz?
gipt es ine restoh-rong owf dem kamping-plats

where can I empty the chemical toilet?
wo kann ich die chemische Toilette entsorgen?
voh kan ikh dee khe-mishe twa-le-te ent-zor-gen

can we camp here overnight?
können wir hier über Nacht campen?
kur'-nen veer heer oober nakht kampen

talking talking talking

launderette services

complete dry-cleaning — Vollreinigung

household - linen washing — Haushaltwäsche-annahme

carpet cleaning — Teppichreinigung

leather cleaning — Lederreinigung

we offer — Unser Angebot

shoe repairs — Schuh-Reparatur

alterations — Änderungsschneiderei

carpet-cleaner rental — Ausleih von Geräten zur Teppichreinigung

launderette

inc. washing powder

inkl. WASCHPULVER

Collection point for dry-cleaning and laundry service.

ANNAHMESTELLE
FÜR REINIGUNG U. WÄSCHEREI
HERBORN

where is the nearest launderette?
wo ist der nächste Waschsalon?
*voh ist der **naykh**-ste **vash**-salong*

where can I do some washing?
wo kann ich hier Wäsche waschen?
*voh kan ikh heer **ve**-she **va**shen*

can I have my laundry washed here?
kann ich hier Wäsche waschen lassen?
*kan ikh heer **ve**-she **va**shen **las**sen*

where is the nearest dry-cleaner?
wo ist die nächste Reinigung?
*voh ist dee **naykh**-ste **rye**-nee-goong*

how does this work?
wie funktioniert das?
*vee foonk-tsyo-**neert** das*

can I borrow an iron?
kann ich ein Bügeleisen borgen?
*kan ikh ine **boo**gel-eye-zen **bor**-gen*

when will my things be ready?
wann sind meine Sachen fertig?
*van zint **mine**-e **zakh**-en **fer**tikh*

talking

Special Needs

*Facilities are generally good for the disabled. There is wheelchair access almost everywhere. On the trains you can call 01805 512 512 to arrange in advance help with getting on and off trains and changing trains. At the station speak to the **Service Point**. They will arrange help for you. All long-distance trains have places and toilets for wheelchair-bound passengers.*

Parking space for disabled.

this symbol is generally used to show facilities for the disabled

Button to press to have the floor of the bus or tram lowered.

Lift for the disabled.

Disabled seat symbol on public transport.

are there any disabled toilets?
gibt es hier Toiletten für Behinderte?
gipt es heer twa-le-ten foor be-hin-der-te

is there a wheelchair-accessible entrance?
gibt es einen Eingang für Rollstuhlfahrer?
gipt es ine-en ine-gang foor roll-shtool-fahrer

is it possible to visit ... with a wheelchair?
kann man ... im Rollstuhl besuchen?
kan man ... im roll-shtool be-zookhen

is there a reduction for the disabled?
gibt es Ermäßigung für Behinderte?
gipt es er-may-sigoong foor be-hin-der-te

I need a bedroom on the ground floor
ich brauche ein Zimmer im Erdgeschoss
ikh brow-khe ine tsimmer im ert-geshoss

I use a wheelchair
ich sitze im Rollstuhl
ikh zit-se im roll-shtool

where is the lift?
wo ist der Aufzug?
voh ist der owf-tsook

talking talking

With Kids

i School in Germany starts at 8am so children go to bed quite early. Very young children (generally under 5) travel free on public transport and pay half price up to 14 (but check with the local operator). Children must use a booster seat in the car if under 12 and under 1.5m in height. Children under 12 cannot travel in the front seat of the car.

Kinderteller
kin-der-**tel**-ler
child's portion

Kindersitz
kin-der-sits
baby seat

Kinderstuhl
kin-der-shtool
high chair

Kinderbett
kin-der-bett
cot

Spielplatz
shpeel-plats
play park

Windeln
vin-deln
nappies

Play park for children under 12 years.

Mother and child changing room.

tokens for using this facility are available from the children's clothing cash desk or at 'Le Buffet'.

is there a baby changing room?
gibt es hier einen Wickelraum?
gipt es heer ine-en **vi**kel-rowm

where can I change the baby?
wo kann ich das Baby wickeln?
voh kan ikh das **ba**by **vik**-eln

do you have...?
haben Sie...?
hah-ben zee...

a high chair
einen Kinderstuhl
ine-en **kin**-der-shtool

a cot
ein Kinderbett
ine **kin**-der-bett

do you sell nappies?
verkaufen Sie Windeln?
fer-**kow**fen zee **vin**-deln

baby wipes
Babytücher
baby-tookher

baby food
Babynahrung
baby-nahroong

is there a children's menu?
gibt es eine Karte für Kinder?
gipt es ine-e **kar**-te foor **kin**-der

a small portion
eine kleine Portion
ine-e **kline**-e port-**syon**

is there a play park near here?
gibt es hier in der Nähe einen Spielplatz?
gipt es heer in der **nay**-e ine-en **shpeel**-plats

Health

*The E111 (health insurance) form has been replaced by a new European Health Insurance card. Apply at the post office or online at **www.dh.gov.uk** to make sure you're covered. For minor ailments, ask the pharmacist for advice. You can consult a specialist for a reasonable price without a doctor's referral.*

sign for the pharmacy
If you know roughly what is wrong with you, speak to a pharmacist. They can help with advising treatment.

HIRSCH
APOTHEKE

Rota for the duty chemist shows which chemist is open.

NOTDIENST
DER APOTHEKEN

MO	COSMOS-APOTHEKE Dotzheimer Str. 14-16 Tel. 303470	PARACELSUS-APOTHEKE Schulthreidter 32 a Tel. 502729
DI	DAIMLER-APOTHEKE Daimlerstr. 20 Tel. 421602	WELLRITZ-APOTHEKE Schwalbacher Str. 50 Tel. 409565
MI	APOTHEKE AM SÜDBAHNHOF Didierstr 6 A Tel. 66306	APOTHEKE IM RAD Dotzheimer Str. 150 Tel. 444885
DO	KUR-APOTHEKE A. d. Quellen 1 Tel. 306331	APOTHEKE AM SEDANPLATZ Sedangelat 7 Tel. 400114
FR	MARIEN-APOTHEKE Kanestraße Tel. 527979	KAISER-FRIEDRICH APOTHEKE Schierstraße 15 Tel. 609697
SA	BAHNHOF-APOTHEKE Tel. 370995	RUSSEL-APOTHEKE
SO	APOTHEKE AM MARKT Markt 9	CARL-GUSTAV APOTHEKE

In Germany, many doctors (not only GPs, but also specialists) have their own practices. They are usually closed on Wednesday afternoons. Doctors on duty (**Notdienst**) at weekends and on public holidays are listed in the local papers.

where is the nearest chemist?
wo ist die nächste Apotheke?
*voh ist dee **naykh**-ste apo-**teh**-ke*

have you something for...?
haben Sie etwas gegen...?
*hah-ben zee et-vas **gay**-gen...*

sunburn	**diarrhoea**
Sonnenbrand	Durchfall
*zon*nen-brant	*doorkh*-fall

I need painkillers
ich brauche Schmerztabletten
*ikh **brow**-khe **shmerts**-tab-le-ten*

an upset stomach
Magenverstimmung
mahgen-fer-shtimoong

a headache
Kopfschmerzen
kopf-shmert-sen

I need antibiotics
ich brauche Antibiotika
*ikh **brow**-khe anti-bee-o-tika*

talking

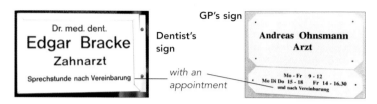

Dr. med. dent.
Edgar Bracke
Zahnarzt
Sprechstunde nach Vereinbarung

Dentist's
sign

GP's sign

Andreas Ohnsmann
Arzt

Mo - Fr   9 - 12
Mo Di Do 15 - 18   Fr 14 - 16.30
und nach Vereinbarung

*with an
appointment*

talking talking talking talking talking

I am not well
mir geht es nicht gut
meer gayt es nikht goot

he/she is not well
ihm/ihr geht es nicht gut
eem/eer gayt es nikht goot

I need to see a doctor
ich brauche einen Arzt
*ikh **brow**-khe ine-en artst*

we need a doctor to come out
wir brauchen einen Hausbesuch
*veer **brow**-khen ine-en **hows**-be-zookh*

please call the doctor
bitte rufen Sie einen Arzt
*bi-te **roo**-fen zee ine-en artst*

my child is ill
mein Kind ist krank
mine kint ist krank

I have a pain here
es tut hier weh
es toot heer veh

I am on this medication
ich nehme dieses Medikament
*ikh **nay**-me **dee**-zes medeeka**ment***

I'm pregnant
ich bin schwanger
*ikh bin **shvan**ger*

I am on the pill
ich nehme die Pille
*ikh **nay**-me dee **pil**-le*

I'm breastfeeding
ich stille mein Baby
*ikh **shti**-le mine **ba**by*

I have cystitis
ich habe eine Blasenentzündung
*ikh **hah**-be ine-e **blah**zen-entsoon-doong*

I'm diabetic
ich bin Diabetiker
*ikh bin dee-a-**beh**-tiker*

I am allergic to...
ich bin allergisch gegen...
*ikh bin a-**ler**-gish **gay**-gen...*

I have high blood pressure
ich habe zu hohen Blutdruck
*ikh **hah**-be tsoo **hoh**-hen **bloot**-drook*

my blood group is...
meine Blutgruppe ist...
*mine-e **bloot**-groo-pe ist...*

I need a receipt for my insurance
ich brauche eine Quittung für meine Versicherung
*ikh **brow**-khe ine-e **kvi**-toong foor mine-e fer-**zikh**eroong*

I need a dentist
ich brauche einen Zahnarzt
*ikh **brow**-khe ine-en **tsahn**artst*

I have toothache
ich habe Zahnschmerzen
*ikh **hah**-be **tsahn**-shmer-tsen*

my crown has come out
meine Krone ist herausgefallen
*mine-e **kroh**-ne ist he**rows**-ge-fal-len*

can your repair my dentures?
können Sie mein Gebiss reparieren?
*kur'-nen zee mine ge**biss** raypa-**ree**ren*

I need a temporary filling
ich brauche eine provisorische Füllung
*ikh **brow**-khe ine-e provi-**zori**-she **foo**loong*

I have an abscess
ich habe einen Abszess
*ikh **hah**-be ine-en ap-**sess***

*Hospital (**Krankenhaus**) visiting hours vary. If you are admitted you will be in a room with about three or four other people. You can hire a telephone and although it is expensive to make calls, it means you will also be able to receive them. You have to pay a daily hospital charge for the first 14 days of your stay. This is non-refundable.*

Road sign for hospital;
Klinik also means hospital.

hospital

accident & emergency

If you need to go to hospital

will I/he/she have to go to hospital?
muss ich/er/sie ins Krankenhaus?
*moos ikh/er/zee ins **kran**ken-hows*

where is the hospital?
wo ist das Krankenhaus?
*voh ist das **kran**ken-hows*

where is the nearest A & E department?
wo ist das nächste Krankenhaus mit Notaufnahme?
*voh ist das **naykh**-ste **kran**ken-hows mit **noht**-owf-nah-me*

please take me to the nearest hospital
bitte bringen Sie mich zum nächsten Krankenhaus
*bi-te **brin**-gen zee mikh tsoom **naykh**-sten **kran**ken-hows*

I need to go to casualty
ich muss zur Notaufnahme
*ikh moos tsoor **noht**-owf-nah-me*

when are visiting hours?
wann ist die Besuchszeit?
*van ist dee be**zookhs**-tsite*

which ward?
welche Station?
vel**-khe shtah-**tsyohn

can you explain what is the matter with me?
können Sie mir erklären, was ich habe?
***kur'**-nen zee meer er-**kleh**-ren vas ikh **hah**-be*

Emergency

i *The emergency number for the police is 110. They must be called to any accident whether there are injuries or not. The fire brigade and ambulance service can be contacted on 112.*

help!
Hilfe!
hil-fe

can you help me?
können Sie mir helfen?
kur'-nen zee meer hel-fen

please call...
bitte rufen Sie...
bi-te roo-fen zee...

the police
die Polizei
dee poli-tsy

an ambulance
einen Krankenwagen
ine-en kran-ken-vahgen

help! Fire!
Hilfe! Feuer!
hil-fe! foy-er!

please call the fire brigade!
bitte rufen Sie die Feuerwehr!
bi-te roo-fen zee dee foy-er-vehr

my ... has been stolen
mein/meine ... ist gestohlen worden
mine/mine-e ... ist geshtoh-len vorden

my car has been stolen
mein Auto ist gestohlen worden
mine owto ist geshtoh-len vorden

here are my insurance details
hier sind meine Versicherungsangaben
heer zint mine-e fer-zikheroongs-angaben

where is the police station/the hospital?
wo ist die Polizeistation/das Krankenhaus?
voh ist dee poli-tsy-shta-tsee-ohn/das kran-ken-hows

I would like to phone...
ich möchte ... anrufen
ikh mur'kh-te ... an-roofen

I want to report a theft
ich möchte einen Diebstahl melden
ikh mur'kh-te ine-en deep-shtahl mel-den

please give me your insurance details
bitte geben Sie mir Ihre Versicherungsangaben
bi-te gay-ben zee meer ee-re fer-zikheroongs-angaben

I need a report for my insurance
ich brauche einen Bericht für meine Versicherung
ikh brow-khe ine-en berikht foor mine-e fer-zikheroong

talking talking talking talking talking

Food
&
Drink

German Food

i   The Germans take everything to do with food or drink with the utmost seriousness, and as a result all the products are handled very carefully in order to meet the highest standards of hygiene and quality control. Care and pride are taken in the preparation of meals. The food is hearty and warming and geared to satisfy large appetites. So be warned! Portions are large.

In Germany the main meal of the day is usually **Mittagessen**, lunch. It starts with soup, followed by the main dish (meat with vegetables or salad and potato or rice, etc) and an optional dessert or fruit.

Dinner (**Abendessen**) consists of platters of cold meats and cheeses. On occasions Germans also have a hot meal, but not a heavy one.

Breakfast (**Frühstück**) generally consists of a variety of cold meats and cheeses, with different kinds of bread and jam and fresh coffee.

sausage stall

Germany has a huge variety of sausages which are served at all times of the day. By law they are made with 100% meat.

In butcher's shops there is often an area for a quick meal (generally eaten standing) such as this dish: **Wiener Würstchen mit Kartoffelsalat** (boiled frankfurter with potato salad).

One of the unusual places where one can eat in Germany (and eat well) is the town hall (**Rathaus**), which normally has a restaurant open to the public (usually in the basement), called the **Ratskeller** (council's cellar). This one is a winebar which normally has a buffet.

durchgehend warme Küche — *hot meals served all day*

beer garden

Beer is usually served with large Pretzels.

A **Stehcafé** is a good place for a coffee and cake, generally standing only. They are often attached to a baker's and the 7am opening means you can get breakfast.

where can we have a snack?
wo können wir einen Snack bekommen?
voh kur'-nen veer ine-en snack be-kommen

can you recommend a good local restaurant?
können Sie ein gutes Restaurant am Ort empfehlen?
kur'-nen zee ine gootes restoh-rong am ort em-faylen

are there any vegetarian restaurants?
gibt es hier vegetarische Restaurants?
gipt es heer vaygay-tarish-e restoh-rongs

do we need to book?
müssen wir einen Tisch reservieren?
moos-sen veer ine-en tish rayzer-veeren

what dishes should we try?
welche Gerichte sollten wir probieren?
vel-khe ge-rikh-te zoll-ten veer pro-bee-ren

how do we get to the restaurant?
wie kommen wir zu dem Restaurant?
vee kommen veer tsoo dem restoh-rong

talking talking talking

i Snacks can be bought at various **Imbiss** places. The local market or shopping area serve typical snacky food such as **Bratwurst** (fried sausage), **Bockwurst** (boiled sausage) and **Buletten** (thick hamburger). German standards of food hygiene are high.

keywords

Bockwurst
bok-voorst
boiled sausage

Bratwurst
braht-voorst
roast sausage

Kartoffelsalat
kartof-fel-zalaht
potato salad

Bulette
boo-le-te
thick hamburger

Getränke
ge-tren-ke
drinks

Imbiss stall
These serve snacks: soup, hamburgers, sausages, barbecued chicken and chips. Most serve beer.

Bratwurst

Wiener Würstchen

talking talking

I'd like a ... please
ich möchte einen/eine/ein ... bitte
ikh mur'kh-te ine-en/ine-e/ine ... bi-te

a white coffee
einen Kaffee mit Milch
ine-en kafay mit milkh

a large white coffee
einen großen Milchkaffee
ine-en groh-sen milkh-kafay

a decaff coffee
einen entkoffeinierten Kaffee
ine-en ent-kof-fe-eeneerten kafay

a hot chocolate
eine heiße Schokolade
ine-e hay-se shoko-lah-de

a tea with milk
einen Tee mit Milch
ine-en tay mit milkh

a half lager
ein kleines Pils
ine kline-es pils

an orange juice
einen Orangensaft
ine-en oronjen-zaft

an apple juice
einen Apfelsaft
ine-en ap-fel-zaft

a red wine
einen Rotwein
ine-en rohtvine

a white wine
einen Weißwein
ine-en vicevine

a bottle of mineral water
eine Flasche Mineralwasser
ine-e fla-she mineral-vasser

fizzy	still
sprudelnd	still
shproodelnt	*shtill*

snack board

Unsere
Augebote:
Sandwich ——— sandwiches
Bel. Brötchen ——— bread roll with meat
or cheese
Suppen ——— soup
Süßwaren ——— sweets

Sign in front of a restaurant

Mittagstisch
von 12-16⁰⁰
von Montag
bis Samstag
WARSTEINER

*lunch menu
from 12–4pm
Monday to Saturday*

You can find a great
variety of cakes at a
Café Konditorei.

Pfefferminz
pfe-fer-mints
mint

Himbeere
him-beh-re
raspberry

Erdbeere
ert-beh-re
strawberry

Johannisbeere
yohanis-beh-re
blackcurrant

Zitrone
tsitroh-ne
lemon

Ananas
ana-nas
pineapple

Pfirsich
pfeer-zikh
peach

Pistazie
pis-ta-tsee-e
pistacchio

Haselnuss
hah-zel-noos
hazelnut

Weintraube
vine-trow-be
grape

keywords keywords keywords keywords

---

can we eat here?
können wir hier essen?
kur'-nen veer heer es-sen

do you have a dish of the day?
haben Sie ein Tagesgericht?
hah-ben zee ine tah-ges-gerikht

what sandwiches do you have?
was für Sandwiches haben Sie?
vas foor sandwiches hah-ben zee

I would like ice-cream
ich möchte Eis
ikh mur'kh-te ice

what can we eat?
was können wir essen?
vas kur'-nen veer es-sen

what is the dish of the day?
was ist das Tagesgericht?
vas ist das tah-ges-gerikht

what cakes do you have?
was für Kuchen haben Sie?
vas foor koo-khen hah-ben zee

what flavours do you have?
was für Eissorten haben Sie?
vas foor ice-sor-ten hah-ben zee

talking

i) *In smaller towns restaurants tend to shut one day (generally Mondays). As a rule, eating places (including restaurants) have a menu with prices outside, so you will be prepared for the cost before going in. Restaurants usually offer set-price meals.*

Some hotels offer special deals. Check what is included in the price.

price includes aperitif and parking

Restaurants usually offer set-price meals.

closed on Mondays

You will find a good variety of Chinese and Italian restaurants. Turkish food tends to be sold in snackbars rather than restaurants.

I would like to book a table
ich möchte einen Tisch reservieren
ikh **mur'kh**-te *i*ne-en tish rayzer-**vee**ren

for tonight
für heute Abend
foor **hoy**-te **ah**bent

for lunch
zum Mittagessen
tsoom **mi**tahk-es-sen

at 7.30
um sieben Uhr dreißig
oom **zee**ben oor **dry**-sikh

smoking/non-smoking
Raucher/Nichtraucher
row-kher/**nikht**-row-kher

for 4 people
für vier Personen
foor feer per-**zohn**en

for tomorrow night
für morgen Abend
foor **morgen ah**bent

at 12.30
um zwölf Uhr dreißig
oom tsvur'lf oor **dry**-sikh

at 8 o'clock
um acht Uhr
oom akht oor

in the name of...
auf den Namen...
owf den **nah**-men...

Look out for different restaurant offers.

SYRISCH · LIBANESISCHE · SPEZIALITÄTEN

Restaurant Palmyra

Und nach dem Theater - wohin ?
Kennen Sie schon unseren

THEATERTELLER
(ab 22.00 Uhr)

... acht verschiedene kalte und warme
Kompositionen der syrisch-libanesischen
Küche mit Fladenbrot
(auf Wunsch auch vegetarisch)

EUR 10,-

Taunusstraße 15 · 65183 Wiesbaden
Tägl. 12.00–24.00 Uhr durchgehend geöffnet
Telefon 06 11 / 52 21 21
Außer Haus & Partyservice

post-theatre menu (from 10pm)

Syrian and Lebanese dishes with pitta bread

vegetarian dishes on request

open from 12 noon to midnight

take-away and party catering

---

the menu please
die Speisekarte bitte
dee shpy-ze-kar-te bi-te

the wine list please
die Weinkarte bitte
dee vine-kar-te bi-te

do you have a children's menu?
haben Sie eine Kinderkarte?
hah-ben zee ine-e kin-der-kar-te

for a starter I will have...
als Vorspeise nehme ich...
als for-shpy-ze nay-me ikh...

for a main dish I will have...
als Hauptgericht nehme ich...
als howpt-gerikht nay-me ikh...

what vegetarian dishes do you have?
welche vegetarischen Gerichte haben Sie?
vel-khe vaygay-tarish-en gerikh-te hah-ben zee

what desserts do you have?
welche Nachspeisen haben Sie?
vel-khe nakh-shpy-zen hah-ben zee

some tap water please
etwas Leitungswasser bitte
et-vas lye-toongs-vasser bi-te

some more bread please
noch etwas Brot bitte
nokh et-vas broht bi-te

the bill please
zahlen bitte
tsahlen bi-te

we would like to pay separately
wir möchten getrennt bezahlen
veer mur'kh-ten ge-trent be-tsahlen

talking talking talking talking talking

Service and VAT are included (**Alle Preise inklusive Bedienung und Mehrwertsteuer**). Tipping is optional.

snack menu

chicken broth with egg and bread roll

KLEINE SPEISEKARTE	EUR
Hühnerbrühe mit Brötchen	**2,15**
Hühnerbrühe mit Ei und Brötchen	**2,40**
Köingspastete	**4,85**
Ragout fin	**4,85**
Schinkenbrot	**3,65**
Salamibrot	**3,65**
Käsebrot	**3,65**
Bockwurst mit Brot	**2,30**

chicken broth with bread roll

vol au vent filled with chicken in white sauce

vol au vent filled with meat sauce

ham open sandwich

salami open sandwich

cheese open sandwich

boiled sausage with bread

Germany has a huge variety of bread. It is generally served at breakfast or with a light evening meal. Butter is usually served with bread. Note that German butter is unsalted.

You will find a wonderful selection of mouth-watering cakes at **Café Konditorei**, generally served with cream (**mit Sahne**).

*Don't be overwhelmed by German words – they may be long, but they are made up of smaller bits of words. Try and work out what the item is by identifying what makes up the long word. So **Tomatencremesuppe** is cream of tomato soup. You will also come across English terms such as **Snacks** and **Fingerfood**. There are also usually children's menus. Remember, German portions are quite large!*

SPEISEKARTE *menu*

FRÜHSTÜCK *breakfast*

SUPPEN *soups*

VORSPEISEN *starters*

EIERSPEISEN *egg dishes*

SALATE *salads*

HAUPTGERICHTE *main dishes*

NUDELGERICHTE *pasta dishes*

FISCH und MEERESFRÜCHTE *fish and seafood*

FLEISCHGERICHTE *meat dishes*

BEILAGEN *side dishes*

SPEZIALITÄTEN *special dishes*

GEMÜSE *vegetables*

NACHSPEISEN *sweets*

KUCHEN *cakes*

WARME GETRÄNKE *hot drinks*

ALKOHOLFREIE GETRÄNKE *alcohol-free drinks*

FRUCHTSÄFTE *fruit juice*

i If you are a beer lover, Germany is the place to be. There are
over 1,000 breweries with more than half of them in Bavaria.
Many cities have at least one brewpub. Wheat beers are a speciality
of Bavaria along with smoked beer. It is best to sample the local beer
in the place it has been brewed. In Cologne you should try the pale
refreshing **Kölsch** and in Düsseldorf sample the darkish malty **Altbier**.

Pilsner

A typical lager available all over
Germany.

Hefe-Weißbier

A speciality beer from Bavaria with
a fruity, slightly smoked aroma.

Kölsch

A pale-coloured, light-textured,
fruity-flavoured beer brewed
in Cologne. Best drunk in
a brewpub.

Weißbier

The Bavarians also brew dark
versions of their wheat beers.
These may contain some malted
wheat that has been darkened by
roasting. **Dunkel** means *dark*.

Pilsner
pils-ner
pils lager

Weißbier
vice-beer
wheat beer

Fassbier
fass-beer
draught

Rauchbier
rowkh-beer
smoked beer

Radler
rad-ler
lager shandy

Helles
hel-les
lager

Dunkles
doonk-les
ale

ein Großes
ine **groh**-ses
large

ein Kleines
ine **kline**-es
small

what beers do you have?
was für Biere haben Sie?
vas foor bee-re hah-ben zee

can you recommend a local beer?
können Sie ein Bier aus dieser Gegend empfehlen?
kur'-nen zee ine beer ows deezer gaygent em-faylen

I would like to try a speciality beer
ich möchte eine Bierspezialität probieren
ikh mur'kh-te ine-e beer-sphay-tsya-litayt pro-bee-ren

do you have alcohol-free beers?
haben Sie alkoholfreie Biere?
hah-ben zee alko-hol-fry-e bee-re

a large beer
ein großes Bier
ine groh-ses beer

a small beer
ein kleines Bier
ine kline-es beer

a litre glass of beer
eine Maß Bier
ine-e mahs beer

what bottled beer do you have?
was für Flaschenbiere haben Sie?
vas foor flashen-bee-re hah-ben zee

*Wines are usually categorised according to three criteria: the overall growing area, the village or even the vineyard where they are produced, and the type of grape they are made from. Major grape varieties include **Riesling**, **Edelzwicker**, **Gewürztraminer** and **Müller-Thurgau**. The names of the villages and vineyards producing wines are innumerable. The name of the wine is often the name of the village (e.g. **Nierstein**) plus the name of the particular vineyard (e.g. **Gutes Domtal**) which combined become **Niersteiner Gutes Domtal**.*

Qualitätsweine mit Prädikat
This is the mark of the highest quality wine. If you want a good German wine, choose this rather than **Tafelwein**, **Landwein** or **QbA** (wine from a specified region).

bottled at source

Qualitätswein b. A.
This indicates that the grapes are from one region; in this case, Rheinhessen.

Note this wine's lower alcoholic content. In general drier wines benefit from some bottle age, and lower alcohol or sweeter wines are good for instant drinking.

Halbtrocken medium dry

German *Riesling* is one of the best, most rewarding wines in the world. The finest examples contrive to be tangy, steely, minerally, densely fruity and bone-dry all at once. It is worth trying those from *Rheinhessen*, *Pfalz*, *Nahe* or *Rheingau* regions.

This is a good medium dry wine. If you are choosing a wine from a cool area like the *Mosel*, select a *Riesling Kabinett* that is only moderate in alcohol, say 8 or 9%, so that the fruit sweetness remains to counter the cool-climate acidity. Other *Rieslings* are better at 12% alcohol upwards.

Weißwein
vice-vine
white wine

Roséwein
rohzay-vine
rosé wine

Rotweine
rohtvine
red wine

Sekt
zekt
sparkling wine

trocken
tro-ken
dry

halbtrocken
halp-tro-ken
medium dry

lieblich
leeb-likh
sweet

Tafelwein
tahfel-vine
table wine

keywords keywords keywords

---

the wine list please
die Weinkarte bitte
dee vinekar-te bi-te

what wines do you have?
was für Weine haben Sie?
vas foor vine-e hah-ben zee

is there a local wine?
gibt es einen Wein aus dieser Gegend?
gipt es ine-en vine ows dee-zer gaygent

can you recommend a good wine?
können Sie mir einen guten Wein empfehlen?
kur'-nen zee mee ine-en goo-ten vine em-fay-len

a glass of red wine please
ein Glas Rotwein bitte
ine glahs roht-vine bi-te

a glass of white wine please
ein Glas Weißwein bitte
ine glahs vice-vine bi-te

a bottle of wine
eine Flasche Wein
ine-e fla-she vine

red wine
Rotwein
roht-vine

white wine
Weißwein
vice-vine

a carafe of house wine
eine Karaffe Hauswein
ine-e kara-fe hows-vine

a glass of wine
ein Glas Wein
ine glahs vine

talking talking talking

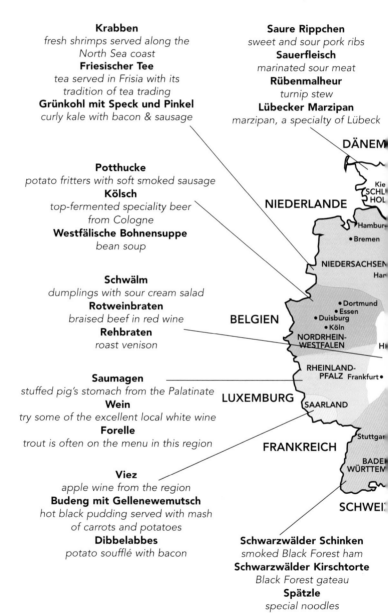

Flavours of Germany

Krabben
*fresh shrimps served along the
North Sea coast*
Friesischer Tee
*tea served in Frisia with its
tradition of tea trading*
Grünkohl mit Speck und Pinkel
curly kale with bacon & sausage

Saure Rippchen
sweet and sour pork ribs
Sauerfleisch
marinated sour meat
Rübenmalheur
turnip stew
Lübecker Marzipan
marzipan, a specialty of Lübeck

DÄNEM

Potthucke
potato fritters with soft smoked sausage
Kölsch
*top-fermented speciality beer
from Cologne*
Westfälische Bohnensuppe
bean soup

Kie
SCHL
HOL

NIEDERLANDE

Hambur

• Bremen

NIEDERSACHSEN

Ha

Schwälm
dumplings with sour cream salad
Rotweinbraten
braised beef in red wine
Rehbraten
roast venison

BELGIEN

• Dortmund
• Essen
• Duisburg
• Köln
NORDRHEIN-
WESTFALEN

H

RHEINLAND-
PFALZ Frankfurt •

Saumagen
stuffed pig's stomach from the Palatinate
Wein
try some of the excellent local white wine
Forelle
trout is often on the menu in this region

LUXEMBURG

SAARLAND

Stuttgar

FRANKREICH

BADE
WÜRTTEM

Viez
apple wine from the region
Budeng mit Gellenewemutsch
*hot black pudding served with mash
of carrots and potatoes*
Dibbelabbes
potato soufflé with bacon

SCHWEI

Schwarzwälder Schinken
smoked Black Forest ham
Schwarzwälder Kirschtorte
Black Forest gateau
Spätzle
special noodles

Himmel und Erde
stew made with apples and potato
Grützwurst
sausage similar to black pudding
Mecklenburger Rippenbraten
*rib roast best served with potatoes
and red cabbage*
Tollatschen
sweet and sour meat

Currywurst
*roast sausage served in a
spicy sauce*
Spreewälder Gurken
*pickled cucumbers from the
Spreewald region*
Zinnaer Klosterbruder
a dark herb liqueur

Arme Ritter
*'poor knights': white bread steeped
in egg and fried*
Baumkuchen
*'tree cake':cake made up of many
layers with filling inbetween*
Nordhäuser Doppelkorn
local rye schnapps

Quarkkeulchen
curd cheese dough fried and sliced
Sauerbraten
*marinated beef roast often served
with dumplings and red cabbage*
Rinderrouladen
beef olives

Thüringer Bratwurst
*the famous Thuringian roasted
sausage*
Thüringer Klöße
*Thuringian dumplings, among the
most famous in Germany*
Rotkäppchen-Sekt
a locally produced sparkling wine

Weißwurst
veal sausage
Brez'n
large pretzel
Leberkäse
*fine meat loaf, served warm in a
bread roll at snackbars*

Rostock
MECKLENBURG-
VORPOMMERN

POLEN

BRANDENBURG
Berlin•

SACHSEN-
ANHALT

•Leipzig
Dresden•
THÜRINGEN SACHSEN

TSCHECHIEN

•Nürnberg

BAYERN

•München

ÖSTERREICH

There are times when you cannot eat some things. It is as well warning the waiter before making your choice.

I'm vegetarian
ich bin Vegetarier
ikh bin vaygay-taree-er

I don't eat meat/pork
ich esse kein Fleisch/Schweinefleisch
ikh es-se kine flysh/shvy-ne-flysh

I don't eat fish/shellfish
ich esse keinen Fisch/keine Meeresfrüchte
ikh es-se kye-nen fish/kye-ne mehres-frur'kh-te

I'm allergic to shellfish
ich bin allergisch gegen Meeresfrüchte
ikh bin a-ler-gish gay-gen mehres-frur'kh-te

I am allergic to peanuts
ich bin allergisch gegen Erdnüsse
ikh bin a-ler-gish gay-gen ert-noos-se

I can't eat raw eggs
ich kann kein rohes Ei essen
ikh kan kine roh-es eye es-sen

I can't eat liver
ich kann keine Leber essen
ikh kan kye-ne lay-ber es-sen

I am on a diet
ich bin auf Diät
ikh bin owf dee-ayt

I don't drink alcohol
ich trinke keinen Alkohol
ikh trin-ke kye-nen alko-hol

what is in this?
was ist darin enthalten?
vas ist da-rin ent-halten

is it raw?
ist das roh?
ist das roh

is it made with unpasteurised milk?
ist das mit nicht pasteurisierter Milch gemacht?
ist das mit nikht pastur'-ree-zeer-ter milkh gemakht

gebraten
ge-brah-ten
fried

gekocht
ge-kokht
boiled

gedämpft
ge-dempft
steamed

geröstet
ge-rur's-tet
roast

am Spieß
am shpees
kebab

gefüllt
ge-foolt
stuffed

gegrillt
ge-grilt
grilled

geräuchert
ge-roy-khert
smoked

geschmort
ge-shmohrt
stewed/braised

mariniert
maree-neert
marinated

eingelegt
ine-ge-lehgt
pickled

pochiert
po-kheert
poached

gezuckert
ge-tsoo-kert
sugared

gesalzen
ge-zalt-sen
salted

Aal *eel*
  Aalsuppe *eel soup*
Allgäuer Emmentaler *whole-milk hard cheese from the Allgäu*
Allgäuer Käsespätzle *cheese noodles from the Allgäu*
Alpzirler *cow's milk cheese from Austria*
Alsterwasser *lager shandy*
Altbier *top-fermented beer from the lower Rhine*
Ananas *pineapple*
Apfel *apple*
  Apfelkorn *apple brandy*
  Apfelkuchen *apple cake*
  Apfelmus *apple puree*
  Apfelsaft *apple juice*
  Apfelsalami *salami with apple*
  Apfelstrudel *flaky pastry filled with apples and spices*
  Apfelwein *cider (apple wine)*
Aprikose *apricot*
Arme Ritter *French toast*
Art *style or fashion of e.g. 'nach Art des Hauses' => à la maison*
Artischocken *artichokes*
Aubergine *aubergine*
Auflauf *baked dish, can be sweet or savoury*
Aufschnitt *sliced cold meats*
Austern *oysters*
Bäckerofen *'baker's oven', pork and lamb bake from Saarland*

Apfelstrudel

Backpflaumen *prunes*
Banane *banana*
Bandnudeln *ribbon pasta*
Barack *apricot brandy*
Barsch *perch*
Bauernfrühstück *scrambled eggs, bacon, cooked diced potatoes, onions, tomatoes*
Baunzerl *little bread roll with distinctive cut on top (Austria)*
Bayrisch Kraut *shredded cabbage cooked with sliced apples, wine and sugar*
Beilage *side dish*
Bereich Bernkastel *area along the Moselle producing crisp white wines*
Bergkäse *cheese from the Alps*
Berliner *doughnut filled with jam*
Berliner Weiße *fizzy beer with fruit syrup added*

Aufschnitt

Berner Erbsensuppe *soup made of dried peas with pig's trotters*
Bienenstich *type of cake, baked on a tray with a coating of almonds and sugar and a cream filling*
Bierschinken *beer sausage with ham*
Bierteig *pastry made with beer*
Bierwurst *beer sausage*
Birchermüsli *muesli with yoghurt (Switzerland)*
Birne *pear*
Birnen, Bohnen und Speck *(Northern Germany) pears, green beans and bacon*
Birne Helene *dessert with vanilla ice cream, pear and chocolate sauce*
Birnenmost *pear wine*
Birnensekt *sparkling pear wine*
Blätterteig *puff pastry*
Blätterteigpastete *vol-au-vent*
Blattsalat *green salad*
blau *rare (meat); poached (fish)*
Blauschimmelkäse *blue cheese*
Blumenkohl *cauliflower*
Blunz'n *black pudding (South Germany and Austria)*
Blutwurst *black pudding*
Bockbier *strong beer (light or dark), drunk especially in Bavaria*
Bockwurst *boiled sausage. A popular snack served with a bread roll*
Böhmische Knödel *sliced dumpling*
Bohnen *beans*
Bohnensalat *bean salad*
Bohnensuppe *thick bean and bacon soup*

Bosniakerl *wholemeal roll with caraway seeds*
Brathähnchen *roast chicken*
Brathering *fried herring (eaten cold)*
Bratkartoffeln *fried potatoes*
Bratwurst *fried sausage. A popular snack served with a bread roll*
Brauner *strong black coffee with a little milk*
Bremer Kükenragout *Bremen chicken fricassée*
Brezel *(or in Bavaria:* **Brezn***) pretzel*
Broiler *spit-roasted chicken (East German)*
Brombeeren *blackberries*
Bröselknödel *soup with little dumplings prepared with bone marrow and breadcrumbs*
Brot *bread*
Brötchen *bread roll*
Brühe *clear soup*
Brühwurst *thick frankfurter*
B'soffene *pudding soaked in mulled wine*
Buletten *thick hamburgers (but without the bread)*
Buletten mit Kartoffelsalat *thick hamburgers with potato salad*
Bündnerfleisch *raw beef smoked and dried, served thinly sliced*
Burgenländische Krautsuppe *thick cabbage and vegetable soup*
Butter *butter*
Butterbrot *open sandwich*
Butterkäse *high-fat cheese*

Bockwurst

*Eisbein mit Bockwurst
und Sauerkraut*

Cervelat *fine beef and pork salami*
Chindbettering *ring of bread*
Cremeschnitten *cream slices*
Champagner *champagne*
Champignons *button mushrooms*
Cordon bleu *veal cutlet filled
with boiled ham and cheese,
covered in breadcrumbs*
Currywurst *sausage served with
a spicy sauce. A popular snack
originally from Berlin*
Damenkäse *mild buttery cheese*
Dampfnudeln *hot yeast dumplings
with vanilla sauce*
Danziger Goldwasser *schnapps
containing tiny bits of gold leaf*
Datteln *dates*
Deutsches Beefsteak *thick
hamburger (but without the bread)*
dicke Bohnen *broad beans*
Doppelbockbier *like **Bockbier**,
but still stronger*
Dorsch *cod*
Dresdner Suppentopf
*Dresden vegetable soup
with dumplings (East German)*
Dunkles *dark beer*
Ei *egg*
  Eier im Glas *soft boiled eggs
served in a glass*
Eierkuchen *pancakes*
Eierschwammerln *chanterelles*
Eierspeispfandl *special Viennese
omelette*
eingelegt *pickled*
Einmachsuppe *chicken or veal*

broth with cream and egg
Einspänner *coffee with whipped
cream served in a glass (Austria)*
Eintopf *stew*
Eis *ice cream*
Eisbecher *knickerbocker glory*
Eisbein *boiled pork knuckle often
served with sauerkraut*
Eiskaffee *iced coffee served with
vanilla ice cream*
Eiswein *a rich, naturally sweet,
white wine made from grapes
which are harvested only after a
period of frost*
Emmentaler *Swiss Emmental,
whole-milk hard cheese*
Ennstaler *blue cheese from
mixed milk*
Ente *duck*
Erbach *area producing scented
white wines mainly from Riesling
grape*
Erbsen *peas*
  Erbsenpüree
  *green pea
  purée*
  Erbsensuppe
  pea soup
Erdäpfel
*potatoes
(Austria)*
  Erdäpfelgulasch
  *spicy sausage and
  potato stew*

Erbsen

Erdäpfelknödel *potato and
semolina dumplings*
Erdäpfelkren *relish with potato
and horseradish (Austria)*
Erdäpfelnudeln *fried, boiled
potato balls tossed in fried
breadcrumbs*

Erdbeeren *strawberries*
Erdnüsse *peanuts*
erster Gang *first course*
Essig *vinegar*
Export Bier *premium beer*
Falscher Hase *baked mince meatloaf*
Fasan *pheasant*
Feigen *figs*
Fenchel *fennel*
fettarm *low in fat*
Fisch *fish*
  Fischfilet *fish fillet*
  Fischgerichte *fish and seafood*
  Fischklöße *fish dumplings*
  Fischsuppe *fish soup*
flambiert *flambé*
Fledermaus *boiled beef in horseradish cream browned in the oven*
Fleisch *meat*
  Fleischgerichte *meat dishes*
  Fleischklößchen *meatballs*
  Fleischlaberln *highly seasoned meat cake (Austria)*
  Fleischpflanzerl *thick hamburgers (without the bread)*
  Fleischsalat *sausage salad with onions*
  Fleischsuppe *meat soup served with dumplings*
Flunder *flounder*
Fondue *melted cheese with wine and bread for dipping*

Erdbeeren

Forelle *trout*
Forelle blau *steamed trout with potatoes and vegetables*
  Forelle Müllerin *trout fried in batter with almonds*
  Forelle Steiermark *trout fillet with bacon in white sauce*
  Frikadelle *thick hamburger (without the bread)*
frisch *fresh*
Fritattensuppe *beef broth with strips of pancake (Austria)*
frittiert *fried*
Froschschenkel *frogs' legs*
Frucht *fresh fruit*
Früchtetee *fruit tea*
Fruchtsaft *fruit juice*
Fünfkernbrot *wholemeal bread made with five different cereals*
Gang *course*
Gans *goose*
  Gänseleber *foie gras*
  Gänseleberpastete *goose liver pâté*
Gebäck *pastries*
gebacken *baked*
gebackene Leber *liver fried in breadcrumbs*
gebraten *roasted/fried*
gedämpft *steamed*
Geflügel *poultry*
gefüllt *stuffed/filled*
  gefüllte Kalbsbrust *stuffed breast of veal*
  gefüllte Paprika *peppers filled with mince*
    gegrillt *grilled*
      gegrillter Lachs *grilled salmon*
        Gehacktes *mince*
        gekocht *boiled*
        gekochtes Rindfleisch mit grüner Soße *boiled beef with green sauce*

Feigen

gemischter Salat *mixed salad*
Gemüse *vegetables*
  Gemüse und Klöße *vegetables and dumplings*
  Gemüselasagne *vegetable lasagne*
  Gemüseplatte *mixed vegetables*
  Gemüsesuppe *vegetable soup*
geräuchert *smoked*
Gericht *dish*
geschmort *braised*
Geschnetzeltes *thinly sliced meat in sauce served with potatoes or rice*
Geselchtes *smoked meats (Austria)*
Gespritzter *spritzer, white wine and soda water*
Gewürzgurken *gherkins*
Gitziprägel *baked rabbit in batter (a Swiss dish)*
Glühwein *mulled wine*
Goldbarsch *redfish*
Graf Görz *Austrian soft cheese*
Grammeln *croissant stuffed with bacon*
Grießklößchensuppe *soup with semolina dumplings*
Grießtaler *gnocchi*
Grog *hot rum*
grüne Bohnen *green beans*
grüne Veltlinersuppe *green wine soup*
grüner Salat *green salad*
Grükohl *kale*
Gruyère *gruyère cheese*
  Güggeli *roast chicken with onions and mushrooms in white wine sauce (Switzerland)*

Gulasch

Gulasch *stewed diced beef and pork with paprika served with dumplings and red cabbage*
Gulaschsuppe *spicy meat soup with paprika*
Gulyas *beef stew with paprika*
Gumpoldskirchner *spicy white wine from Austria*
Gurke *cucumber*
  Gurkensalat *cucumber salad*
gutbürgerliche Küche *traditional German cooking*
Gyros *kebab*
Hackbraten *mincemeat roast*
Hackepeter auf Schrippen mit Zwiebeln *spiced minced pork on rolls, with onions*
Hackfleisch *mince*
Hähnchen *chicken*
  Hähnchenbrust *chicken breast*
  halbtrocken *medium-dry*
  Hamburger Rundstück *Hamburg meat roll*
Hammel *mutton*
Hartkäse *hard cheese*

grüne Bohnen

Himbeeren

Hase hare

Hasenbraten roast hare

Hasenpfeffer peppered rabbit stew

Hauptgericht main course

Hausbrauerei house brewery

hausgemacht home-made

Hausmannskost good traditional home cooking

Hawaitoast toast with cooked ham, pineapple slice and melted cheese

Hecht pike

Hefeweizen wheat beer

Heidschnuckenragout lamb stew

heiß hot

Helles light beer

Hering herring
  Heringsschmaus herring in creamy sauce

Herz heart

Heuriger new wine

Himbeeren raspberries
  Himbeergeist raspberry brandy

Hirn brain

Hirsch venison

Hockheim strong white wines from the Rheingau

Honig honey

Hühnchen chicken

Hühnerfrikasse chicken fricassée

Hühnerschenkel chicken drumsticks

Hühnerleber chicken liver

Hummer lobster

Ingwer ginger

Jägerschnitzel cutlet served with mushrooms and wine sauce

Jogurt yoghurt

Johannisbeeren currants (can be red, black or white)

Jura Omelette bacon, potato and onion omelette

Kabeljau cod

Kaffee coffee
  Kaffee komplett coffee with milk and sugar
  Kaffee mit Milch coffee with milk
  Koffeinfreier Kaffee decaf

Kaisermelange black coffee with an egg yolk

Kaiserschmarren strips of pancake served with raisins, sugar and cinnamon

Kakao cocoa

Kalb veal
  Kalbsbraten roast veal

Karotten

Kalbshaxe *knuckle of veal*
  Kalbskoteletts *veal cutlets*
  Kalbsleber *calf's liver*
  Kalbsschnitzel *veal escalope*
kalt *cold*
  kalte Platte *cold meat platter*
Kaninchen *rabbit*
Kapuziner *Austrian equivalent to a cappuccino which is black coffee with a drop of milk*
Karotten *carrots*
Karpfen *carp*
  Karpfen blau *poached carp*
  Karpfen in Bier *carp poached in beer with herbs*
Kartoffeln *potatoes*
  Kartoffelklöße *potato dumplings*
  Kartoffelpuffer *potato pancakes. A popular snack*
  Kartoffelpüree *mashed potatoes*
  Kartoffelsalat *potato salad*
  Kartoffelsuppe *potato soup*
Käse *cheese*
  Käsebrötchen *roll with small bacon pieces in the dough and melted cheese on top*
  Käsefondue *dish made from melted cheese and flavoured with wine and kirsch into which you dip bread*
  Käsekuchen *cheesecake*
  Käsenudeln *noodles served with cheese*
  Käseplatte *cheese platter with various cheeses*
  Käsesuppe *cheese soup*
Kasseler *smoked pork*
  Kasseler Rippe mit Sauerkraut *smoked pork rib with sauerkraut*
Kastanienroulade *roulade with chestnut filling*
Katenspeck *streaky bacon*
Kaviar *caviar*
Kekse *biscuits*
Kirschen *cherries*
Kirschwasser *cherry schnapps*
Kirtagssuppe *soup with caraway seed thickened with potato (Austria)*

Kartoffelsuppe

Klops *rissole*
Klöße *dumplings*
Knackwurst *hot spicy sausage. A popular snack served with bread*
Knoblauch *garlic*
Knödel *dumpling*
  Knödelbeignets *fruit dumplings*
Knöderl *dumplings (Austria)*
Kohl *cabbage*
Kohlrouladen *stuffed cabbage*
Kohlsprossen *Brussels sprouts*
Kölsch *top-fermented beer from Cologne*
Kompott *stewed fruit*
Konfitüre *jam*

Kassler mit Rotkohl und Spätzle

*Knödelbeignets mit
Pflaumenkompott*

Königsberger Klopse meatballs
served in thick white sauce with
capers

Kopfsalat lettuce salad

Korn rye spirit

Kotelett pork chop/cutlet dipped
in breadcrumbs and deep fried

Krabben prawns
  Krabbencocktail prawn cocktail

Kraftbrot wheatgerm bread

Kraftfleisch corned beef

Kraftsuppe consommé

Krapfen doughnut

Kräuter herbs

Kräutertee herbal tea

Krautwickerl stuffed cabbage

Krebs crawfish, crab

Kren horseradish

Kristallweizen a kind of
sparkling beer

Kroketten croquettes

Kucken cake

Kürbis pumpkin

Labskaus cured pork,
herring and potato stew

Lachs salmon
  Lachsbrot smoked salmon
  with bread

Lamm lamb

Lammkeule leg of lamb

Languste spiny lobster

Lasagne lasagne

Lauch leeks

Leber liver

Leberkäse pork liver meatloaf

Leberknödelsuppe light soup
with chicken liver dumplings

Leberpastete liver paté

Leberwurst liver sausage

Lebkuchen gingerbread

Leinsamenbrot wholemeal
bread with linseed

Leipziger Allerlei vegetable
dish made from peas, carrots,
cauliflower and cabbage
(East German)

Lendenbraten roast loin

Lieblich sweet (wine)

Likör liqueur

Limburger strong cheese
flavoured with herbs

Limonade lemonade

Linsen lentils
  Linsenspecksalat lentil salad
  with bacon
  Linsensuppe lentil and
  sausage soup

Linzer Torte latticed tart with
jam topping

Liptauer Quark cream cheese
with paprika and herbs

Lunge lungs

Mais sweetcorn

Maiskolben corn on the cob

Lammkeule mit Rotkohl und Klößen

Makrele *mackerel*

Malzbier *dark malt beer*

Mandarine *tangerine*

Mandeln *almonds*

Marillenknödel *apricot dumplings (Austria)*

Marmelade *jam*

Maronitorte *chestnut tart*

Märzenbier *stronger beer brewed for special occasions*

Mastochsenhaxe *knuckle of beef (with sauce) from Sachsen-Anhalt (East German)*

Maß *a litre of beer*

Matjes *herring*

Maultaschen *ravioli-like pasta filled with pork, veal and spinach mixture*

Meeresfrüchte *seafood*

Meerrettich *horseradish*

Mehrkornbrötchen *rolls made with several kinds of wholemeal flour*

Melange *milky coffee*

Melone *melon*

Menü *combination of items from the menu at a special price, usually consisting of three courses*

Mettenden *sausage with a filling similar to mince*

Milch *milk*
  Milchrahmstrudel *strudel filled with egg custard and soft cheese*
  Milchreis *rice pudding*
  Milchshake *milk shake*

Mineralwasser *mineral water*
  Mit/ohne Kohlensäure *carbonated/non-carbonated*

Mirabellen *small yellow plums*

Mischbrot *grey bread made with rye and wheat flour*

Mittagstisch *lunch menu*

Mohn *poppy seed*
  Mohnnudeln *noodles with poppy seeds, cinnamon, sugar and butter*
  Mohntorte *gâteau with poppy seeds*

Möhren *carrots*
  Möhrensalat *carrot salad*

Mohr im Hemd *chocolate pudding*

Most *fruit juice; (in the South) fruit wine*

Münchener *a kind of dark lager from Munich*

Muscheln *mussels*

Nachspeisen *desserts*

Nachtisch *dessert*

Nieren *kidneys*

Nierstein *village on the Rhine producing medium to sweet white Rheinwein*

Nockerln *small dumplings*

Nudeln *noodles*
Nudelsuppe *noodle soup*

Nüsse *nuts*
Nusskuchen *nut cake*
Nusstorte *nut gâteau*

Obst *fruit*
Obstkuchen *fruit cake*
Obstsalat *fruit salad*

Ochsenschwanz *oxtail*
Ochsenschwanzsuppe *oxtail soup*

Öl *oil*

Oppenheim *village on the Rhine producing fine white wines*

Orange *orange*

Orangensaft *orange juce*

Palatschinken *pancakes filled with curd mixture or jam or ice cream*

Pampelmuse *grapefruit*

paniert *coated with breadcrumbs*

Paprika *peppers*

Pellkartoffeln *small jacket potatoes served with their skins, often accompanied by Quark*

Peperoni *hot chilli pepper*

Petersilie *parsley*

Pfannkuchen *pancakes*

Pfeffer *pepper*

Pfefferkäse mit Schinken *ham and pepper cheese log*

Pfifferlinge *chanterelles*

Pfirsich *peach*

Pflaumen *plums*

Pflaumenkuchen *plum tart*

Pils, Pilsner *a strong, slightly bitter lager*

Pilze *mushrooms*

Pilzsuppe *mushroom soup*

Pommes frites *chips*

Portion *portion, serving*

Powidltascherl *ravioli-like pasta filled with plum jam (Austria)*

Preiselbeeren *cranberries*

Pumpernickel *very dark bread made with wholemeal coarse rye flour*

Punschpudding *pudding containing alcohol*

Pute *turkey*
Puten-schnitzel *turkey breast in breadcrumbs*

Quark *curd cheese*

Raclette *melted cheese and potatoes*

Radieschen *radish(s)*

Radler *beer with lemonade (Bavaria)*

Ragout *stew*

Rahm *sour cream*

Rahmschnitzel *cutlet with a creamy sauce*

Rahmsuppe *creamy soup*

Räucherkäse mit Schinken *smoked cheese with bacon pieces in it*

Räucherkäse mit Walnüssen *smoked cheese with pieces of walnut in it*

Räucherlachs *smoked salmon*

Räucherspeck *smoked bacon*

Reh *venison*
  Rehrücken *roast saddle of venison*

Reibekuchen *potato cakes*

Reis *rice*

Remoulade, Remouladensauce *tartar sauce*

Rhabarber *rhubarb*

Riesling *Riesling wine*
  Rieslingsuppe *wine soup made with Riesling*

Rind(fleisch) *beef*
  Rinderbraten *roast beef*
  Rinderrouladen *rolled beef (beef olives)*

Rippenbraten *roast spare ribs*

Risi lisi, Risibisi *rice with peas*

Roh *raw*

Rollmops *marinated herring fillets rolled up with small pieces of onion, gherkins and white peppercorns*

Rinderbraten

Rosenkohl *Brussels sprouts*

Roséwein *rosé wine*

Rosinen *raisins*

Rösti *fried diced potatoes, onions and bacon*

Rotbarsch *rosefish*

rote Bete *beetroot*

rote Grütze *raspberry, red currant and wine jelly served with fresh cream*

rote Rübe *beetroot*

Rotkohl *red cabbage*

Rotwein *red wine*

Roulade *beef olive*

Rübe *turnip*

Rührei *scrambled eggs*

Sachertorte *rich chocolate gâteau*

Saft *juice*

Sahne *cream*

Saison *season e.g. je nach Saison depending on the season*

Salat *salad*
  Gemischter Salat *mixed salad*
  Salatbeilage *side salad*
  Salz *salt*
  Salzkartoffeln *boiled potatoes*

Sardellen *anchovies*

Sardinen *sardines*

Rotkohl

Sauerbraten mit Rotkohl und Klößen

Sauerbraten *braised pickled beef served with dumplings and vegetables*
Sauerkraut *shredded pickled white cabbage*
Scampi *scampi*
Schafskäse *ewe's milk cheese*
scharf *spicy*
Schaschlik *shish kebab*
Schellfisch *haddock*
Schnaps *strong spirit*
Schinken *ham*
  Schinkenkipferl *ham-filled croissant ·*
  Schinkenwurst *ham sausage*
Schlachtplatte *mixture of cold sausages and meat*

Sauerkraut mit Bockwurst

Schlagsahne *whipped cream*
Schmelzkäse *cheese spread*
Schmorgurken *hotpot with cucumber and meat*
Schnecke *snail*
Schnittlauch *chives*
  Schnittlauchbrot *chives on bread*
Schnitzel *escalope served with potatoes and vegetables*
Schokolade *chocolate*
Schokoladentorte *chocolate gateaux*
Scholle *plaice*
Schorle *wine and sparkling water*
Schwäbischer Apfelkuchen *apple cake from Swabia*
Schwammerlgulasch *mushroom stew*
Schwarzbrot *rye bread*
schwarze Johannisbeeren *blackcurrants*
schwarzer Tee *black tea*

Schwarzwälder Kirschtorte

Schwarzwälder Kirschtorte *Black Forest cherry gâteau*
Schwarzwälder Schinken *Black Forest ham*
Schwarzwälder Torte *fruit compote flan with cream*
Schwein *pork*
  Schweinebraten *roast pork*

Schweinefleisch *pork*
Schweinehaxe *knuckle of pork*
Schweinekotelett *pork chop*
Schweinsrostbraten *roast pork*

Schwertfisch *swordfish*

Seezunge *sole*

Sekt *sparkling wine like champagne*

Selters(wasser) *sparkling mineral water*

Semmeln *bread rolls*

Semmelknödel *whole roll dumpling*

Senf *mustard*

Seniorenteller *small portion of a dish for senior citizens*

Sesam *sesame*

Scampi *scampi*

Slivovitz *plum schnapps*

Sonnenblumenbrot *wholemeal bread with sunflower seeds*

Soße *sauce*

Spanferkel *suckling pig*

Spargel *asparagus*
　Spargelcremesuppe *cream of asparagus soup*
　Spargelsalat *asparagus salad*

Spätzle *home-made noodles*

Speck *bacon (fat)*

Speisekarte *(printed) menu*

Spezialität des Hauses *speciality of the house/chef's special*

Spiegelei *fried egg, sunny side up*

Spieß *kebab style*

Spinat *spinach*

Sprudel *sparkling mineral water*

Stachelbeeren *gooseberries*

Stachelbeertorte *gooseberry tart*

Stangl *croissant covered with cheese*

Starkbier *strong beer*

Steinbutt *turbot*

Stollen

Steinpilze *wild mushroom found in the woods*

Steirischer Selchkäse *ewe's milk cheese (Austria)*

Steirisches Lammkarree mit Basilikum *lamb baked with basil (Austria)*

Sterz *Austrian polenta*

Stollen *spiced loaf with candied peel traditionally eaten at Christmas*

Strudel *strudel*

Sulz/Sülze *meat in aspic*

Spinat

Suppen soups
süß sweet
süßsauer sweet-and-sour
Tafelspitz boiled beef of various cuts
Tafelspitzsulz beef in aspic
Tagesgericht dish of the day
Tagesspuppe soup of the day
Tee tea
  Tee mit Milch tea with milk
  Tee mit Zitrone tea with lemon
  Eine Tasse Tee a cup of tea
  Ein Kännchen Tee a (little) pot of tea
Thunfisch tuna fish
Thüringer Rostbratwurst sausages from Thuringia, grilled or fried
Tilsiter savoury cheese with sharpish taste
Tintenfisch squid
Tomaten tomatoes
  Tomatensaft tomato juice
  Tomatensoße tomato sauce
Topf stew
Topfen curd cheese (Austria)
  Topfenknödel curd cheese dumplings
  Topfennudeln pasta with cheese
  Topfenstrudel flaky pastry strudel with curd-cheese filling
Torte gateau

Trauben grapes
  Traubensaft grape juice
Trocken dry (wine)
Truthahn turkey
Türkischer Turkish coffee
überbacken baked in the oven with cheese on top
vegetarische Gerichte vegetarian dishes
Vollkorn wholemeal
Vollkornbrot wholemeal bread
Vorspeisen starters
Wacholder juniper
Waldpilze wild mushrooms
Walnüsse walnuts
warm warm
  warmer Krautsalat salad with warm cabbage and crunchy bacon
Wasser water
Weichkäse cream cheese
Wein vine
Weinbrand brandy
Weinkarte wine list
Weißbrot wheat bread
Weiße golden wheat beer
Weißkohl white cabbage

Trauber

Tomaten

Weißwein white wine
Weißwurst white sausage (veal and pork with herbs)
Weizenbier wheat beer
Wels catfish
Westfälischer Schinken Westphalian ham
Wiener frankfurters
Wiener Backhendl roast chicken covered in breadcrumbs
Wiener Fischfilets fish fillets baked in sour cream sauce
Wiener Hofburgtorte chocolate gâteau
Wiener Kartoffelsuppe potato soup with mushrooms
Wiener Sachertorte Viennese chocolate cake
Wiener Schnitzel veal escalope fried in breadcrumbs
Wiener Würstchen frankfurter
Wild game
Wildbraten roast venison
Wildgulasch game stew
Wildschwein wild boar
Wirsingkohl Savoy cabbage
Wurst sausage
Würstchen frankfurter

Würzfleisch strips of meat roasted in a spicy sauce
Zander pike-perch
Ziegenkäse goat's milk cheese
Ziegett mixed milk cheese
Zigeunerschnitzel cutlet in paprika sauce
Zillertaler cow's cheese from the Zillertal
Zimt cinnamon
Zitrone lemon
Zitronentee lemon tea
Zopf braided bread loaf
Zucchini courgette
Zucker sugar
Zuger Köteli baked dace with herbs and wine
Zunge tongue
Zürcher Geschnetzeltes thinly sliced meat (veal or turkey), served with a wine sauce and mushrooms (and side dish such as Rösti) (Switzerland)
Zwetschgen plums
Zwetschgendatschi damson tart
Zwetschgenknödel plum dumplings
Zwiebeln onions
Zwiebelkuchen onion flan
Zwiebelrostbraten large steak with onions
Zwiebelsalami salami with onion
Zwiebelsuppe onion soup

Wurst

A

a *(with der words)* ein
  (with die words) eine
  (with das words) ein
abbey die Abtei
able: to be able können
abortion die Abtreibung
about *(concerning)* über
  about 4 o'clock ungefähr vier Uhr
above *(overhead)* oben
  (higher than) über
abroad im Ausland
abscess der Abszess
accelerator das Gaspedal
to accept akzeptieren
accident der Unfall
accident and emergency department
  die Notaufnahme
accommodation die Unterkunft
to accompany begleiten
account *(bill)* die Rechnung
  (in bank) das Konto
account number die Kontonummer
to ache: it aches es tut weh
acid die Säure
actor der Schauspieler
adaptor der Adapter
address die Adresse
  what is the address? wie lautet die
  Adresse?
address book das Adressbuch
adhesive tape das Klebeband
admission fee der Eintrittspreis
adult der/die Erwachsene
  for adults für Erwachsene
advance: in advance im Voraus
advertisement *(in paper)* die Anzeige
to advise raten
A&E die Notaufnahme
aeroplane das Flugzeug
aerosol die Spraydose
afraid: to be afraid of Angst haben vor
after *(afterwards)* danach
  after lunch nach dem Mittagessen
afternoon der Nachmittag
  this afternoon heute Nachmittag
  tomorrow afternoon morgen
  Nachmittag
  in the afternoon am Nachmittag
aftershave das Rasierwasser
again wieder
against gegen
age das Alter
agency die Agentur
ago: a week ago vor einer Woche
to agree vereinbaren

agreement die Vereinbarung
AIDS das Aids
air das Luft
air ambulance *(helicopter)* der
  Rettungshubschrauber
airbag der Airbag
airbed die Luftmatratze
air conditioning die Klimaanlage
air-conditioning unit die Klimaanlage
air freshener der Lufterfrischer
airline die Fluggesellschaft
air mail: by air mail per Luftpost
airplane das Flugzeug
airport der Flughafen
airport bus der Flughafenbus
air ticket das Flugticket
aisle der Gang
alarm die Alarmanlage
alarm call der Weckruf
alarm clock der Wecker
alcohol der Alkohol
alcohol-free alkoholfrei
alcoholic alkoholisch
all alle
allergic: to be allergic to allergisch sein
  gegen
  I'm allergic to... ich bin allergisch
  gegen...
allergy die Allergie
to allow erlauben
  to be allowed dürfen
all right *(agreed)* in Ordnung
  are you all right? geht es Ihnen gut?
almost fast
alone allein
Alps die Alpen
already schon
also auch
altar der Altar
aluminium foil die Alufolie
always immer
a.m. vormittags
am: I am ich bin
amber *(traffic lights)* das Gelb
ambulance der Krankenwagen
America Amerika
American *adj* amerikanisch
  m/f der/die Amerikaner(in)
amount: total amount die Gesamtsumme
anaesthetic die Narkose
  local anaesthetic die örtliche Betäubung
  general anaesthetic die Vollnarkose
anchor der Anker
and und
angina die Angina

angry zornig
animal das Tier
ankle der Knöchel
anniversary der Jahrestag
to announce bekannt geben
announcement die Bekanntmachung
annual jährlich
another (additional) noch ein/
noch eine/noch ein
(different) ein anderer/eine andere/
ein anderes
another beer please noch ein Bier bitte
answer die Antwort
to answer antworten
answerphone der Anrufbeantworter
antacid das säurebindende Mittel
antibiotic das Antibiotikum
antifreeze das Frostschutzmittel
antihistamine das Antihistamin
anti-inflammatory das entzündungs-
hemmende Mittel
antiques die Antiquitäten
antique shop der Antiquitätenladen
antiseptic das Antiseptikum
any jegliche(r/s)
have you any apples? haben Sie Äpfel?
anybody jeder
anything irgendetwas
anywhere irgendwo
apartment das Appartement
appendicitis die Blinddarmentzündung
apple der Apfel
appointment der Termin
I have an appointment ich habe einen
Termin
approximately ungefähr
apricot die Aprikose
April der April
apron die Schürze
architect der/die Architekt(in)
are sind ; seid ; bin
arm der Arm
armbands (to swim) die Schwimmflügel
armchair der Sessel
to arrange vereinbaren
to arrest verhaften
arrival die Ankunft
to arrive ankommen
art die Kunst
art gallery die Kunsthalle
arthritis die Arthritis
artichokes die Artischocken
artificial künstlich
artist der/die Künstler(in)
ashtray der Aschenbecher

to ask (question) fragen
(for something) bitten um
asleep: to be asleep schlafen
to fall asleep einschlafen
asparagus der Spargel
aspirin das Aspirin
asthma das Asthma
I have asthma ich habe Asthma
at: at the hotel im Hotel
at home zu Hause
at 8 o'clock um acht Uhr
at once sofort
at night am Abend
ATM der Geldautomat
to attack angreifen
attractive attraktiv
aubergine die Aubergine
auction die Auktion
audience das Publikum
August der August
aunt die Tante
au pair das Au-pair-Mädchen
Australia Australien
Australian adj australisch
m/f der/die Australier(in)
Austria Österreich
Austrian adj österreichisch
m/f der/die Österreicher(in)
author der/die Autor(in)
automatic automatisch
automatic car das Automatikauto
auto-teller der Geldautomat
autumn der Herbst
available erhältlich
avalanche die Lawine
avenue die Allee
average der Durchschnitt
to avoid (obstacle) ausweichen
(person) meiden
awake wach
away weg
awful schrecklich
awning (caravan) das Vorzelt
(on house) die Markise
axe die Axt
axle (car) die Achse

B
baby das Baby
baby food die Babynahrung
baby milk die Babymilch
baby's bottle die Babyflasche
baby seat (in car) der Kindersitz
babysitter der/die Babysitter(in)
baby wipes die Babytücher
back (of body, hand) der Rücken

backpack der Rucksack
bacon der Speck
bad *(weather, news)* schlecht
(fruit, vegetables) verdorben
bag die Tasche
baggage das Gepäck
baggage allowance das Freigepäck
baggage reclaim die Gepäckausgabe
bait *(for fishing)* der Köder
baked gebacken
baker's die Bäckerei
balcony der Balkon
ball der Ball
ballet das Ballett
balloon der Ballon
Baltic Sea die Ostsee
banana die Banane
band *(musical)* die Band
bandage der Verband
bank die Bank
(river) das Ufer
bank account das Bankkonto
banknote der Geldschein
bar die Bar
barbecue der Grill
to have a barbecue eine Grillparty
geben
barber der Herrenfriseur
to bark bellen
barn die Scheune
basement das Untergeschoss
basket der Korb
basketball der Basketball
Basle Basel
bat *(racquet)* der Schläger
bath das Bad
tub die Badewanne
to have a bath ein Bad nehmen
bathing cap die Badekappe
bathroom das Badezimmer
with bathroom mit Bad
battery die Batterie
bay *(along coast)* die Bucht
B&B Übernachtung mit Frühstück
to be sein
beach der Strand
private beach der Privatstrand
sandy beach der Sandstrand
nudist beach der FKK-Strand
beach hut der Strandkorb
beans die Bohnen
beard der Bart
beautiful schön
because weil
to become werden

bed das Bett
double bed das Doppelbett
single bed das Einzelbett
twin beds zwei Einzelbetten
bed and breakfast Übernachtung mit
Frühstück
bedclothes die Bettwäsche
bedroom das Schlafzimmer
bee die Biene
beef das Rindfleisch
beer das Bier
before vor
before breakfast vor dem Frühstück
to begin beginnen
behind hinter
beige beige
to believe glauben
bell *(church)* die Glocke
(door) die Klingel
to belong to gehören zu
below unterhalb
belt der Gürtel
bend *(in road)* die Kurve
berth *(train, ship)* die Kabine
beside *(next to)* neben
best: the best der/die/das beste
bet die Wette
to bet on wetten auf
better besser
better than besser als
between zwischen
bib *(baby's)* das Lätzchen
bicycle das Fahrrad
by bicycle mit dem Fahrrad
bicycle pump die Luftpumpe
bicycle repair kit das Fahrradflickzeug
big groß
bigger than größer als
bike *(push bike)* das Fahrrad
(motorbike) das Motorrad
bike lock das Fahrradschloss
bikini der Bikini
bill *(account)* die Rechnung
bin *(dustbin)* der Mülleimer
bin liner der Müllbeutel
binoculars das Fernglas
bird der Vogel
biro der Kugelschreiber
birth die Geburt
birth certificate die Geburtsurkunde
birthday der Geburtstag
happy birthday! alles Gute zum
Geburtstag!
my birthday is on... ich habe am ...
Geburtstag
birthday card die Geburtstagskarte

birthday present das Geburtstagsgeschenk
biscuits die Kekse
bit *(piece)* das Stück
　a bit *(a little)* ein bisschen
bite *(by insect)* der Biss
　(of food) der Bissen
to bite beißen
　(insect) stechen
bitten *(by insect)* gestochen
　I've been bitten ich bin gestochen worden
bitter *(taste)* bitter
black schwarz
black ice das Glatteis
blank *(disk, tape)* leer
　blank CD or DVD der Rohling
bleach das Bleichmittel
to bleed bluten
blender der Mixer
blind *(person)* blind
blind *(for window)* das Rollo
blister die Blase
blocked *(pipe, road)* verstopft
blond *(person)* blond
blood das Blut
blood group die Blutgruppe
blood pressure der Blutdruck
blood test der Bluttest
blouse die Bluse
to blow-dry föhnen
blowout *(tyre)* die Reifenpanne
　(bicycle) der Platten
blue blau
　dark blue dunkelblau
　light blue hellblau
blunt *(knife, blade)* stumpf
boar das Wildschwein
to board *(plane, train, etc)* einsteigen
boarding card/pass die Bordkarte
boarding house die Pension
boat *(large)* das Schiff
　(small) das Boot
boat trip die Bootsfahrt
body der Körper
　(dead) die Leiche
to boil kochen
boiled gekocht
boiler der Boiler
bomb die Bombe
bone der Knochen
　fish bone die Gräte
bonnet *(car)* die Motorhaube
book das Buch
　book of tickets die Mehrfahrtenkarte
to book buchen

booking *(in hotel, train, etc)* die Reservierung
booking office *(train)* der Fahrkartenschalter
bookshop die Buchhandlung
boot *(car)* der Kofferraum
boots *(long)* die Stiefel
　(ankle) die Schnürschuhe
border *(country)* die Grenze
boring langweilig
born: I was born in 1960 ich bin neunzehn-hundertsechzig geboren
to borrow borgen
boss der/die Chef(in)
both beide
bottle die Flasche
　a bottle of wine eine Flasche Wein
　a half-bottle eine kleine Flasche
bottle opener der Flaschenöffner
bowl *(soup, etc)* die Schüssel
bow tie die Fliege
box *(of wood)* die Kiste
　(of cardboard) der Karton
box office die Kasse
boy der Junge
boyfriend der Freund
bra der BH
bracelet das Armband
to brake bremsen
brake cable *(bicycle)* der Bremszug
　(car) das Bremsseil
brake fluid die Bremsflüssigkeit
brake light das Bremslicht
brake pads die Bremsbeläge
brakes die Bremsen
branch *(of tree)* der Ast
　(of bank, etc) die Filiale
brand *(make)* die Marke
brass das Messing
brave mutig
bread das Brot
　brown bread das Schwarzbrot
　French bread das Baguette
　sliced bread geschnittenes Brot
　white bread das Weißbrot
bread roll das Brötchen
to break *(object)* zerbrechen
breakable zerbrechlich
breakdown *(car)* die Panne
breakdown van die Pannenhilfe
breakfast das Frühstück
　when is breakfast? wann gibt es Frühstück?
breast die Brust
to breast-feed stillen
to breathe atmen

113

brick der Ziegel
bride die Braut
bridegroom der Bräutigam
bridge die Brücke
briefcase die Aktentasche
to bring bringen
Britain Großbritannien
British britisch
broadband die Breitband
  broadband connection die Breitband-
  Verbindung
brochure die Broschüre
broken gebrochen
broken down *(car, etc)* kaputt
bronchitis die Bronchitis
bronze die Bronze
brooch die Brosche
broom der Besen
brother der Bruder
brother-in-law der Schwager
brown braun
bruise der Bluterguss
brush die Bürste
  (for floor) der Besen
bubble bath das Schaumbad
bucket der Eimer
buffet das Buffet
buffet car der Speisewagen
to build bauen
building das Gebäude
bulb *(electric)* die Glühbirne
bumbag die Gürteltasche
bumper die Stoßstange
bunch *(flowers)* der Blumenstrauß
  (grapes) die Weintraube
bureau de change die Wechselstube
burger der Hamburger
burglar der/die Einbrecher(in)
burn die Brandwunde
to burn verbrennen
bus der Bus
bus station der Busbahnhof
bus stop die Bushaltestelle
bus ticket der Busfahrschein
bus tour die Busfahrt
business das Geschäft
  on business geschäftlich
business address die Geschäftsadresse
business card die Visitenkarte
business centre das Geschäftszentrum
businessman/woman der
  Geschäftsmann/die Geschäftsfrau
business trip die Dienstreise ;
  die Geschäftsreise
busy beschäftigt

but aber
butcher's die Fleischerei
butter die Butter
button der Knopf
to buy kaufen
by *(beside)* bei
  (via) über
  by bus mit dem Bus
  by car mit dem Auto
  by ship mit dem Schiff
  by train mit dem Zug
bypass die Umgehungsstraße

C

cab *(taxi)* das Taxi
cabaret das Varieté
cabin *(on ship)* die Kabine
  inside cabin Innenkabine
  outside cabin Außenkabine
cabin crew die Besatzung
cable car die Seilbahn
café das Café
  internet café das Internet-Café
cake der Kuchen
cake shop die Konditorei
calculator der Taschenrechner
calendar der Kalender
call *(on phone)* der Anruf
to call *(on phone)* anrufen
calm *(person)* ruhig
  (weather) windstill
camcorder der Camcorder
camera die Kamera
camera phone das Foto-Handy
camera shop das Fotogeschäft
to camp campen
camping gas das Campinggas
camping mat die Isomatte
camping stove der Campingkocher
campsite der Campingplatz
can die Dose
can opener der Dosenöffner
can *(to be able)* können
  I can/we can ich kann/wir können
Canada Kanada
Canadian *adj* kanadisch
  m/f der/die Kanadier(in)
canal der Kanal
to cancel stornieren
cancellation die Stornierung
cancer der Krebs
candle die Kerze
canoe das Kanu
cap *(hat)* die Mütze
  (diaphragm) das Diaphragma
capital *(city)* die Hauptstadt

car das Auto
car alarm die Autoalarmanlage
car ferry die Autofähre
car hire die Autovermietung
car insurance die Kfz-Versicherung
car keys die Autoschlüssel
car park der Parkplatz
car parts die Ersatzteile
car port der Einstellplatz
car radio das Autoradio
car seat *(children's)* der Kindersitz
car wash die Waschanlage
caravan der Wohnwagen
carburettor der Vergaser
card *(greetings)* die (Glückwunsch)karte
  (playing) die Spielkarte
cardboard die Pappe
cardigan die Strickjacke
careful vorsichtig
  be careful! passen Sie auf!
carpet der Teppich
carriage *(railway)* der Wagen
carrot die Karotte
to carry tragen
carton der Karton
case *(suitcase)* der Koffer
cash das Bargeld
to cash *(cheque)* einlösen
cash desk die Kasse
cash machine der Geldautomat
cashier der/die Kassierer(in)
cashpoint der Geldautomat
casino das Kasino
casserole dish die Kasserolle
cassette die Kassette
cassette player der Kassettenrekorder
castle das Schloss
  (medieval fortress) die Burg
casualty department die Unfallstation
cat die Katze
cat food das Katzenfutter
catalogue der Katalog
catalytic converter *(car)* der Katalysator
to catch *(bus, train)* nehmen
cathedral der Dom
Catholic katholisch
cauliflower der Blumenkohe
cave die Höhle
cavity *(in tooth)* das Loch
CD die CD
CD ROM die CD-ROM
CD player der CD-Spieler
ceiling die Decke
celery der Sellerie

cellar der Keller
cellphone das Handy
cemetery der Friedhof
cent *(euro)* der Cent
centimetre der Zentimeter
central zentral
central heating die Zentralheizung
central locking *(car)* die
  Zentralverriegelung
centre das Zentrum
century das Jahrhundert
ceramic die Keramik
cereal *(breakfast)* die Cornflakes
certain *(sure)* sicher
certificate die Bescheinigung
chain die Kette
chair der Stuhl
chairlift der Sessellift
chambermaid das Zimmermädchen
champagne der Champagner
change *(money)* das Wechselgeld
to change *(to alter)* ändern
  (bus, train, etc) umsteigen
  to change money Geld wechseln
  to change clothes sich umziehen
changing room die Umkleidekabine
Channel *(English)* der Kanal
chapel die Kapelle
charcoal die Holzkohle
charge *(fee)* die Gebühr
charge *(rechargeable battery)* der Akku
  (prepaid phone time) das
  Gesprächsguthaben
  (electrical) die Ladung
  I've run out of charge *(phone)* mein
  Akku ist leer
to charge *(battery)* aufladen
  I need to charge my phone ich muss
  mein Handy aufladen
to charge berechnen
  please charge it to my account bitte
  setzen Sie es auf meine Rechnung
charge card *(for mobile phone)*
  die Guthabenkarte
  (store card) die Kundenkarte
charger *(for battery, etc)* das Ladegerät
charter flight der Charterflug
chatroom *(internet)* der Chatroom
cheap billig
cheap rate der Billigtarif
to check überprüfen
  (passports) kontrollieren
to check in einchecken
  (at hotel) sich an der Rezeption anmelden
check-in der Check-in
cheers! *(toast)* Prost!

cheese der Käse
chef der Koch/die Köchin
chemical toilet die chemische Toilette
chemist's die Drogerie
 (for medicines) die Apotheke
cheque der Scheck
cheque book das Scheckheft
cheque card die Scheckkarte
cherry die Kirsche
chest *(body)* die Brust
chewing gum der Kaugummi
chicken das Hühnchen
chickenpox die Windpocken
child das Kind
children die Kinder
 for children für Kinder
chilli der Chili ; die Peperoni
chimney der Schornstein
chin das Kinn
china das Porzellan
chips *(french fries)* die Pommes frites
chiropodist der/die Fußpfleger(in)
chocolate die Schokolade
chocolates die Pralinen
choir der Chor
to choose auswählen
chopping board das Küchenbrett
Christian name der Vorname
Christmas Weihnachten
 merry Christmas! frohe Weihnachten!
Christmas card die Weihnachtskarte
Christmas Eve Heiligabend
church die Kirche
cigar die Zigarre
cigarette die Zigarette
cigarette lighter das Feuerzeug
cigarette papers das Zigarettenpapier
cinema das Kino
circle *(theatre)* der Rang
circuit breaker der Unterbrecher
 (for protection) der Schutzschalter
cistern *(of toilet)* der Spülkasten
city die Stadt
city centre das Stadtzentrum
class: first class erste Klasse
 second class zweite Klasse
clean sauber
to clean säubern
cleaning lady die Putzfrau
clear klar
client der Kunde/die Kundin
cliff *(along coast)* die Klippe
 (in mountains) der Felsen
to climb *(mountains)* klettern
climbing boots die Bergschuhe

clingfilm® die Frischhaltefolie
clinic die Klinik
cloakroom die Garderobe
clock die Uhr
to close schließen
closed geschlossen
cloth *(rag)* der Lappen
 (fabric) der Stoff
clothes die Kleider
clothes line die Wäscheleine
clothes peg die Wäscheklammer
clothes shop das Bekleidungsgeschäft
cloudy bewölkt
club der Club
clutch *(car)* die Kupplung
coach *(bus)* der Bus
coach station der Busbahnhof
coach trip die Busreise
coal die Kohle
coast die Küste
coastguard die Küstenwache
coat der Mantel
coat hanger der Kleiderbügel
cocktail bar die Cocktailbar
cockroach die Kakerlake
cocoa der Kakao
code der Kode
coffee der Kaffee
 black coffee schwarzer Kaffee
 white coffee Kaffee mit Milch
 decaffeinated coffee koffeinfreier Kaffee
coil *(IUD)* die Spirale
coin die Münze
Coke® die Cola
colander das Sieb
cold kalt
 I'm cold mir ist kalt
 it's cold es ist kalt
cold *(illness)* die Erkältung
 I have a cold ich habe mich erkältet
cold sore der Ausschlag
collar der Kragen
collar bone das Schlüsselbein
colleague der Kollege/die Kollegin
to collect *(person)* abholen
 (something) (etwas) sammeln
collection die Sammlung
Cologne Köln
colour die Farbe
colour-blind farbenblind
colour film der Farbfilm
comb der Kamm
to come kommen
 (to arrive) ankommen
to come back zurückkommen

to come in hereinkommen
come in! herein!
comedy die Komödie
comfortable bequem
company *(firm)* die Firma
compartment *(in train)* das Abteil
compass der Kompass
to complain sich beschweren
complaint die Klage ·
complete vollständig
to complete vervollständigen
compulsory obligatorisch
computer der Computer
computer disk *(floppy)* die Diskette
computer game das Computerspiel
computer program das
Computerprogramm
concert das Konzert
concert hall die Konzerthalle
concession die Ermäßigung
concussion die Gehirnerschütterung
conditioner *(hair)* der Conditioner
condom das Kondom
conductor der Schaffner/die Schaffnerin
conference die Konferenz
to confirm bestätigen
please confirm bitte bestätigen Sie
confirmation *(flight, etc)* die Bestätigung
confused verwirrt
congratulations! herzlichen Glückwünsch!
connection *(train, etc)* die Verbindung
constipated verstopft
consulate das Konsulat
contact *(person)* der/die
Ansprechpartner(in)
to contact kontaktieren
contact lens cleaner der
Kontaktlinsenreiniger
contact lenses die Kontaktlinsen
to continue weitermachen
contraceptive das Verhütungsmittel
contract der Vertrag
convenient: *is it convenient?*
passt es so?
convulsions die Krämpfe
to cook kochen
cooked gekocht
cooker der Herd
cookies die Kekse
cool kühl
cool-box *(for picnic)* die Kühlbox
copy *(duplicate)* die Kopie
to copy kopieren
cordless phone das schnurlose Telefon
cork der Korken

corkscrew der Korkenzieher
corner die Ecke
cornflakes die Cornflakes
corridor der Flur
cosmetics die Kosmetikartikel
cost *(price)* die Kosten
to cost kosten
how much does it cost? wie viel
kostet es?
costume *(swimming)* der Badeanzug
cot das Kinderbett
cottage das Ferienhäuschen
cotton die Baumwolle
cotton bud das Wattestäbchen
cotton wool die Watte
couchette der Liegewagen
cough der Husten
to cough husten
cough sweets die Hustenbonbons
counter *(shop, bar)* die Theke
country das Land
countryside die Landschaft
couple *(two people)* das Paar
a couple of... ein paar...
courgettes die Zucchini
courier service der Kurierdienst
course *(of study)* der Kurs
(of meal) der Gang
cousin der Cousin/die Cousine
cover charge *(in restaurant)*
die Gedeckkosten
cow die Kuh
craft fair der Kunsthandwerksmarkt
crafts das Kunsthandwerk
craftsperson der Handwerker/
die Handwerkerin
cramps die Krämpfe
cranberry juice der Preiselbeersaft
crash *(collision)* der Zusammenstoß
to crash einen Unfall haben
crash helmet der Sturzhelm
cream *(lotion)* die Creme
(on milk) die Sahne
soured cream saure Sahne
whipped cream Schlagsahne
cream cheese der Frischkäse
credit *(on mobile phone)* das
Gesprächsguthaben
credit card die Kreditkarte
crime das Verbrechen
crisps die Chips
to cross *(road)* überqueren
cross-channel ferry die Kanalfähre
cross-country skiing der Skilanglauf
crossing *(sea)* die Überfahrt

crossroads die Kreuzung
crossword puzzle das Kreuzworträtsel
crowd die Menge
crowded überfüllt
crown die Krone
cruise die Kreuzfahrt
crutches die Krücken
to cry *(weep)* weinen
crystal das Kristall
cucumber die Gurke
cufflinks die Manschettenknöpfe
cul-de-sac die Sackgasse
cup die Tasse
cupboard der Schrank
curlers die Lockenwickler
currency die Währung
current *(electric)* der Strom
  (water) die Strömung
curtains die Vorhänge
cushion das Kissen
custom *(tradition)* der Brauch
customer der Kunde/die Kundin
customs *(duty)* der Zoll
cut die Schnittwunde
to cut schneiden
cutlery das Besteck
cutlet das Schnitzel
to cycle Rad fahren
cycle track der Radweg
cycling das Radfahren
cyst die Zyste
cystitis die Blasenentzündung

D

daily *(each day)* täglich
dairy products die Milchprodukte
dam der Damm
damage der Schaden
damp feucht
dance der Tanz
to dance tanzen
danger die Gefahr
dangerous gefährlich
dark dunkel
  after dark nach Einbruch der Dunkelheit
date das Datum
date of birth das Geburtsdatum
daughter die Tochter
daughter-in-law die Schwiegertochter
dawn die Morgendämmerung
day der Tag
  every day jeden Tag
  per day pro Tag
dead tot
deaf taub

dear *(in letter)* liebe(r/s)
  (expensive) teuer
debit card die Debitkarte
debts die Schulden
decaffeinated coffee der koffeinfreie
  Kaffee
December der Dezember
deckchair der Liegestuhl
to declare erklären
  nothing to declare nichts zu verzollen
deep tief
deep freeze die Tiefkühltruhe
deer das Reh
to defrost entfrosten
to de-ice enteisen
delay die Verspätung
delayed verspätet
delicatessen das Feinkostgeschäft
delicious köstlich
demonstration die Demonstration
dental floss die Zahnseide
dentist der Zahnarzt/die Zahnärztin
dentures das Gebiss
deodorant das Deo
to depart abfahren
department die Abteilung
department store das Kaufhaus
departure die Abfahrt
  (plane) der Abflug
departure lounge die Abflughalle
deposit die Anzahlung
to describe beschreiben
description die Beschreibung
desk der Schreibtisch
dessert der Nachtisch
details die Details
detergent das Waschmittel
detour der Umweg
to develop *(photos)* entwickeln
diabetes der Diabetes
diabetic person der Diabetiker/
  die Diabetikerin
to dial wählen
dialling code die Vorwahl
dialling tone der Wählton
diamond der Diamant
diarrhoea der Durchfall
diapers die Windeln
diaphragm *(contraception)*
  das Diaphragma
diary der Terminkalender
dice der Würfel
dictionary das Wörterbuch
to die sterben
diesel der Diesel

diet die Diät
  I'm on a diet ich muss eine Diät einhalten
  special diet spezielle Diät
different verschieden
difficult schwierig
digital camera die Digitalkamera
digital radio das Digitalradio
to dilute verdünnen
dinghy *(rubber)* das Schlauchboot
dining room das Esszimmer
dinner *(evening meal)* das Abendessen
  to have dinner zu Abend essen
diplomat der Diplomat/die Diplomatin
direct *(route)* direkt
  (train, etc) durchgehend
directions: to ask for directions nach dem Weg fragen
directory *(phone)* das Telefonbuch
directory enquiries die Auskunft
dirty schmutzig
disability die Behinderung
disabled *(person)* behindert
to disagree nicht zustimmen
to disappear verschwinden
disco die Disko
discount der Rabatt
to discover entdecken
disease die Krankheit
dish die Schale
  (food) das Gericht
dishtowel das Geschirrtuch
dishwasher die Geschirrspülmaschine
disinfectant das Desinfektionsmittel
disk die Diskette
to dislocate auskugeln
disposable wegwerfbar
distance die Entfernung
distilled water das destillierte Wasser
district der Bezirk
to disturb stören
to dive tauchen
diversion die Umleitung
diving das Tauchen
divorced geschieden
DIY shop der Baumarkt
dizzy schwindelig
to do machen
doctor der Arzt/die Ärztin
documents die Dokumente
dog der Hund
dog food das Hundefutter
dog lead die Hundeleine
doll die Puppe
dollar der Dollar

domestic *(flight)* Inlands-
donor card der Organspenderausweis
door die Tür
doorbell die Klingel
dormitory der Schlafsaal *(in hostel)* ;
  das Studentenwohnheim *(student residence)*
double Doppel-
double bed das Doppelbett
double room das Doppelzimmer
doughnut der Berliner
down: to go down nach unten gehen
Down's syndrome das Down-Syndrom
downstairs unten
drain der Abfluss
draught *(of air)* der Durchzug
  there's a draught hier zieht es
draught lager das Fassbier
drawer die Schublade
drawing die Zeichnung
dress das Kleid
to dress *(get dressed)* sich anziehen
dressing *(for food)* die Soße
  (for wound) das Verbandsmaterial
dressing gown der Morgenmantel
drill *(tool)* der Bohrer
drink das Getränk
to drink trinken
drinking water das Trinkwasser
to drive fahren
driver *(of car)* der Fahrer/die Fahrerin
driving licence der Führerschein
to drown ertrinken
drug das Medikament
  (narcotic) die Droge
drunk betrunken
dry trocken
to dry trocknen
dry cleaner's die Reinigung
dryer der Wäschetrockner
due: when's he due? wann soll er ankommen?
dummy *(for baby)* der Schnuller
during während
dust der Staub
duster das Staubtuch
dustpan and brush Schaufel und Handfeger
duty-free zollfrei
duvet die Bettdecke
duvet cover der Bettbezug
DVD die DVD
DVD player der DVD-Spieler
to dye färben
dynamo *(car)* die Lichtmaschine
  (bike) der Dynamo

E

each jede(r/s)
ear das Ohr
earache die Ohrenschmerzen
   I have earache ich habe Ohrenschmerzen
earlier früher
early früh
to earn verdienen
earphones die Kopfhörer
earrings die Ohrringe
earth die Erde
earthquake das Erdbeben
east der Osten
Easter Ostern
easy leicht
to eat essen
ecological ökologisch
economy class die Touristenklasse
eco-tourism der Ökotourismus
egg das Ei
   fried egg das Spiegelei
   hard-boiled egg hart gekochte Ei
   scrambled egg Rührei
   soft-boiled egg weich gekochte Ei
either ... or entweder … oder
elastic band das Gummiband
Elastoplast® das Pflaster
elbow der Ellbogen
electric elektrisch
electric blanket die Heizdecke
electric razor der Elektrorasierer
electric shock der elektrische Schlag
electric toothbrush die elektrische
   Zahnbürste
electrician der Elektriker
electricity meter der Stromzähler
electronic elektronisch
electronic organizer der (elektronische)
   Organizer
elevator der Fahrstuhl
e-mail die E-Mail
to e-mail e-mailen
e-mail address die E-Mail-Adresse
embassy die Botschaft
emergency der Notfall
emergency exit der Notausgang
emery board die Nagelfeile
empty leer
end das Ende
engaged *(to marry)* verlobt
   (toilet, telephone) besetzt
engine der Motor
engineer der Ingenieur/die Ingenieurin
England England
English *adj* englisch

Englishman/woman der Engländer/die
   Engländerin
to enjoy *(to like)* mögen
   enjoy your meal! guten Appetit!
enough genug
   that's enough das reicht
enquiry desk die Auskunft
to enter eintreten
entertainment das Entertainment
entrance der Eingang
entrance fee der Eintrittspreis
envelope der Umschlag
epileptic der Epileptiker/die Epileptikerin
epileptic fit der epileptische Anfall
equal gleich
equipment die Ausrüstung
eraser der Radiergummi
error der Fehler
escalator die Rolltreppe
to escape entkommen
essential wesentlich
estate agent's der Grundstücksmakler
euro der Euro
euro cent der Eurocent
Europe Europa
European europäisch
European Union die Europäische Union
evening der Abend
   this evening heute Abend
   tomorrow evening morgen Abend
   in the evening am Abend
evening dress das Abendkleid
evening meal das Abendessen
every *(each)* jede(r/s)
everyone jeder
everything alles
everywhere überall
examination *(medical)* die Untersuchung
   (school) die Prüfung
example: for example zum Beispiel
excellent ausgezeichnet
except außer
excess baggage das Übergepäck
exchange der Austausch
to exchange tauschen
   (money) wechseln
exchange rate der Wechselkurs
exciting aufregend
excursion der Ausflug
excuse me! *(sorry)* Entschuldigung!
exhaust der Auspuff
exhibition die Ausstellung
exit der Ausgang
expense Account das Spesenkonto
expenses die Spesen

expensive teuer
expert der Experte/die Expertin
to expire *(ticket, etc)* ungültig werden
to explain erklären
explanation die Erklärung
explosion die Explosion
export der Export
to export exportieren
express *(train)* der Schnellzug
express *(parcel, etc)* per Express
extension lead das Verlängerungskabel
extra *(spare)* übrig
  (more) noch ein(e)
  an extra towel ein zusätzliches Handtuch
eye das Auge
eyebrows die Augenbrauen
eye drops die Augentropfen
eye liner der Eyeliner
eye shadow der Lidschatten

F

fabric der Stoff
face das Gesicht
face cloth der Waschlappen
facial die Gesichtspflege
facilities die Einrichtungen
factor *(sunblock)* der (Lichtschutz-)Faktor
  factor 25 (Lichschutz-)Faktor 25
factory die Fabrik
to faint ohnmächtig werden
fainted ohnmächtig
fair *(hair)* blond
  (just) gerecht
fair *(trade fair)* die Messe
  (funfair) der Jahrmarkt
fake unecht
fall *(autumn)* der Herbst
to fall fallen
  I have fallen ich bin hingefallen
false teeth das Gebiss
family die Familie
famous berühmt
fan *(electric)* der Ventilator
  (football, music) der Fan
fan belt der Keilriemen
fancy dress die Verkleidung
far weit
  how far is it? wie weit ist es?
fare *(train, bus, etc)* der Fahrpreis
farm der Bauernhof
farmer der Bauer/die Bäuerin
farmers' market der Wochenmarkt ;
  der Bauernmarkt
farmhouse das Bauernhaus

fashionable modern
fast schnell
  too fast zu schnell
to fasten: *to fasten the seatbelt*
  sich anschnallen
fat *(big)* dick
fat das Fett
  saturated fat gesättigte Fettsäuren
  unsaturated fat ungesättigte Fettsäuren
father der Vater
father-in-law der Schwiegervater
fault *(defect)* der Fehler
  it wasn't my fault das war nicht meine
  Schuld
favour der Gefallen
favourite Lieblings-
fax das Fax
  by fax per Fax
to fax faxen
fax number die Faxnummer
February der Februar
to feed füttern
feeding bottle die Babyflasche
to feel fühlen
  I don't feel well ich fühle mich nicht wohl
  I feel sick mir ist schlecht
feet die Füße
female weiblich
ferry die Fähre
festival das Festival
few: *a few* ein paar
fiancé(e) der/die Verlobte
field das Feld
fig die Feige
to fight kämpfen
file *(nail)* die Feile
  (computer) die Datei
  (for papers) der Ordner
to fill füllen
to fill in *(form)* ausfüllen
to fill up *(tank)* voll tanken
fillet das Filet
filling *(in tooth)* die Plombe
film der Film
Filofax® der Terminplaner
filter der Filter
to find finden
fine *(to be paid)* die Geldstrafe
finger der Finger
to finish beenden
fire das Feuer
fire alarm der Feuermelder
fire brigade die Feuerwehr
fire engine das Feuerwehrauto

fire escape die Feuertreppe
fire exit der Notausgang
fire extinguisher der Feuerlöscher
fireplace der Kamin
fireworks das Feuerwerk
firm *(company)* die Firma
first erste(r/s)
first aid die erste Hilfe
first class *(travel)* erste Klasse
first name der Vorname
fish der Fisch
to fish angeln
fishing permit der Angelschein
fishing rod die Angel
fishmonger's die Fischhandlung
fit *(seizure)* der Anfall
to fit passen
  it doesn't fit es passt nicht
to fix reparieren
  can you fix it? können Sie es reparieren?
fizzy sprudelnd
flag die Fahne
flames die Flammen
flash das Blitzlicht
flashlight *(torch)* die Taschenlampe
flask *(thermos)* die Thermosflasche
flat *(level)* flach
flat die Wohnung
flat battery die leere Batterie
flat tyre die Reifenpanne
flavour der Geschmack
  what flavour? welchen Geschmack?
flaw der Defekt
fleas die Flöhe
flesh das Fleisch
flex die Verlängerungsschnur
flight der Flug
flip-flops die Badelatschen
flippers die Schwimmflossen
flood die Flut
  flash flood die Überschwemmung
floor *(of building)* die Etage
  (of room) der Boden
  which floor? auf welcher Etage?
  on the ground floor im Erdgeschoss
  on the first floor in der ersten Etage
floorcloth der Scheuerlappen
floppy disk die Diskette
flour das Mehl
flowers die Blumen
flu die Grippe
fly die Fliege
to fly fliegen
fly sheet das Überzelt
fog der Nebel

foggy neblig
foil die Folie
to fold falten
to follow folgen
food das Essen
food poisoning die Lebensmittelvergiftung
foot der Fuß
  on foot zu Fuß
football der Fußball
football match das Fußballspiel
football player der Fußballer
footpath der Fußweg
for für
  for me für mich
  for him/her für ihn/sie
forbidden verboten
forehead die Stirn
foreign ausländisch
foreigner der Ausländer/die Ausländerin
forest der Wald
forever für immer
to forget vergessen
fork *(for eating)* die Gabel
  (in road) die Gabelung
form *(document)* das Formular
fortnight zwei Wochen
forward vorwärts
fountain der Brunnen
fox der Fuchs
fracture der Bruch
fragile zerbrechlich
fragrance das Parfüm
frame *(picture)* der Rahmen
France Frankreich
free *(not occupied)* frei
  (costing nothing) umsonst
free-range Freiland-
  free-range eggs Eier aus Freilandhaltung
freezer die Tiefkühltruhe
French *adj* französisch
French beans die grünen Bohnen
French fries die Pommes frites
Frenchman/woman der Franzose/die Französin
frequent häufig
fresh frisch
fresh water das frische Wasser
Friday der Freitag
fridge der Kühlschrank
fried gebraten
friend der Freund/die Freundin
friendly freundlich
frog der Frosch

from von
  from Scotland aus Schottland
  from England aus England
front die Vorderseite
  in front of vor
front door die Eingangstür
frost der Frost
frozen gefroren
fruit das Obst
  dried fruit das Trockenobst
fruit juice der Fruchtsaft
to fry braten
frying pan die Bratpfanne
fuel *(petrol)* das Benzin
fuel gauge die Tankanzeige
fuel pump *(in car)* die Benzinpumpe
  (at petrol station) die Zapfsäule
fuel tank der Tank
full voll
  (occupied) besetzt
  I'm full ich bin satt!
full board die Vollpension
fumes die Abgase
fun der Spaß
funeral die Beerdigung
funfair der Jahrmarkt
funny *(amusing)* komisch
fur der Pelz
furnished möbliert
furniture die Möbel
fuse die Sicherung
fuse box der Sicherungskasten
future die Zukunft

G

gallery die Galerie
game das Spiel
  (meat) das Wild
garage *(private)* die Garage
  (for repairs) die Werkstatt
  (petrol station) die Tankstelle
garden der Garten
garlic der Knoblauch
gas das Gas
gas cooker der Gasherd
gastritis die Gastritis
gate *(airport)* das Gate
gay *(person)* der/die Homosexuelle
gearbox das Getriebe
gear cable *(bike)* der Schaltzug
gears das Getriebe
  first gear der erste Gang
  second gear der zweite Gang
  third gear der dritte Gang
  fourth gear der vierte Gang
  neutral der Leerlauf
  reverse der Rückwärtsgang

generous großzügig
Genetically modified genmanipuliert
gents' *(toilet)* die Herrentoilette
genuine echt
German *adj* deutsch
  m/f der/die Deutsche
German measles die Röteln
Germany Deutschland
to get *(to obtain)* bekommen
  (to fetch) holen
to get in(to) *(bus, etc)* einsteigen
to get off *(bus, etc)* aussteigen
gift das Geschenk
gift shop der Geschenkeladen
girl das Mädchen
girlfriend die Freundin
to give geben
to give back zurückgeben
glacier der Gletscher
glass das Glas
  a glass of water ein Glas Wasser
glasses *(spectacles)* die Brille
glasses case das Brillenetui
gloves die Handschuhe
glue der Klebstoff
gluten das Gluten
  gluten-free glutenfrei
GM-free genfrei
to go *(on foot)* gehen
  (in car) fahren
  I'm going to... ich fahre nach...
  we're going to... wir fahren nach...
  to go home nach Hause fahren
  to go on foot zu Fuß gehen
to go back zurückgehen
to go in hineingehen
to go out ausgehen
God Gott
goggles *(swimming)* die Taucherbrille
  (skiing) die Schneebrille
gold das Gold
golf das Golf
golf ball der Golfball
golf clubs die Golfschläger
golf course der Golfplatz
good gut
  (pleasant) schön
good afternoon guten Tag
goodbye auf Wiedersehen
good day guten Tag
good evening guten Abend
good morning guten Morgen
good night gute Nacht
goose die Gans
GPS *(global positioning system)* das GPS
grandchild das Enkelkind

granddaughter die Enkelin
grandfather der Großvater
grandmother die Großmutter
grandparents die Großeltern
grandson der Enkel
Grapefruit die Grapefruit
grapes die Trauben
grass das Gras
grated *(cheese)* gerieben
gram das Gramm
grater die Reibe
great *(big)* groß
  (wonderful) großartig
Great Britain Großbritannien
green grün
greengrocer's der Gemüseladen
greetings card die Grußkarte
grey grau
grill der Grill
to grill grillen
grilled gegrillt
grocer's der Lebensmittelladen
ground der Boden
ground floor das Erdgeschoss
  on the ground floor im Erdgeschoss
groundsheet der Zeltboden
group die Gruppe
guarantee die Garantie
guard *m/f (on train)* der Schaffner/
  die Schaffnerin
guava die Guave
guest der Gast
guesthouse die Pension
guide *m/f (tour guide)* der
  Fremdenführer/die Fremdenführerin
guidebook der Reiseführer
guided tour die Führung
guitar die Gitarre
gun die Waffe
gym das Fitnesscenter
gym shoes die Turnschuhe
gynaecologist der Gynäkologe/
  die Gynäkologin, der Frauenarzt/
  die Frauenärztin

H

haemorrhoids die Hämorrhoiden
hail der Hagel
hair die Haare
hairbrush die Haarbürste
haircut der Haarschnitt
hairdresser der Friseur
hairdryer der Föhn
hair dye die Tönung
hair gel das Haargel

hairgrip die Haarklemme
hair spray das Haarspray
half halb
  a half bottle eine kleine Flasche
  half an hour eine halbe Stunde
half board die Halbpension
half fare der halbe Fahrpreis
half price der halbe Preis
ham der Schinken
  (cooked) Kochschinken
  (cured) geräucherter Schinken
hamburger der Hamburger
hammer der Hammer
hand die Hand
handbag die Handtasche
handbrake *(car)* die Handbremse
hand-made handgearbeitet
handicapped behindert
handkerchief das Taschentuch
handle der Griff
handlebars der Lenker
hand luggage das Handgepäck
hands-free kit *(for phone)*
  die Freisprecheinrichtung
hands-free phone das Telefon mit
  Freisprechanlage
handsome gut aussehend
hang gliding das Drachenfliegen
hangover der Kater
to hang up auflegen
to happen passieren
  what happened? was ist passiert?
happy glücklich
  happy birthday! alles Gute zum Geburtstag!
harbour der Hafen
hard *(difficult)* schwierig
  (not soft) hart
hardware shop die Eisenwarenhandlung
to harm schädigen
harvest die Ernte
hat der Hut
to have haben
  I have... ich habe...
  we have... wir haben...
  do you have...? haben Sie...?
to have to müssen
hay fever der Heuschnupfen
he er
head der Kopf
headache die Kopfschmerzen
  I have a headache ich habe
  Kopfschmerzen
headlights die Scheinwerfer
headphones die Kopfhörer
health die Gesundheit
health food shop das Reformhaus

healthy gesund
to hear hören
hearing aid das Hörgerät
heart das Herz
heart attack der Herzinfarkt
heartburn das Sodbrennen
to heat up *(food, milk)* aufwärmen
heater das Heizgerät
 (radiator) der Heizkörper
heating die Heizung
heavy schwer
heel der Absatz
heel bar der Schuhreparatur-Service
 (shoemaker) der Schuster
height die Höhe
helicopter der Hubschrauber
hello hallo
helmet *(for bike)* der Schutzhelm
help! Hilfe!
to help helfen
hem der Saum
hepatitis die Hepatitis
her *(with der words)* ihr
 (with das words) ihr
 (with die words) ihre
 to her zu ihr
herbal tea der Kräutertee
herbs die Kräuter
here hier
 here is... hier ist…
hernia der Eingeweidebruch
hi! hallo!
to hide verstecken
high hoch
 (number, speed) groß
high blood pressure der hohe Blutdruck
high chair der Kinderstuhl
high tide die Flut
hill der Hügel
hill-walking das Bergwandern
him ihm
hip die Hüfte
hip replacement die künstliche Hüfte
hire die Vermietung
 car hire die Autovermietung
 bike hire die Fahrradvermietung
 boat hire der Bootsverleih
 ski hire der Skiverleih
to hire mieten
hire car das Mietauto
his *(with der words)* sein
 (with das words) sein
 (with die words) seine
historic historisch
history die Geschichte
to hit schlagen
to hitchhike trampen

hobby das Hobby
to hold halten
 to contain enthalten
hold-up *(traffic jam)* der Stau
hole das Loch
holiday der Feiertag
 holidays der Urlaub
 on holiday in den Ferien
home das Zuhause
 at home zu Hause
homeopathic *(remedy, etc)* homöopathisch
homeopathy die Homöopathie
homepage die Homepage
homesick *(to be)* Heimweh haben
 I'm homesick ich habe Heimweh
homosexual homosexuell
honest ehrlich
honey der Honig
honeymoon die Flitterwochen
hood *(of jacket)* die Kapuze
hook der Haken
to hope hoffen
 I hope so hoffentlich
 I hope not hoffentlich nicht
horn *(car)* die Hupe
hors d'œuvre die Vorspeise
horse das Pferd
horse racing das Pferderennen
to horse ride reiten
hosepipe der Schlauch
hospital das Krankenhaus
hostel das Wohnheim
 (youth hostel) die Jugendherberge
hot heiß
 I'm hot mir ist heiß
 it's hot *(weather)* es ist heiß
hot-water bottle die Wärmflasche
hotel das Hotel
hour die Stunde
 1 hour eine Stunde
 2 hours zwei Stunden
 half an hour eine halbe Stunde
house das Haus
housewife/husband die Hausfrau/
 der Hausmann
house wine der Hauswein
housework die Hausarbeit
how wie
 how much? wie viel?
 how many? wie viele?
 how are you? wie geht es Ihnen?
hungry *(to be)* hungrig
to hunt jagen
hunting permit die Jagderlaubnis
hurry: I'm in a hurry ich habe es eilig
to hurt *(be painful)* weh tun
 my back hurts mir tut der Rücken weh
 that hurts das tut weh

husband der Mann
hut *(beach)* der Strandkorb
  (mountain) die Hütte
hypodermic needle die Spritze

I

I ich
ice das Eis
  with/without ice mit/ohne Eis
ice box die Kühlbox
ice cream das Eis
ice cube der Eiswürfel
ice rink die Eisbahn
to ice-skate Schlittschuh laufen
ice skates die Schlittschuhe
iced: iced coffee der Eiskaffee
  iced tea der Eistee
idea die Idee
identity card der Personalausweis
if wenn
ignition die Zündung
ignition key der Zündschlüssel
ill krank
  I'm ill ich bin krank
illness die Krankheit
immediately sofort
immersion heater der Boiler
immobilizer *(on car)* die Wegfahrsperre
immunisation die Immunisierung
to import importieren
important wichtig
impossible unmöglich
to improve verbessern
in in
  in 2 hours in zwei Stunden
  in Vienna in Wien
in front of vor
included inbegriffen
inconvenient unpassend
to increase vergrößern
indicator *(in car)* der Blinker
indigestion die Magenverstimmung
indigestion tablets die Magentabletten
indoors drinnen
infection die Infektion
infectious ansteckend
information die Auskunft
information desk der
  Informationsschalter
information office das Informationsbüro
ingredients die Zutaten
inhaler *(for medication)* der
  Inhalationsapparat
injection die Spritze

to injure verletzen
injured *(person)* verletzt
injury die Verletzung
ink die Tinte
inn das Gasthaus
inner tube der Schlauch
inquiries die Auskunft
inquiry desk der Auskunftsschalter
insect das Insekt
insect bite der Insektenstich
insect repellent das Insektenschutzmittel
inside in
instant coffee der Pulverkaffee
instead of anstelle von
insulin das Insulin
insurance die Versicherung
to insure versichern
insured versichert
to intend to vorhaben
interesting interessant
international international
  (arrivals, departures) Ausland
internet das Internet
**internet access: do you have internet
  access?** haben Sie Internet-Anschluss?
internet café das Internet-Café
interpreter der Dolmetscher/
  die Dolmetscherin
interval die Pause
into in
  into town in die Stadt
  into the centre ins Zentrum
to introduce vorstellen
invitation die Einladung
to invite einladen
invoice die Rechnung
iPod® der iPod
Ireland Irland
Irish *adj* irisch
Irishman/woman der Ire/die Irin
iron *(for clothes)* das Bügeleisen
  (metal) das Eisen
to iron bügeln
ironing board das Bügelbrett
ironmonger's die Eisenwarenhandlung
is ist
island die Insel
it er/sie/es
Italian *adj* italienisch
  m/f der Italiener/die Italienerin
Italy Italien
to itch jucken
item das Ding
IUD das Intrauterinpessar ; die Spirale

J

jack *(for car)* der Wagenheber
jacket die Jacke
jacuzzi der Whirlpool
jam *(food)* die Marmelade
jammed blockiert
January der Januar
jar *(honey, jam, etc)* das Glas
jaundice die Gelbsucht
jaw der Kiefer
jealous eifersüchtig
jeans die Jeans
jellyfish die Qualle
jet ski das Wassermotorrad
jetty die Mole
Jew der Jude/die Jüdin
jeweller's der Juwelier
jewellery der Schmuck
Jewish jüdisch
job *(employment)* die Stelle
to jog joggen
to join *(club)* beitreten
to join in mitmachen
joint *(of body)* das Gelenk
to joke scherzen
joke der Witz
journalist der Journalist/die Journalistin
journey die Reise
judge der Richter/die Richterin
jug der Krug
juice der Saft
  carton of juice der Saftkarton
July der Juli
to jump springen
jumper der Pullover
jump leads *(for car)* das Starthilfekabel
junction *(road)* die Kreuzung
June der Juni
just: *just two* nur zwei
  I've just arrived ich bin gerade
  angekommen

K

to keep *(retain)* behalten
kettle der Wasserkocher
key der Schlüssel
keycard die Schlüsselkarte
keyring der Schlüsselring
to kick *(ball)* schießen
  (person) treten
kidneys die Nieren
to kill töten
kilo das Kilo
kilometre der Kilometer

kind *(person)* nett
kind *(sort)* die Art
kiosk der Kiosk
kiss der Kuss
to kiss küssen
kitchen die Küche
kitchen paper das Küchenpapier
kite der Drachen
kiwi fruit die Kiwi
knee das Knie
kneehighs die Kniestrümpfe
knickers der Slip
knife das Messer
to knit stricken
to knock stoßen
to knock down *(in car)* überfahren
to knock over *(object)* umstoßen
knot der Knoten
to know *(facts)* wissen
  (be acquainted with) kennen
  I don't know ich weiß nicht
to know how to können
kosher koscher

L

label das Schild
lace *(shoe)* der Schnürsenkel
ladder die Leiter
ladies' *(toilet)* die Damentoilette
lady die Dame
lager das helle Bier
  bottled lager das Flaschenbier
  draught lager das Fassbier
lake der See
lamb das Lammfleisch
lamp *(for table)* die Lampe
to land landen
landlady die Vermieterin
landlord der Vermieter
landslide der Erdrutsch
lane die Gasse
  (of motorway/road) die Spur
language die Sprache
language school die Sprachenschule
laptop der Laptop
laptop bag die Laptop-Tasche
large groß
last *(final)* letzte(r/s)
  the last bus der letzte Bus
  last night gestern Abend
  last time letztes Mal
late spät
  the train is late der Zug hat Verspätung
later später
to laugh lachen

launderette der Waschsalon
laundry service der Wäschereiservice
lavatory die Toilette
law das Gesetz
lawn der Rasen
lawyer der Rechtsanwalt/die Rechtsanwältin
laxative das Abführmittel
layby die Haltebucht
lazy faul
lead (metal) das Blei
to lead führen
lead-free bleifrei
leaf das Blatt
leak (of gas, liquid) das Leck
to leak: *it's leaking* es hat ein Leck
to learn lernen
learning disability: *he/she has a learning disability* er/sie hat eine Lernschwäche
lease (rental) der Mietvertrag
leather das Leder
to leave (a place) weggehen/wegfahren
  when does the train leave? wann fährt der Zug ab?
leek der Lauch
left: *on the left* links
  to the left nach links
left-luggage locker das Schließfach
left-luggage office die Gepäckaufbewahrung
leg das Bein
lemon die Zitrone
lemongrass das Zitonengras
lemon tea der Zitronentee
lemonade die Limonade
to lend leihen
length (size) die Länge
  (duration) die Dauer
lens die Linse
lenses (contact) die Kontaktlinsen
lesbian lesbisch
less weniger
  less than weniger als
lesson die Unterrichtsstunde
to let (to allow) erlauben
  (room, house) vermieten
letter (written) der Brief
  (of alphabet) der Buchstabe
letterbox der Briefkasten
lettuce der Kopfsalat
library die Bibliothek
lid der Deckel
lie (untruth) die Lüge
to lie down sich hinlegen
lifebelt der Rettungsring

lifeboat das Rettungsboot
lifeguard der Rettungsschwimmer/ die Rettungsschwimmerin
life insurance die Lebensversicherung
life jacket die Schwimmweste
life raft die Rettungsinsel
lift (elevator) der Aufzug
  can I have a lift? können Sie mich mitnehmen?
lift pass der Liftpass
light (not heavy) leicht
light das Licht
  have you a light? haben Sie Feuer?
light bulb die Glühbirne
lighter das Feuerzeug
lighthouse der Leuchtturm
lightning der Blitz
like (preposition) wie
to like mögen
  I like coffee ich trinke gern Kaffee
  I don't like... ich mag ... nicht
  we'd like... wir möchten...
lilo® die Luftmatratze
lime (fruit) die Limone
line (row, of railway) die Linie
  (telephone) die Leitung
linen das Leinen
lingerie die Unterwäsche
lips die Lippen
lip-reading das Lippenlesen
lipstick der Lippenstift
liqueur der Likör
list die Liste
to listen to zuhören
litre der Liter
  litre of milk ein Liter Milch
litter (rubbish) der Abfall
little (small) klein
  a little... ein bisschen...
to live (exist) leben
  (reside) wohnen
  I live in London ich wohne in London
liver die Leber
living room das Wohnzimmer
loaf of bread das Brot
local (wine, speciality) hiesig
lock das Schloss
to lock zuschließen
locker (luggage) das Schließfach
locksmith der Schlosser
log (for fire) der Holzscheit
log book (car) die Zulassung
  (vehicle registration document) die (Kfz-)Zulassung

long lang
  for a long time lange Zeit
long-sighted weitsichtig
to look after sich kümmern um
to look at anschauen
to look for suchen
loose *(screw, tooth)* locker
  it's come loose es hat sich gelockert
lorry der Lastwagen
to lose verlieren
lost *(object)* verloren
  I've lost my wallet ich habe meine
  Brieftasche verloren
  I'm lost *(on foot)* ich habe mich verlaufen
  I'm lost *(in car)* ich habe mich verfahren
lost property office das Fundbüro
lot: *a lot* viel
lotion die Lotion
lottery das Lotto
loud laut
loudspeaker der Lautsprecher
lounge *(hotel/airport)* die Lounge
  (in house) das Wohnzimmer
love die Liebe
to love lieben
  I love you ich liebe dich
  I love swimming ich schwimme gern
lovely schön
low niedrig
low-alcohol alkoholarm
low-fat fettarm
low tide die Ebbe
luck das Glück
lucky glücklich
luggage das Gepäck
luggage rack die Gepäckablage
luggage tag der Kofferanhänger
luggage trolley der Gepäckwagen
lump *(swelling)* die Beule
lunch das Mittagessen
lunch break die Mittagspause
lung die Lunge
luxury der Luxus

M

machine die Maschine
mad verrückt
magazine die Zeitschrift
magnet der Magnet
magnifying glass die Lupe
maid *(in hotel)* das Zimmermädchen
maiden name der Mädchenname
mail die Post
  by mail per Post
main *(principal)* Haupt-

main course *(of meal)* das Hauptgericht
main road die Hauptstraße
to make machen
  (meal) zubereiten
make-up das Make-up
male männlich
man der Mann
  men die Männer
manager der Geschäftsführer/
  die Geschäftsführerin
mango die Mango
manicure die Maniküre
manual *(gear change)* das Schaltgetriebe
many viele
map die Karte
  (of region, country) die Landkarte
  (of town) der Stadtplan
March der März
margarine die Margarine
marina der Jachthafen
mark *(stain)* der Fleck
market der Markt
market place der Marktplatz
marmalade die Orangenmarmelade
married verheiratet
  I'm married ich bin verheiratet
  are you married? sind Sie verheiratet?
to marry heiraten
mascara die Wimperntusche
mass *(in church)* die Messe
massage die Massage
mast der Mast
matches die Streichhölzer
material das Material
matter: *it doesn't matter* das macht nichts
  what's the matter? was ist los?
mattress die Matratze
May der Mai
mayonnaise die Mayonnaise
maximum das Maximum
Mb *(megabyte)* MB
me *(direct object)* mich
  (indirect object) mir
meal das Essen
to mean bedeuten
  what does this mean? was bedeutet das?
measles die Masern
to measure messen
meat das Fleisch
  I don't eat meat ich esse kein Fleisch
mechanic der Mechaniker/
  die Mechanikerin
medical insurance die
  Krankenversicherung

medical treatment die medizinische Behandlung
medicine die Medizin
medieval mittelalterlich
medium rare *(meat)* halb durch
to meet *(by chance)* treffen
  (arranged) sich treffen mit
  pleased to meet you! sehr erfreut!
meeting das Treffen
  (business) die Besprechung
megabyte das Megabyte
  128 megabytes 128 Megabyte
melon die Melone
to melt schmelzen
member *(of club, etc)* das Mitglied
memory das Gedächtnis
memory card die Speicherkarte
memory stick *(for camera, etc)* der Memorystick
men die Männer
to mend reparieren
meningitis die Hirnhautentzündung
menu die Speisekarte
  set menu die Tageskarte
message die Nachricht
metal das Metall
meter der Zähler
metre der Meter
metro die U-Bahn
metro station die U-Bahn-Station
micro-brewery die Hausbrauerei
microphone das Mikrophon
microwave oven die Mikrowelle
midday der Mittag
  at midday am Mittag
middle die Mitte
middle-aged in den mittleren Jahren
midge die Mücke
midnight die Mitternacht
  at midnight um Mitternacht
migraine die Migräne
  I have a migraine ich habe Migräne
mile die Meile
milk die Milch
  fresh milk frische Milch
  full cream milk Vollfettmilch
  hot milk heiße Milch
  long-life milk H-Milch
  powdered milk das Milchpulver
  semi-skimmed milk Halbfettmilch
  skimmed milk Magermilch
  soya milk die Sojamilch
  with/without milk mit/ohne Milch
millimetre der Millimeter
mince *(meat)* das Hackfleisch
mind: *do you mind if...?* haben Sie etwas dagegen, wenn...?
  I don't mind es ist mir egal

mineral water das Mineralwasser
minibar die Minibar
minidisk die Minidisk
minimum das Minimum
minister *(church)* der Pfarrer/die Pfarrerin
  (political) der Minister/die Ministerin
mint *(herb)* die Minze
  (sweet) das Pfefferminzbonbon
minute die Minute
mirror der Spiegel
miscarriage die Fehlgeburt
to miss *(train, etc)* verpassen
Miss Fräulein
missing *(object)* verschwunden
  my son's missing mein Sohn ist weg
mistake der Fehler
misty dunstig
misunderstanding das Missverständnis
to mix mischen
mixer der Mixer
mobile *(phone)* das Handy
mobile number die Handynummer
modem das Modem
modern modern
moisturizer die Feuchtigkeitscreme
mole *(on skin)* das Muttermal
moment: *just a moment* einen Moment, bitte
monastery das Kloster
Monday der Montag
money das Geld
  I have no money ich habe kein Geld
moneybelt die Gürteltasche
money order die Postanweisung
month der Monat
  this month diesen Monat
  last month letzten Monat
  next month nächsten Monat
monthly monatlich
monument das Denkmal
moon der Mond
mooring der Anlegeplatz
mop *(floor)* der Mopp
moped das Moped
more mehr
  more than mehr als
  more wine noch etwas Wein
morning der Morgen
  in the morning am Morgen
  this morning heute Morgen
morning-after pill die Pille danach
mosque die Moschee
mosquito die Stechmücke
mosquito net das Moskitonetz
mosquito repellent das Insektenschutzmittel

most: *most of* das meiste von
moth *(clothes)* die Motte
mother die Mutter
mother-in-law die Schwiegermutter
motor der Motor
motorbike das Motorrad
motorboat das Motorboot
motorway die Autobahn
mould der Schimmel
mountain der Berg
mountain bike das Mountainbike
mountain rescue die Bergwacht
mountaineering das Bergsteigen
mouse die Maus
moustache der Schnurrbart
mouth der Mund
to move bewegen
 it isn't moving es bewegt sich nicht
movie der Kinofilm
to mow mähen
MP3 player der MP3-Spieler
Mr Herr
Mrs Frau
Ms Frau
much viel
 too much zu viel
muddy schlammig
mugging der Überfall
mumps der Mumps
Munich München
muscle der Muskel
museum das Museum
mushrooms die Pilze
music die Musik
musical das Musical
mussel die Muschel
must müssen
 I must ich muss
 we must wir müssen
 you musn't du darfst nicht
mustard der Senf
my *(with der words)* mein
 (with das words) mein
 (with die words) meine

N

nail *(fingernail)* der Fingernagel
 (metal) der Nagel
nailbrush die Nagelbürste
nail file die Nagelfeile
nail polish/varnish der Nagellack
nail polish remover der
 Nagellackentferner
nail scissors die Nagelschere

name der Name
 what is your name? wie ist Ihr Name?
nanny das Kindermädchen
napkin die Serviette
nappy die Windel
narrow eng
national national
nationality die Nationalität
natural natürlich
nature die Natur
nature reserve das Naturschutzgebiet
navy blue marineblau
near *(place, time)* nahe
 near the bank in der Nähe der Bank
 is it near? ist es in der Nähe?
necessary notwendig
neck der Hals
necklace die Halskette
nectarine die Nektarine
to need brauchen
 I need... ich brauche...
 we need... wir brauchen...
 I need to go ich muss gehen
needle die Nadel
 needle and thread Nadel und Faden
neighbour der Nachbar/die Nachbarin
nephew der Neffe
net das Netz
 the Net das Internet
never nie
 I never drink wine Wein trinke ich nie
new neu
news die Nachrichten
newsagent's der Zeitungsladen
newspaper die Zeitung
newsstand der Zeitungskiosk
New Year (1 Jan) Neujahr
 happy New Year! ein gutes neues Jahr!
New Year's Eve Silvester
New Zealand Neuseeland
next nächste(r/s)
 next to neben
 next week nächste Woche
 the next bus der nächste Bus
nice *(person)* nett
 (place, holiday) schön
niece die Nichte
night die Nacht
 at night am Abend
 last night gestern Abend
 per night pro Nacht
 tonight heute Abend
night club der Nachtklub
nightdress das Nachthemd
no nein
 no thanks nein danke
 no problem kein Problem

(without) ohne
no sugar ohne Zucker
no ice ohne Eis
nobody niemand
noise der Lärm
noisy laut
it's very noisy es ist sehr laut
non-alcoholic alkoholfrei
none keine(r/s)
non-smoker der Nichtraucher
non-smoking Nichtraucher-
north der Norden
Northern Ireland Nordirland
North Sea die Nordsee
nose die Nase
not nicht
I do not know ich weiß nicht
note *(banknote)* der Geldschein
(written) die Notiz
note pad der Notizblock
nothing nichts
nothing else nichts weiter
notice *(sign)* das Schild
novel der Roman
November der November
now jetzt
nowhere nirgends
nuclear nuklear
nudist beach der FKK-Strand
number die Zahl
number plate das Nummernschild
nurse die Krankenschwester/
der Krankenpfleger
nursery die Kinderbetreuung
nursery school die Vorschule
nut *(to eat)* die Nuss
(for bolt) die Schraubenmutter

O

oar das Ruder
oats der Hafer
to obtain erhalten
occupation *(work)* der Beruf
ocean der Ozean
October der Oktober
odd *(strange)* seltsam
of von
a glass of water ein Glas Wasser
made of... aus...
off *(light, radio, etc)* aus
(rotten) schlecht
office das Büro
off-season die Nebensaison
often oft
how often? wie oft?
oil das Öl

oil filter der Ölfilter
ointment die Salbe
OK okay
old alt
how old are you? wie alt sind Sie?
I'm... years old ich bin... Jahre alt
old age pensioner der Rentner/
die Rentnerin
on *(light, radio, etc)* an
on auf
on the table auf dem Tisch
on time pünktlich
once einmal
at once sofort
onion die Zwiebel
only nur
open geöffnet
to open öffnen
opera die Oper
operation *(surgical)* die Operation
operator *(phone)* die Vermittlung
opposite gegenüber
opposite the bank gegenüber der Bank
quite the opposite ganz im Gegenteil
optician's der Optiker
or oder
orange *(colour)* orange
orange *(fruit)* die Orange
orange juice der Orangensaft
orchestra das Orchester
order *(in restaurant)* die Bestellung
to order *(food)* bestellen
organic organisch
to organize organisieren
other: the other one der/die/das andere
have you got any others? haben Sie
noch andere?
our *(with der words)* unser
(with das words) unser
(with die words) unsere
out *(light, etc)* aus
she's out sie ist nicht da
out of order kaputt
outdoor *(pool, etc)* im Freien
outside draußen
oven der Herd
ovenproof dish die feuerfeste Form
over *(on top of, above)* über
to overbook überbuchen
to overcharge zu viel berechnen
overdone *(food)* verkocht
overdose die Überdosis
to overheat überhitzen
to overload überladen
to oversleep verschlafen
to overtake überholen

to owe schulden
I owe you... ich schulde Ihnen...
you owe me... Sie schulden mir...
owner der Besitzer/die Besitzerin
oxygen der Sauerstoff

P

pace das Tempo
pacemaker der Herzschrittmacher
to pack *(luggage)* packen
package das Paket
package tour die Pauschalreise
packet das Paket
padded envelope der gefütterte Umschlag
paddling pool das Planschbecken
padlock das Vorhängeschloss
page die Seite
paid bezahlt
I've paid ich habe bezahlt
pain der Schmerz
painful schmerzhaft
painkiller das Schmerzmittel
to paint malen
painting *(picture)* das Bild
pair das Paar
palace der Palast
pale blass
palmtop computer der Palmtop
pan *(saucepan)* der Kochtopf
(frying pan) die Bratpfanne
pancake der Pfannkuchen
panniers *(for bike)* die Satteltaschen
panties die Unterhose
pants *(underwear)* der Slip
panty liner die Slipeinlage
paper das Papier
paper hankies die Papiertaschentücher
paper napkins die Papierservietten
paralysed gelähmt
paramedic *(in ambulance)* der Sanitäter/die Sanitäterin
parcel das Paket
pardon? wie bitte?
I beg your pardon! Entschuldigung!
parents die Eltern
park der Park
to park parken
parking disk die Parkscheibe
parking fine der Strafzettel
parking meter die Parkuhr
parking ticket *(fine)* der Strafzettel
(to display) der Parkschein

partner *(business)* der Geschäftspartner/die Geschäftspartnerin
(boy/girlfriend) der Partner/die Partnerin
party *(celebration)* die Party
(political) die Partei
pass der Pass
passenger der Passagier
passionfruit die Passionsfrucht
passport der Reisepass
passport control die Passkontrolle
password das Passwort
pasta die Nudeln
pastry der Teig
(cake) das Gebäck
path der Weg
patient *(in hospital)* der Patient/die Patientin
pavement der Bürgersteig
to pay zahlen
I'd like to pay ich möchte zahlen
where do I pay? wo kann ich bezahlen?
payment die Bezahlung
payphone das Münztelefon
PDA *(Personal Digital Assistant)* der PDA ; der (elektronische) Organizer
peace der Frieden
peach der Pfirsich
peak rate der Höchsttarif
peanut allergy die Erdnussallergie
pear die Birne
pearls die Perlen
peas die Erbsen
pedal das Pedal
pedalo *(pedal boat)* das Tretboot
pedestrian der Fußgänger/die Fußgängerin
pedestrian crossing der Fußgängerübergang
to pee austreten
to peel *(fruit)* schälen
peg *(clothes)* die Wäscheklammer
(tent) der Hering
pen der Füller
pencil der Bleistift
penfriend der Brieffreund/die Brieffreundin
penicillin das Penizillin
penis der Penis
penknife das Taschenmesser
pension die Rente
pensioner der Rentner/die Rentnerin
people die Leute
pepper *(spice)* der Pfeffer/die Paprikaschote
per pro
per day pro Tag

per hour pro Stunde
per person pro Person
perfect perfekt
performance die Vorstellung
perfume das Parfüm
perhaps vielleicht
period *(menstruation)* die Periode
perm die Dauerwelle
permit die Genehmigung
person die Person
personal organizer der Terminplaner
personal stereo der Walkman®
pet das Haustier
pet food das Tierfutter
pet shop die Zoohandlung
petrol das Benzin
  4-star petrol Superbenzin
  unleaded petrol bleifreies Benzin
petrol cap der Tankdeckel
petrol pump *(at petrol station)*
  die Tanksäule
  (in car) die Benzinpumpe
petrol station die Tankstelle
petrol tank der Tank
pharmacist der Apotheker/
  die Apothekerin
pharmacy die Apotheke
to phone telefonieren
phone das Telefon
  by phone per Telefon
phonebook das Telefonbuch
phonebox die Telefonzelle
phone call der Anruf
phonecard die Telefonkarte
photocopy die Fotokopie
  I need a photocopy ich brauche eine
  Fotokopie
to photocopy fotokopieren
photocopier das Kopiergerät
photograph das Foto
  to take a photograph fotografieren
phrase book der Sprachführer
piano das Klavier
to pick *(choose)* auswählen
  (pluck) pflücken
pickpocket der Taschendieb
picnic das Picknick
  to have a picnic ein Picknick machen
picture *(painting)* das Bild
  (photo) das Foto
pie *(sweet)* der Obstkuchen
  (savoury) die Pastete
piece das Stück
pier die Pier
pig das Schwein

pill die Pille
  to be on the Pill die Pille nehmen
pillow das Kopfkissen
pillowcase der Kopfkissenbezug
pilot der Pilot/die Pilotin
pin die Stecknadel
PIN number die Geheimzahl
pineapple die Ananas
pink rosa
pipe *(smoker's)* die Pfeife
  (drain, etc) das Rohr
pitch *(for tent/caravan)* der Stellplatz
pity: what a pity wie schade
pizza die Pizza
place der Platz
place of birth der Geburtsort
plain *(unflavoured)* einfach
plait der Zopf
plane *(airplane)* das Flugzeug
plant die Pflanze
plaster *(sticking)* das Pflaster
  (for broken limb) der Gips
plastic *(made of)* Plastik-
plastic bag der Plastikbeutel
plate der Teller
platform *(at station)* der Bahnsteig
  which platform? welcher Bahnsteig?
play *(theatre)* das Stück
to play spielen
play area die Spielecke
playground der Spielplatz
play park der Spielplatz
playroom das Spielzimmer
please bitte
pleased erfreut
  pleased to meet you sehr erfreut
pliers die Zange
plug *(electrical)* der Stecker
  (in sink) der Stöpsel
to plug in einstecken
plum die Pflaume
plumber der Klempner
plumbing die Installationen
  (water pipes) die Wasserleitungen
p.m. nachmittags
poached *(egg, fish)* pochiert
pocket die Tasche
points *(in car)* die Unterbrecherkontakte
poison das Gift
poisonous giftig
police *(force)* die Polizei
policeman/woman der Polizist/
  die Polizistin
police station das Polizeirevier

polish (shoe) die Schuhcreme
  (furniture) die Möbelpolitur
pollen der Pollen
polluted verschmutzt
pony das Pony
pony trekking das Ponyreiten
pool der Swimmingpool
pool attendant der Bademeister
poor arm
pop socks die Kniestrümpfe
popular beliebt
pork das Schweinefleisch
port (seaport) der Hafen
porter (for door) der Portier
  (station) der Gepäckträger
portion die Portion
portrait das Portrait
possible möglich
post: by post per Post
to post aufgeben
postbox der Briefkasten
postcard die Ansichtskarte
postcode die Postleitzahl
postman der Briefträger/die Briefträgerin
post office das Postamt
poster das Poster
to postpone verschieben
pot (cooking) der Topf
potato die Kartoffel
  baked potato die Folienkartoffel
  boiled potatoes die Salzkartoffeln
  fried potatoes die Bratkartoffeln
  mashed potatoes das Kartoffelpüree
  roast potatoes die Bratkartoffeln
  sautéed potatoes die Röstkartoffeln
potato peeler der Kartoffelschäler
potato salad der Kartoffelsalat
pothole das Schlagloch
pottery die Töpferwaren
pound das Pfund
to pour eingießen
powder: in powder form pulverförmig
powdered milk die Trockenmilch
power (electricity) der Strom
power cut der Stromausfall
pram der Kinderwagen
to pray beten
to prefer vorziehen
pregnant schwanger
  I'm pregnant ich bin schwanger
to prepare vorbereiten
to prescribe verschreiben
prescription das Rezept
present (gift) das Geschenk
president der Präsident

pressure: tyre pressure der Reifendruck
  blood pressure der Blutdruck
pretty hübsch
price der Preis
price list die Preisliste
priest der Priester
print (photo) der Abzug
printer der Drucker
printout der Ausdruck
prison das Gefängnis
private privat
prize der Preis
probably wahrscheinlich
problem das Problem
professor der Professor/die Professorin
programme das Programm
prohibited verboten
to promise versprechen
to pronounce aussprechen
  how's it pronounced? wie spricht man
  das aus?
protein das Eiweiß
Protestant protestantisch
to provide zur Verfügung stellen
public öffentlich
public holiday der gesetzliche Feiertag
pudding die Nachspeise
to pull ziehen
  to pull a muscle sich einen Muskel zerren
to pull over (car) anhalten
pullover der Pullover
pump (bike, etc) die Luftpumpe
  (in petrol station) die Tanksäule
puncture die Reifenpanne
puncture repair kit das Reifenflickzeug
puppet die Puppe
puppet show das Puppenspiel
purple violett
purpose der Zweck
  on purpose absichtlich
purse der Geldbeutel
to push stoßen
pushchair die Kinderkarre
to put (place) stellen
to put back verschieben
pyjamas der Pyjama

Q

quality die Qualität
quantity die Quantität
quarantine die Quarantäne
to quarrel streiten
quarter das Viertel
quay der Kai
queen die Königin

query die Frage
question die Frage
queue die Schlange
to queue anstehen
quick(ly) schnell
quiet ruhig
quilt die Bettdecke
quite *(rather)* ziemlich
  it's quite good es ist ganz gut
  it's quite expensive es ist ziemlich teuer
quiz show das Quiz

R

rabbit das Kaninchen
rabies die Tollwut
race das Rennen
race course die Rennbahn
racquet der Schläger
radiator *(car)* der Kühler
  (heater) der Heizkörper
radio das Radio
radishes die Radieschen
railcard die Bahncard
railway die Eisenbahn
railway station der Bahnhof
rain der Regen
to rain regnen
  it's raining es regnet
raincoat der Regenmantel
raisins die Rosinen
rake die Harke
rape die Vergewaltigung
to rape vergewaltigen
rare *(unique)* selten
  (steak) blutig
raspberry die Himbeere
rash *(skin)* der Ausschlag
rate *(price)* der Preis
rate of exchange der Wechselkurs
raw roh
razor der Rasierapparat
razor blades die Rasierklingen
to read lesen
ready fertig
  to get ready sich fertig machen
real echt
to realize erkennen
rearview mirror der Rückspiegel
receipt die Quittung
receiver der Hörer
reception *(desk)* der Empfang ;
  die Rezeption
receptionist der Empfangschef/
  die Empfangsdame
to recharge *(battery)* wieder aufladen

recipe das Rezept
to recognize erkennen
to recommend empfehlen
to record aufnehmen
to recover genesen
to recycle recyceln
red rot
to reduce reduzieren
reduction die Ermäßigung
refund die Rückerstattung
to refund rückerstatten
to refuse ablehnen
region das Gebiet
to register *(at hotel)* sich anmelden
registered letter das Einschreiben
registration form das Anmeldeformular
to reimburse entschädigen
relation *(family)* der/die Verwandte
to remain *(to stay)* bleiben
to remember sich erinnern
  I don't remember ich kann mich nicht
  erinnern
remote control die Fernbedienung
to remove entfernen
rent die Miete
to rent mieten
repair die Reparatur
to repair reparieren
to repeat wiederholen
to reply antworten
report der Bericht
to report berichten
request die Bitte
to request erbitten
to require benötigen
to rescue retten
reservation die Reservierung ;
  die Buchung
to reserve reservieren ; buchen
reserved reserviert
residence permit die
  Aufenthaltsgenehmigung
rest *(repose)* die Ruhe
  (remainder) der Rest
to rest ruhen
restaurant das Restaurant
restaurant car der Speisewagen
retired pensioniert
to return *(in car)* zurückfahren
  (on foot) zurückgehen
  (return something) zurückgeben
return ticket *(train)* die Rückfahrkarte
  (plane) das Rückflugticket
to reverse *(car)* rückwärts fahren

to reverse the charges ein R-Gespräch führen
reverse charge call das R-Gespräch
reverse gear der Rückwärtsgang
rheumatism der Rheumatismus
rib die Rippe
ribbon das Band
rice der Reis
rich (person) reich
  (food) reichhaltig
to ride (horse) reiten
right (correct) richtig
right: on the right rechts
  to the right nach rechts
right of way die Vorfahrt
ring der Ring
to ring klingeln
  it's ringing es klingelt
  to ring s.o. jemanden anrufen
ripe reif
river der Fluss
road die Straße
road map die Straßenkarte
road sign das Straßenschild
roast Rost-
roll (bread) das Brötchen
roller blades die Rollerblades
romantic romantisch
roof das Dach
roof-rack der Dachgepäckträger
room (in house, hotel) das Zimmer
  (space) der Platz
  double room das Doppelzimmer
  family room das Familienzimmer
  single room das Einzelzimmer
room number die Zimmernummer
room service der Zimmerservice
root die Wurzel
rope das Seil
rose (flower) die Rose
rotten (fruit, etc) verfault
round rund
roundabout (traffic) der Kreisverkehr
row (in theatre, etc) die Reihe
to row (boat) rudern
rowing (sport) das Rudern
rubber (eraser) der Radiergummi
  (material) das Gummi
rubber gloves die Gummihandschuhe
rubbish der Abfall
rubella die Röteln
rucksack der Rucksack
ruin (eg castle) die Ruine
ruler (measuring) das Lineal
to run rennen

rush hour die Rushhour
rusty rostig
rye bread das Roggenbrot

S

sad traurig
saddle der Sattel
safe (for valuables) der Safe
safe ungefährlich
  is it safe? ist das ungefährlich?
safety die Sicherheit
safety belt der Sicherheitsgurt
safety pin die Sicherheitsnadel
sail das Segel
to sail segeln
sailboard das Segelbrett
sailing (sport) das Segeln
sailing boat das Segelboot
salad der Salat
  green salad grüner Salat
  mixed salad gemischter Salat
  potato salad Kartoffelsalat
  tomato salad Tomatensalat
salad dressing die Salatsoße
salary das Gehalt
sale (in general) der Verkauf
  (seasonal bargains) der Schlussverkauf
salesperson der Verkäufer/die Verkäuferin
salt das Salz
salt water das Salzwasser
salty salzig
same gleich
sand der Sand
sandals die Sandalen
sandwich das Sandwich
sanitary pads die Damenbinden
satellite dish die Satellitenschüssel
satellite TV das Satellitenfernsehen
satnav (satellite navigation system, for car) das SatNav
Saturday der Samstag
sauce die Soße
  tomato sauce die Tomatensoße
saucepan der Kochtopf
sauna die Sauna
sausage die Wurst
to save (person) retten
  (money) sparen
savoury pikant
to say sagen
scales die Waage
to scan einscannen
scarf (headscarf) das Kopftuch
  (round neck) das Halstuch
scenery die Landschaft

schedule der Plan
school die Schule
  primary school die Grundschule
  secondary school die Oberschule
scissors die Schere
score der Endstand
Scot der Schotte/die Schottin
Scotland Schottland
Scottish schottisch
screen der Bildschirm
screen wash das Scheibenputzmittel
screw die Schraube
screwdriver der Schraubenzieher
search engine die Suchmaschine
security check die Sicherheitskontrolle
sedative das Beruhigungsmittel
to see sehen
to select auswählen
selection die Auswahl
self-catering für Selbstversorger
self-employed freiberuflich
self-service die Selbstbedienung
to sell verkaufen
  do you sell...? verkaufen Sie...?
sell-by date das Haltbarkeitsdatum
Sellotape® der Tesafilm®
to send schicken
senior citizen der Rentner/die Rentnerin
separated *(couple)* getrennt
September der September
septic tank die Klärgrube
serious schlimm
to serve *(dish)* servieren
service *(in shop, etc)* die Bedienung
  is service included? ist die Bedienung
  inbegriffen?
service station die Raststätte
set menu die Tageskarte
settee das Sofa
several verschiedene
to sew nähen
sex das Geschlecht
  (intercourse) der Sex
shade der Schatten
  in the shade im Schatten
to shake schütteln
shallow *(water)* seicht
shampoo das Shampoo
shampoo and set Waschen und Föhnen
to share teilen
sharp scharf
to shave rasieren
shaver der Rasierapparat
she sie
sheep das Schaf

sheet *(on bed)* das Betttuch
shell *(seashell)* die Muschel
  (egg, nut) die Schale
sheltered geschützt
to shine scheinen
shingles die Gürtelrose
ship das Schiff
shirt das Hemd
shock der Schock
shock absorber der Stoßdämpfer
shoe der Schuh
shoelaces die Schnürsenkel
shoe polish die Schuhcreme
shoe shop der Schuhladen
shop der Laden
to shop einkaufen
shop assistant der Verkäufer/
  die Verkäuferin
shopping das Einkaufen
  to go shopping einkaufen gehen
shopping centre das Einkaufszentrum
shore das Ufer
short kurz
shortage der Mangel
short circuit der Kurzschluss
short cut die Abkürzung
shorts die Shorts
short-sighted kurzsichtig
shoulder die Schulter
to shout rufen
show *(theatrical)* die Aufführung
to show zeigen
shower *(bath)* die Dusche
  (of rain) der Schauer
shower cap die Duschhaube
shower gel das Duschgel
to shrink einlaufen
shut *(closed)* geschlossen
to shut schließen
shutter *(on window)* der Fensterladen
sick *(ill)* krank
  (nauseous) übel
  I feel sick mir ist schlecht
sick bag die Spucktüte
side die Seite
side dish die Beilage
sidelight das Standlicht
sidewalk der Bürgersteig
sight die Sehenswürdigkeit
sightseeing tour die Besichtigungstour
sign *(notice)* das Schild
to sign unterschreiben
signature die Unterschrift
signpost der Wegweiser
silk die Seide

silver das Silber
to sing singen
single *(unmarried)* ledig
 (not double) Einzel-
 (ticket) einfach
single bed das Einzelbett
single room das Einzelzimmer
sink *(kitchen)* das Spülbecken
sister die Schwester
sister-in-law die Schwägerin
to sit sitzen
 sit down please! bitte setzen Sie sich!
site *(website)* die Website
SIM card die SIM-Karte
size *(clothes, shoes)* die Größe
to skate *(on ice)* Schlittschuh laufen
skates *(ice)* die Schlittschuhe
 (roller) die Rollschuhe
skateboard das Skateboard
skating rink die Eisbahn
ski der Ski
to ski Ski fahren
ski boots die Skistiefel
skiing das Skilaufen
ski instructor der Skilehrer/die
 Skilehrerin
ski jump die Sprungschanze
ski lift der Skilift
ski pants die Skihose
ski pass der Skipass
ski run/piste die Abfahrt
ski stick/pole der Skistock
ski suit der Skianzug
skin die Haut
skirt der Rock
sky der Himmel
sledge der Schlitten
to sleep schlafen
 to sleep in verschlafen
 to sleep late ausschlafen
sleeper *(on train)* der Schlafwagen
sleeping bag der Schlafsack
sleeping car der Schlafwagen
sleeping pills die Schlaftabletten
slice die Scheibe
slide *(photograph)* das Dia
to slip rutschen
slippers die Hausschuhe
slow(ly) langsam
to slow down langsamer werden
small klein
smaller than kleiner als
smell der Geruch
 (unpleasant) der Gestank
to smell riechen

smile das Lächeln
to smile lächeln
smoke der Rauch
to smoke rauchen
 I don't smoke ich bin Nichtraucher(in)
smoke alarm der Feuermelder
smoked *(food)* geräuchert
smokers *(sign)* Raucher
smooth weich
SMS message die SMS
snack der Snack
 to have a snack einen Imbiss essen
snack bar die Snackbar
snake die Schlange
snake bite der Schlangenbiss
to sneeze niesen
snorkel der Schnorchel
snow der Schnee
to snow: *it's snowing* es schneit
to snowboard Snowboard fahren
snow chains die Schneeketten
snow tyres die Winterreifen
snowed up eingeschneit
soap die Seife
soap powder das Waschmittel
socket die Steckdose
socks die Socken
soda water das Soda
sofa das Sofa
sofa bed das Sofabett
soft weich
soft drink das alkoholfreie Getränk
soldier der Soldat
sole *(of shoe)* die Sohle
soluble löslich
some einige
someone irgendjemand
something etwas
son der Sohn
son-in-law der Schwiegersohn
song das Lied
soon bald
 as soon as possible so bald wie möglich
sore throat die Halsschmerzen
sorry: *I'm sorry!* tut mir leid!
sort die Sorte
 what sort? welche Sorte?
soup die Suppe
sour sauer
soured cream die saure Sahne
south der Süden
souvenir das Souvenir
spa das Bad
space der Platz
spade der Spaten

Spain Spanien
spam (email) der Spam
Spanish adj spanisch
spanner der Schraubenschlüssel
spare parts die Ersatzteile
spare room das Gästezimmer
spare tyre der Ersatzreifen
spare wheel das Ersatzrad
sparkling perlend
  sparkling water das Sprudelwasser
  sparkling wine der Schaumwein
spark plugs die Zündkerzen
to speak sprechen
  do you speak English? sprechen Sie
  Englisch?
speaker (loudspeaker) der Lautsprecher ;
  die Box
special speziell
**special needs: people with special
  needs** Behinderte
special offer das Sonderangebot
specialist der Spezialist/die Spezialistin
speciality die Spezialität
speed die Geschwindigkeit
speed limit die Geschwindigkeitsbegrenzung
  to exceed the speed limit
  die Geschwindigkeitsbegrenzung
  überschreiten
speedometer der Tachometer
to spell: how's it spelt? wie buchstabiert
  man das?
to spend ausgeben
SPF (sun protection factor) LSF (or SF)
  SPF 30 LSF (or SF) 30
spice das Gewürz
spicy würzig
to spill verschütten
spinach der Spinat
spin dryer die Wäscheschleuder
spine das Rückgrat
splinter der Splitter
spoilt verdorben
sponge der Schwamm
spoon der Löffel
sport der Sport
sports centre das Fitnesscenter
sports shop das Sportgeschäft
spot der Fleck
sprain die Verstauchung
spring (season) der Frühling
  (metal) die Feder
spring onions die Frühlingszwiebeln
square (in town) der Platz
stadium das Stadion
staff das Personal

stain der Fleck
stairs die Treppe
stale (bread) trocken
stalls (in theatre) das Parkett
stamp die Briefmarke
to stand stehen
star der Stern
  (film) der Star
to start (begin) anfangen
starter (in meal) die Vorspeise
  (in car) der Anlasser
station der Bahnhof
stationer's die Schreibwarenhandlung
statue die Statue
stay der Aufenthalt
  enjoy your stay! angenehmen
  Aufenthalt!
to stay (to remain) bleiben
steak das Steak
to steal stehlen
steamed gedünstet
steel der Stahl
steep steil
steeple der Kirchturm
step der Schritt
stepdaughter die Stieftochter
stepfather der Stiefvater
stepmother die Stiefmutter
stepson der Stiefsohn
stereo die Stereoanlage
sterling das Pfund Sterling
steward/stewardess der Steward/
  die Stewardess
to stick (with glue) kleben
sticking plaster das Heftpflaster
still (yet) noch
  (motionless) still
  still water stilles Wasser
sting der Stachel
to sting stechen
stitches: the wound needs stitches
  die Wunde muss genäht werden
stock cube der Brühwürfel
stockings die Strümpfe
stolen gestohlen
stomach der Magen
stomach ache die Magenschmerzen
stone der Stein
stop (sign) das Stoppschild
to stop halten
stopover die Zwischenlandung
store (shop) das Geschäft
storey das Geschoss
storm der Sturm
story die Geschichte

straight away sofort
straight on geradeaus
strange (odd) seltsam
straw (for drinking) der Strohhalm
strawberries die Erdbeeren
stream der Bach
street die Straße
street map der Stadtplan
strength die Stärke
stress der Stress
strike (of workers) der Streik
string die Schnur
striped gestreift
stroke der Schlaganfall
  to have a stroke einen Schlaganfall haben
strong stark
  strong coffee starker Kaffee
  strong tea starker Tee
stuck: it's stuck es klemmt
student der Student/die Studentin
student discount die Studentenermäßigung
stuffed gefüllt
stung gestochen
stupid dumm
subscription (fee) der Beitrag
subsidiary die Tochtergesellschaft
subtitles die Untertitel
subway die Unterführung
suddenly plötzlich
suede das Wildleder
sugar der Zucker
sugar-free zuckerfrei
to suggest vorschlagen
suit (man's) der Anzug
  (woman's) das Kostüm
suitcase der Koffer
sum die Summe
summer der Sommer
summer holidays die Sommerferien
summit der Gipfel
sun die Sonne
to sunbathe sonnenbaden
sunblock die Sonnencreme
sunburn der Sonnenbrand
suncream die Sonnencreme
Sunday der Sonntag
sunglasses die Sonnenbrille
sunny sonnig
sunrise der Sonnenaufgang
sunroof das Sonnendach
sunscreen das Sonnenschutzmittel
sunset der Sonnenuntergang
sunshade der Sonnenschirm

sunstroke der Sonnenstich
suntan die Sonnenbräune
suntan lotion das Sonnenöl
supermarket der Supermarkt
supper das Abendessen
supplement (to pay) der Zuschlag
to supply zur Verfügung stellen
sure: I'm sure ich bin mir sicher
to surf surfen
  to surf the Net im Internet surfen
surfboard das Surfbrett
surgery die Operation
surname der Nachname
surprise die Überraschung
to survive überleben
suspension (in car) die Aufhängung
to swallow verschlucken
to sweat schwitzen
sweater der Pullover
sweatshirt das Sweatshirt
sweet (not savoury) süß
sweetener der Süßstoff
sweets die Süßigkeiten
to swell anschwellen
to swim schwimmen
swimming costume der Badeanzug
swimming pool das Schwimmbad
swimsuit der Badeanzug
swing (for children) die Schaukel
swipecard die Magnetkarte
Swiss adj schweizerisch
  m/f der Schweizer/die Schweizerin
switch der Schalter
to switch off (light) ausschalten
  (machine) abschalten
  (gas, water) abstellen
to switch on (light, machine) einschalten
  (gas, water) anstellen
Switzerland die Schweiz
swollen geschwollen
synagogue die Synagoge
syringe die Spritze

T

table der Tisch
tablecloth die Tischdecke
tablet (pill) die Tablette
table tennis das Tischtennis
table wine der Tafelwein
to take nehmen
  (medicine) einnehmen
  how long does it take? wie lange dauert es?
take-away food das Essen zum Mitnehmen

to take off abfliegen
talc der Körperpuder
to talk to sprechen mit
tall groß
tampons die Tampons
tangerine die Mandarine
tank *(petrol)* der Tank
  (fish) das Aquarium
tap der Wasserhahn
tap water das Leitungswasser
tape die Kassette
tape measure das Maßband
tape recorder der Kassettenrekorder
target das Ziel
taste der Geschmack
to taste probieren
  can I taste it? darf ich es probieren?
tax die Steuer
taxi das Taxi
taxi driver der Taxifahrer/die Taxifahrerin
taxi rank der Taxistand
tea der Tee
  herbal tea Kräutertee
  tea with milk Tee mit Milch
tea bag der Teebeutel
teapot die Teekanne
teaspoon der Teelöffel
tea towel das Geschirrtuch
to teach unterrichten
teacher der Lehrer/die Lehrerin
team das Team
tear *(in material)* der Riss
teat *(on bottle)* der Sauger
teenager der Teenager
teeth die Zähne
telegram das Telegramm
telephone das Telefon
to telephone telefonieren
telephone box die Telefonzelle
telephone call der Anruf
telephone card die Telefonkarte
telephone directory das Telefonbuch
telephone number die Telefonnummer
television das Fernsehen
to tell erzählen
temperature die Temperatur
  to have a temperature Fieber haben
temporary provisorisch
tenant der Mieter
tendon die Sehne
tennis das Tennis
tennis ball der Tennisball
tennis court der Tennisplatz

tennis racket der Tennisschläger
tent das Zelt
tent peg der Hering
terminal das Terminal
terrace die Terrasse
to test testen
testicles die Hoden
tetanus injection die Tetanusimpfung
text message die SMS
  to text eine SMS schreiben
  I'll text you ich schreibe Ihnen/dir eine SMS
than als
to thank danken
  thank you danke
  thanks very much vielen Dank
that das
  that one das dort
the der, die, das
theatre das Theater
theft der Diebstahl
their *(with der words)* ihr
  (with das words) ihr
  (with die words) ihre
them ihnen
there *(over there)* dort
there is/there are es gibt
these diese
  these ones diese hier
they sie
thick *(not thin)* dick
thief der Dieb
thigh der Oberschenkel
thin dünn
thing das Ding
  my things meine Sachen
to think denken
thirsty durstig
  to be thirsty Durst haben
this dies
  this one das hier
thorn der Dorn
those jene
  those ones jene dort
thread der Faden
throat die Kehle
throat lozenges die Halspastillen
through durch
to throw away wegwerfen
thumb der Daumen
thunder der Donner
thunderstorm das Gewitter
Thursday der Donnerstag
ticket die Karte
  (train, bus, etc) die Fahrkarte

(entrance fee) die Eintrittskarte
a single ticket eine einfache Fahrkarte
a return ticket eine Rückfahrkarte
ticket inspector der Schaffner/
die Schaffnerin
ticket office der Fahrkartenschalter
tide die Gezeiten
high tide die Flut
low tide die Ebbe
tidy ordentlich
to tidy up aufräumen
tie die Krawatte
tight eng
tights die Strumpfhose
tile die Fliese
till (cash desk) die Kasse
till (until) bis
till 2 o'clock bis zwei Uhr
time (of day) die Zeit
what time is it? wie spät ist es?
timer die Schaltuhr
timetable der Fahrplan
tin (can) die Dose
tinfoil die Alufolie
tin-opener der Dosenöffner
to tip Trinkgeld geben
tip (to waiter, etc) das Trinkgeld
tipped (cigarettes) Filter-
tired müde
tissues die Papiertaschentücher
to zu (zum/zur)
(with names of places) nach
to London nach London
to the airport zum Flughafen
toadstool der Giftpilz
toast der Toast
tobacco der Tabak
tobacconist's die Tabakwarenhandlung
today heute
toddler das Kleinkind
toe die Zehe
together zusammen
toilet die Toilette
disabled toilet die Behindertentoilette
toilet brush die Toilettenbürste
toilet paper das Toilettenpapier
toiletries die Toilettenartikel
toll (motorway) die Maut
tomato die Tomate
tinned tomatoes die Dosentomaten
tomato juice der Tomatensaft
tomorrow morgen
tomorrow morning morgen früh
tomorrow afternoon morgen Nachmittag
tomorrow evening morgen Abend
tongue die Zunge

tonic water das Tonic
tonight heute Abend
tonsillitis die Mandelentzündung
too (also) auch
too big zu groß
too small zu klein
too noisy zu laut
tools das Werkzeug
toolkit der Werkzeugkasten
tooth der Zahn
toothache die Zahnschmerzen
I have toothache ich habe
Zahnschmerzen
toothbrush die Zahnbürste
toothpaste die Zahnpasta
toothpick der Zahnstocher
top: *the top floor* das oberste Stockwerk
top (of mountain) der Gipfel
(lid) der Deckel
(clothing) das Oberteil
on top of... oben auf...
topless oben ohne
torch (flashlight) die Taschenlampe
torn zerrissen
total (amount) die Endsumme
to touch anfassen
tough (meat) zäh
tour die Fahrt
guided tour die Führung
tour guide der Reiseführer/
die Reiseführerin
tour operator der Reiseveranstalter
tourist der Tourist/die Touristin
tourist information die Touristeninformation
tourist office das Fremdenverkehrsbüro
tourist route die Touristenroute
tourist ticket die Touristenkarte
to tow (car) abschleppen
towbar (car) die Abschleppstange
tow rope das Abschleppseil
towel das Handtuch
tower der Turm
town die Stadt
town centre das Stadtzentrum
town hall das Rathaus
town plan der Stadtplan
toxic giftig
toy das Spielzeug
toy shop der Spielzeugladen
tracksuit der Jogginganzug
traditional traditionell
traffic der Verkehr
traffic jam der Stau
traffic lights die Ampel
traffic policeman der Verkehrspolizist

T english > german

trailer der Anhänger
train der Zug
by train mit dem Zug
trainers die Turnschuhe
tram die Straßenbahn
tranquilliser das Beruhigungsmittel
to translate übersetzen
to travel reisen
travel agent's das Reisebüro
travel documents die Reisepapiere
travel guide der Reiseführer
travel insurance die Reiseversicherung
travel sickness die Reisekrankheit
traveller's cheques die Reiseschecks
tray das Tablett
tree der Baum
trip der Ausflug
trolley *(luggage)* der Gepäckwagen
(shopping) der Einkaufswagen
trousers die Hose
truck der Laster
true wahr
trunk der Koffer
trunks die Badehose
to try versuchen
to try on anprobieren
T-shirt das T-Shirt
Tuesday der Dienstag
tumble dryer der Wäschetrockner
tuna der Tunfisch
tunnel der Tunnel
to turn *(right/left)* abbiegen
to turn around umdrehen
to turn off *(light)* ausmachen
(TV, radio, etc) ausschalten
(tap) zudrehen
to turn on *(light)* anmachen
(TV, radio, etc) anschalten
(tap) aufdrehen
turnip die Steckrübe
turquoise *(colour)* türkis
tweezers die Pinzette
twice zweimal
twin-bedded room das Zweibettzimmer
twins die Zwillinge
to type Maschine schreiben
typical typisch
tyre der Reifen
tyre pressure der Reifendruck
Tyrol das Tirol

U

ugly hässlich
ulcer das Geschwür
umbrella der Regenschirm
(sun) der Sonnenschirm

uncle der Onkel
uncomfortable unbequem
unconscious bewusstlos
under unter
undercooked nicht gar
underground die U-Bahn
underpants die Unterhose
underpass die Unterführung
understand verstehen
I don't understand ich verstehe nicht
underwear die Unterwäsche
unemployed arbeitslos
to unfasten aufmachen
United Kingdom das Vereinigte Königreich
United States die Vereinigten Staaten
university die Universität
unleaded petrol das bleifreie Benzin
unlikely unwahrscheinlich
to unlock aufschließen
to unpack auspacken
unpleasant unangenehm
to unplug herausziehen
to unscrew aufschrauben
until bis
unusual ungewöhnlich
up: to get up aufstehen
upside down verkehrt herum
upstairs oben
urgent dringend
urine der Urin
us uns
to use benutzen
useful nützlich
username der Benutzername
usual(ly) gewöhnlich
U-turn die Wende

V

vacancy *(in hotel)* Zimmer frei
vacant frei
vacation der Urlaub
vaccination die Impfung
vacuum cleaner der Staubsauger
vagina die Vagina
valid gültig
valuable wertvoll
valuables die Wertsachen
value der Wert
valve das Ventil
van der Lieferwagen
vase die Vase
VAT die Mehrwertsteuer (MWST)
vegan: *I'm vegan* ich bin Veganer

144

vegetables das Gemüse
vegetarian vegetarisch
  I'm vegetarian ich bin Vegetarier
vehicle das Fahrzeug
vein die Ader
Velcro® das Klettband
vending machine der Automat
venereal disease die Geschlechtskrankheit
ventilator der Ventilator
very sehr
vest das Unterhemd
vet der Tierarzt
via über
to video *(from TV)* auf Video aufnehmen
  (to film) filmen
video das Video
video camera die Videokamera
video cassette/tape die Videokassette
video game das Videospiel
video recorder der Videorekorder
Vienna Wien
view die Aussicht
villa die Villa
village das Dorf
vinegar der Essig
vineyard der Weinberg
virus der Virus
visa das Visum
  to apply for a visa ein Visum beantragen
visit der Besuch
to visit *(person)* besuchen
  (place) besichtigen
visiting hours *(hospital)* die Besuchszeit
visitor der Besucher
vitamin das Vitamin
voice die Stimme
voicemail die Voicemail ;
  die Sprachmitteilung
volcano der Vulkan
volleyball der Volleyball
voltage die Spannung
to vomit erbrechen
voucher der Gutschein

W

wage der Lohn
waist die Taille
waistcoat die Weste
to wait for warten auf
waiter/waitress der Kellner/die Kellnerin
waiting room der Warteraum
to wake up aufwachen
Wales Wales
walk der Spaziergang
  to go for a walk einen Spaziergang
  machen

to walk spazieren gehen
  (go on foot) zu Fuß gehen
walking boots die Wanderschuhe
walking stick der Wanderstock
Walkman® der Walkman®
wall die Mauer
wallet die Brieftasche
to want wollen
  I want... ich möchte...
  we want... wir möchten...
war der Krieg
ward *(hospital)* die Station
wardrobe der Kleiderschrank
warehouse die Lagerhalle
warm warm
  it's warm es ist warm
to warm up *(milk, etc)* aufwärmen
warning triangle das Warndreieck
to wash waschen
  (to wash oneself) sich waschen
wash and blow dry Waschen und
  Föhnen
washing machine die Waschmaschine
washing powder das Waschpulver
washing-up bowl die Abwaschschüssel
washing-up liquid das Spülmittel
wasp die Wespe
wasp sting der Wespenstich
waste bin der Abfalleimer
to watch zuschauen
watch die Armbanduhr
water das Wasser
  hot water warmes Wasser
  cold water kaltes Wasser
  drinking water Trinkwasser
  mineral water Mineralwasser
  sparkling water Sprudelwasser
  still water stilles Wasser
water heater das Heißwassergerät
watermelon die Wassermelone
waterproof wasserdicht
water sports der Wassersport
to water ski Wasserski fahren
water wings die Schwimmflügel
waves *(on sea)* die Wellen
way der Weg
way in *(entrance)* der Eingang
way out *(exit)* der Ausgang
we wir
weak schwach
  (tea, coffee) dünn
to wear tragen
weather das Wetter
weather forecast die Wettervorhersage
website die Webseite

website address die Internetadresse
wedding die Hochzeit
wedding anniversary der Hochzeitstag
wedding present das Hochzeitsgeschenk
Wednesday der Mittwoch
week die Woche
  last week letzte Woche
  next week nächste Woche
  this week diese Woche
weekday der Werktag
weekend das Wochenende
weekly wöchentlich
weekly ticket das Wochenticket
to weigh wiegen
weight das Gewicht
welcome willkommen
well gut
  he's not well ihm geht es nicht gut
well *(for water)* der Brunnen
well-done *(steak)* durch
wellington boots die Gummistiefel
Welsh *adj* walisisch
  m/f der Waliser/die Waliserin
west der Westen
wet nass
wetsuit der Taucheranzug
what was
wheat der Weizen
wheel das Rad
wheelchair der Rollstuhl
wheel clamp die Parkkralle
when wann
where wo
which: *which man?* welcher Mann?
  which woman? welche Frau?
  which book? welches Buch?
while während
  in a while bald
white weiß
who wer
whole vollständig
wholemeal bread das Vollkornbrot
whose wessen
why warum
wide breit
widow die Witwe
widower der Witwer
wife die Frau
wig die Perücke
to win gewinnen
wind der Wind
windmill die Windmühle
window das Fenster
  (of shop) das Schaufenster
windscreen die Windschutzscheibe

windscreen wipers die Scheibenwischer
to windsurf surfen
windy: *it's windy* es ist windig
wine der Wein
  dry wine trockener Wein
  house wine Hauswein
  red wine Rotwein
  rosé wine Roséwein
  sparkling wine Schaumwein
  sweet wine süßer Wein
  white wine Weißwein
wine list die Weinkarte
wing der Flügel
wing mirror der Seitenspiegel
winter der Winter
wire der Draht
wireless internet die kabellose Internet-Verbindung
with mit
without ohne
to withdraw cash Geld abheben
witness der Zeuge
woman die Frau
wonderful wunderbar
wood *(material)* das Holz
wooden hölzern
woods *(forest)* der Wald
wool die Wolle
word das Wort
work die Arbeit
work permit die Arbeitsgenehmigung
to work *(person)* arbeiten
  (machine) funktionieren
world die Welt
worried besorgt
worse schlechter
worth: *it's worth £50* es ist fünfzig Pfund wert
to wrap up einwickeln
wrapping paper das Geschenkpapier
wrist das Handgelenk
to write schreiben
  please write it down bitte schreiben Sie das auf
writing paper das Briefpapier
wrong falsch
  what's wrong? was stimmt nicht?

X

X-ray die Röntgenaufnahme
to x-ray röntgen

Y

yacht die Jacht
year das Jahr
  this year dieses Jahr

next year nächstes Jahr
last year letztes Jahr
yearly jährlich
yellow gelb
Yellow Pages die Gelben Seiten
yes ja
yesterday gestern
yet: *not yet* noch nicht
yoghurt der Jogurt
plain yoghurt Naturjogurt
yolk das Eigelb
you *(polite sing. and pl.)* Sie
(familiar sing.) du ; ihr *(pl.)*
young jung

your dein/Ihr
(with der words) dein/Ihr
(with das words) dein/Ihr
(with die words) deine/Ihre
youth hostel die Jugendherberge

Z

zebra crossing der Zebrastreifen
zero null
zip der Reißverschluss
zone die Zone
zoo der Zoo
zoom lens der Zoom

A

Aal *m* eel
ab off ; from
  ab 8 Uhr from 8 o'clock
  ab Mai from May onward
abbestellen to cancel
abbiegen to turn *(right/left)*
Abbildung *f* illustration
abblenden to dip *(lights)*
Abblendlicht *nt* dipped headlights
Abend *m* evening
Abendessen *nt* evening meal
abends in the evening(s)
aber but
abfahren to depart ; to leave
Abfahrt *f* departures
Abfahrtszeit *f* departure time
Abfall *m* rubbish
Abfertigungsschalter *m* check-in desk
abfliegen to take off
Abflug *m* flight departures
  Abflug Inland domestic departures
  Abflug Ausland international departures
Abflughalle *f* departure lounge
Abflugzeit *f* departure time
Abfluss *m* drain
Abführmittel *nt* laxative
abholen to fetch ; to claim *(baggage, etc)*
  abholen lassen to send for
Abkürzung *f* short cut
abladen to dump ; to offload
ablaufen to expire
ablehnen to refuse
Abonnement *nt* subscription
Abreise *f* departure
absagen to cancel
Absatz *m* heel
abschalten to switch off *(machine)*
abschicken to dispatch
Abschleppdienst *m* breakdown service
abschleppen to tow *(car)*
Abschleppseil *nt* towrope
Abschleppstange *f* towbar
Abschleppwagen *m* breakdown van
Absender *m* sender
abstellen to turn off ; to park car
Abszess *m* abscess
Abtei *f* abbey
Abteil *nt* compartment
Abteilung *f* department
Abtreibung *f* abortion
Abtreibungspille *f* abortion pill
Abzug *m* print *(photo)*
Achse *f* axle

achten auf to pay attention to
Achtung *f* caution ; danger
Ader *f* vein
Adler *m* eagle
Adressbuch *nt* address book
Adresse *f* address
adressieren to address
Affe *m* monkey
ähnlich similar
Akku charge *(rechargeable battery)*
  Gesprächsguthaben prepaid phone time
  Ladung electrical
  mein Akku ist leer I've run out of charge
  (phone)
Aktentasche *f* briefcase
Akzent *m* accent *(pronunciation)*
akzeptieren to accept
Alarmanlage *f* alarm
Alge *f* seaweed
Alkohol *m* alcohol
alkoholfrei non-alcoholic
alkoholisch alcoholic *(drink)*
alle all ; everybody ; everyone
  alle zwei Tage every other day
Allee *f* avenue
allein alone
Allergie *f* allergy
allergisch gegen allergic to
Allerheiligen *nt* All Saints' Day
alles everything ; all
allgemein general ; universal
Alpen *pl* Alps
alt old
Altar *m* altar
Altbier *nt* top-fermented dark beer
Alter *nt* age *(of person)*
ältere(r/s) older ; elder
Altglascontainer *m* bottle bank
Alufolie *f* aluminium foil
am at ; in ; on
  am Bahnhof at the station
  am Abend in the evening
  am Freitag on Friday
Ameise *f* ant
Amerika *nt* America
Amerikaner(in) *m/f* American
amerikanisch *adj* American
Ampel *f* traffic light
Amtszeichen *nt* dialling tone
Amüsierviertel *nt* nightclub district
an at ; on *(light, radio, etc)* ; near
  Frankfurt an 1300 arriving Frankfurt at 1300
  an/aus on/off
Ananas *f* pineapple
anbauen to grow *(cultivate)*

anbieten to offer
andere(r/s) other
ändern to change (to alter)
Änderung f change
Anfall m fit (seizure)
Anfang m start (beginning)
anfangen to begin ; to start
Anfänger(in) m/f beginner
Anfängerhügel m nursery slope
Anfrage f enquiry
Angaben pl details ; directions (to a place)
angeben to give
Angebot nt offer
  im Angebot on offer
Angehörige(r) m/f relative
angeln to fish
Angeln nt fishing ; angling
  Angeln verboten no fishing
Angelrute f fishing rod
Angelschein m fishing permit
angenehm pleasant
Angestellte(r) m/f employee
Angina f angina
angreifen to attack
Angst haben vor to be afraid of
Anhänger m trailer ; fan (supporter)
Anker m anchor
ankommen to arrive
ankündigen to announce
Ankunft f arrivals
Anlage f park ; grounds ; facilities
  öffentliche Anlage public park
Anlasser m starter (in car)
Anlegeplatz m mooring
Anlegestelle f landing stage ; jetty
anmachen to turn on
Anmeldeformular nt registration form
Anmeldung f registration ; reception (place)
Annahme f acceptance ; reception
annehmen to assume ; to accept
anprobieren to try on
Anruf m phone call
Anrufbeantworter m answerphone
anrufen to phone
anschalten to turn on
anschauen to look at
Anschlagbrett nt notice board
Anschluss m connection (train, etc)
Anschlussflug m connecting flight
anschnallen to fasten
Anschrift f address
anschwellen to swell
Ansicht f view
Ansichtskarte f picture postcard

Ansprechpartner(in) m/f contact person
anstatt instead of
ansteckend infectious
anstehen to queue
anstellen to switch on (gas, water)
Anteil m share (part)
Antenne f aerial
Antibiotikum nt antibiotic
antik ancient
Antiquitäten pl antiques
Antiquitätenladen m antique shop
Antiseptikum nt antiseptic
Antwort f answer ; reply
antworten to answer ; to reply
Anweisungen pl instructions
Anzahl f number
Anzahlung f deposit
Anzeige f advertisement ; report (to police)
Anzug(-züge) m suit(s) (man's)
anzünden to light ; to set fire to
Apfel (Äpfel) m apple(s)
Apfelsaft m apple juice
Apfelsine(n) f orange(s)
Apfelwein m cider
Apotheke f pharmacy
Apotheker (Apothekerin) pharmacist
Apparat m appliance ; camera ; extension
Aprikose(n) f apricot(s)
April m April
Aquarium nt fish tank
Arbeit f employment ; work
arbeiten to work (person)
arbeitslos unemployed
Architekt(in) m/f architect
Architektur f architecture
arm poor
Arm m arm
Armband nt bracelet
Armbanduhr f watch
Ärmelkanal m English Channel
Art f type ; sort ; manner
Arthritis f arthritis
Artikel m article ; item
Artischocke f artichoke
Arznei f medicine
Arzt (Ärztin) m/f doctor
Aschenbecher m ashtray
Aspirin nt aspirin
Ast m branch (of tree)
Asthma nt asthma
Atlantik m Atlantic Ocean
atmen to breathe
attraktiv attractive
Aubergine f aubergine

auch also ; too ; as well
auf onto ; on ; upon ; on top of
 auf Deutsch in German
 auf Wiedersehen goodbye
aufdrehen to turn on *(tap)*
Aufenthalt *m* stay ; visit
Aufenthaltsgenehmigung *f* residence permit
Aufenthaltsraum *m* lounge
Auffahrt *f* slip-road
Aufführung *f* performance ; show
aufgeben to quit ; to post ; to check in *(baggage)*
aufhalten to delay ; to hold up
 sich aufhalten to stay
aufladen to charge *(battery)*
 ich muss mein Handy aufladen I need to charge my phone
auflegen to hang up
aufmachen to open *(shop, bank etc)* ; to unfasten
 sich aufmachen to set off
aufregend exciting
aufschließen to unlock
aufschrauben to unscrew
aufschreiben to write down
aufstehen to get up
Aufstieg *m* ascent
aufwachen to wake up
aufwärmen to heat up *(food, milk)*
Aufzug *m* lift/elevator
Auge(n) *nt* eye(s)
Augenblick *m* moment ; instant
Augentropfen *pl* eye drops
August *m* August
Auktion *f* auction
Au-pair-Mädchen *nt* au pair
aus off *(light, radio, etc)* ; made of... ; from ; out of
Ausdruck *m* expression ; print-out ; term *(word)*
Ausfahrt *f* exit *(motorway)*
Ausfall *m* failure *(mechanical)*
Ausflug(-flüge) *m* trip(s) ; excursion(s)
Ausfuhr *f* export(s)
ausführen to export ; to carry out *(job)*
ausfüllen to fill in *(form)*
 bitte nicht ausfüllen please leave blank *(on form)*
Ausgabe *f* issue *(of magazine)* ; issuing counter
Ausgaben *pl* expenses
Ausgang *m* exit ; gate *(at airport)*
ausgeben to spend *(money)*
ausgehen to go out *(for amusement)*
ausgeschaltet off *(radio)*

ausgestellt issued at *(passport)*
ausgezeichnet excellent
auskugeln to dislocate *(joint)*
Auskunft *f* information
Ausland *nt* foreign countries ; abroad ; international
 aus dem Ausland from overseas
Ausländer(in) *m/f* foreigner
ausländisch foreign
Auslandsgespräch *nt* international call
auslassen to leave out ; to omit
auslaufen to sail *(ship)*
ausmachen to turn off *(light)* ; to put out *(fire, etc)*
Ausnahme *f* exception
auspacken to unpack
Auspuffrohr *nt* exhaust pipe
Ausrüstung *f* kit ; equipment
ausschalten to switch off *(light, TV, radio)*
Ausschank *m* bar ; drinks
Ausschlag *m* cold sore ; skin rash
ausschließlich excluding ; exclusive(ly)
Außenkabine *f (on ferry)* outside cabin
Außenseite *f* outside
Außenspiegel *m* outside mirror
außer Betrieb out of order
äußerlich exterior
Aussicht *f* view ; prospect
aussprechen to pronounce
Ausstattung *f* equipment *(of car)*
aussteigen to get out of *(vehicle)*
Ausstellung *f* show ; exhibition
Ausstellungsdatum *nt* date of issue
Austausch *m* exchange
Australien *nt* Australia
Australier(in) *m/f* Australian
australisch *adj* Australian
Ausverkauf *m* sale
ausverkauft sold out
Auswahl *f* choice
auswählen to choose
auswärts essen to eat out
ausweichen to avoid
Ausweis *m* identity card ; pass *(permit)*
auszahlen to pay
Auto(s) *nt* car(s)
Autobahn *f* motorway
Autobahngebühr *f* toll
Autofähre *f* car-ferry
Autokarte *f* road map
Automat *m* vending machine
 Automat wechselt change given
Automatikauto *nt* automatic car
automatisch automatic
Automobilklub *m* automobile association

Autor(in) m/f author
Autoreisezug m motorail service
Autoschlüssel pl car keys
Autovermietung f car hire

B

Baby nt baby
Babyflasche f baby's bottle
Babymilch f baby milk
Babynahrung f baby food
Babyraum m mother and baby room
Babysitter(in) m/f baby-sitter
Babytücher pl baby wipes
Bach m stream
Bäckerei f baker's
Backofen m oven
Bad nt bath ; spa
Badeanzug m swimsuit
Badehose f swimming trunks
Badekappe f bathing cap
Badelatschen pl flip flops
baden to bathe ; to swim
  Baden verboten no swimming
Badewanne f bath(tub)
Badezimmer nt bathroom
Baguette nt French bread
Bahn f railway ; rink
  per Bahn by rail
Bahnhof m station ; depot
Bahnlinie f line (railway)
Bahnsteig m platform
Bahnübergang m level crossing
bald soon
Balkon m balcony
Ball m ball
Ballett nt ballet
Ballon m balloon
Banane(n) f banana(s)
Band (Bänder) nt ribbon(s) ; tape(s)
Band f band (musical)
Bank f bank ; bench
Bankkonto nt bank account
Bar f nightclub ; bar
Bär m bear (animal)
Bargeld nt cash
Bart m beard
Basel Basle
Batterie f battery
Bauarbeiten pl roadworks ; construction work
bauen to build
Bauer (Bäuerin) m/f farmer
Bauernhaus nt farmhouse
Bauernhof m farm(yard)

Bauernmarkt farmers' market
Baum m tree
Baumarkt m DIY shop
Baumwolle f cotton (fabric)
Baustelle f roadworks ; construction site
Bayern nt Bavaria
beachten to observe ; to obey
beantworten to answer
Bedarfshaltestelle f request stop
bedeckt cloudy (weather)
Bedeutung f meaning
bedienen to serve ; to operate
  sich bedienen to help oneself
Bedienung f service charge
Bedingung f condition
Beefsteak nt steak
  deutsches Beefsteak hamburger ; beefburger
beenden to end ; to finish
Beerdigung f funeral
Beere f berry
beginnen to begin
begrüßen to greet ; to welcome
behalten to keep (retain)
Behandlung f treatment
beheizt heated
behindert disabled (person)
  Behinderte special needs: people with special needs
Behindertentoilette f toilet for disabled
Behinderung f obstruction ; handicap
bei near ; by (beside) ; at ; on ; during
beide both
Beilage f side-dish ; vegetables ; side-salad
Bein nt leg
Beisel nt pub (Austria)
Beispiel(e) nt example(s)
  zum Beispiel for example
beißen to bite
Beitrag m contribution ; subscription (to club)
beitreten to join (club)
Bekleidungsgeschäft nt clothes shop
bekommen to get (receive, obtain)
beladen to load (truck, ship)
Belastung f load
belegt no vacancies
Beleuchtung f lighting
Belgien nt Belgium
beliebt popular
Belohnung f reward
benachrichtigen to inform
Benachrichtigung f advice note
benötigen to require

benutzen to use
Benutzername username
Benzin nt petrol
bequem comfortable
Beratungsstelle f advice centre
berechtigt zu entitled to
Berechtigte(r) m/f authorized person
bereit ready
Bereitschaftsdienst m emergency service
Berg(e) m mountain(s)
bergab downhill
bergauf uphill
Bergführer(in) m/f mountain guide
Bergschuhe pl climbing boots
Bergtour f hillwalk ; climb
Bergwacht f mountain rescue
Bergwanderung f hill-walking
Bericht(e) m report(s) ; bulletin(s)
berichten to report
Berliner m doughnut
Beruf m profession ; occupation
beruflich professional
Beruhigungsmittel nt tranquilliser
berühmt famous
berühren to handle ; to touch
beschädigen to damage
beschäftigt busy
Beschäftigung f employment ; occupation
  Bescheinigung f certificate
beschreiben to describe
Beschreibung f description
Besen m brush (for sweeping floor)
besetzt engaged ; occupied
besichtigen to visit (place)
Besichtigungen pl sightseeing
Besichtigungstour f guided tour
Besitzer(in) m/f owner
besondere(r/s) particular ; special
besorgt worried
Besprechung f (business) meeting
besser better
Besserung(en) f improvement(s)
  gute Besserung get well soon
bestätigen to confirm
Bestätigung f confirmation (flight, etc)
beste(r/s) best
Besteck nt cutlery
bestellen to book ; to order
Bestellung f order
Bestimmungen pl regulations
Bestimmungsort m destination
besuchen to visit (person)
Besucher(in) m/f visitor
Besuchszeit f visiting hours

beten to pray
Betrag m amount
  Betrag erhalten payment received
betreten to enter
Betrieb m business
betrunken drunk
Bett(en) nt bed(s)
Bettbezug m duvet cover
Bettdecke f duvet ; quilt
Bettlaken nt sheet (on bed)
Bettzeug nt bedclothes
Beule f lump (swelling)
bewacht guarded
bewegen to move
Bewohner(in) m/f resident
bewölkt cloudy
bewusstlos unconscious
bezahlen to pay ; to settle bill
bezahlt paid
Bezahlung f payment
Bezirk m district
bezüglich concerning
BH m bra
Bibliothek f library
Biene f bee
Bienenstich m bee sting ; type of cream
  cake
Bier nt beer
  Bier vom Fass draught beer
Biergarten m beer garden
Bierkeller m beer cellar
Bierstube f pub that specializes in beer
bieten to offer
Bikini m bikini
Bild(er) nt picture(s)
Bilderrahmen m picture frame
Bildschirm m screen (TV, computer)
billig cheap ; inexpensive
billiger cheaper
Billigtarif m cheap rate
Birne(n) f pear(s) ; lightbulb(s)
bis until ; till
  bis jetzt up till now
  bis zu 6 up to 6
  bis bald see you soon
bisschen: ein bisschen a little ; a bit of
bitte please
bitte? pardon?
bitten um to ask for
bitter bitter (taste)
blass pale
Blase f blister, (anat.) bladder
Blasenentzündung f cystitis
Blatt (Blätter) nt sheet(s) (of paper) ;
  leaf (leaves)

blau blue
Blaue Zone f limited parking zone
(parking disk required)
Blei nt lead (metal)
bleiben to stay (to remain)
Bleichmittel nt bleach
Bleiersatz m lead additive
bleifreies Benzin nt unleaded petrol
Bleistift m pencil
blind blind (person)
Blinddarmentzündung f appendicitis
Blinker m indicator (in car)
Blitz m lightning
Blitzlicht nt flash (for camera)
blockiert jammed (camera, lock)
Blockschrift f block letters
blond fair (hair) ; blond
Blumen pl flowers
Blumenladen m florist's shop
Bluse f blouse
Blut nt blood
Blutdruck m blood pressure
bluten to bleed
Bluterguss m bruise
Blutgruppe f blood group
blutig rare (steak)
Bluttest m blood test
Blutvergiftung f blood poisoning
Bockbier nt strong beer
Boden m floor (of room) ; ground
Bodensee m Lake Constance
Bohnen pl beans
grüne Bohnen French beans
Bohrer m drill (tool)
Boiler m immersion heater
Bombe f bomb
Bonbon nt sweet
Boot nt boat (small)
Bootsfahrt f cruise
Bootsrundfahrt f round boat trip
Bootsverleih m boat hire
Bordkarte f boarding pass
borgen to borrow
Böschung f embankment
botanischer Garten m botanical gardens
Botschaft f embassy
Bowle f punch (drink)
Box loudspeaker
Brandwunde f burn (on skin)
Brat- fried ; roast
braten to fry ; to roast
Bratkartoffeln pl fried potatoes
Bratpfanne f frying pan
Bratwurst f sausage

Brauch m custom (tradition)
brauchen to need
Brauerei f brewery
braun brown
Bräune f suntan
Braut f bride
Bräutigam m bridegroom
Brechreiz m nausea
breit wide
Breitband broadband
Breitband-Verbindung broadband
connection
Bremse(n) f brake(s)
bremsen to brake
Bremsflüssigkeit f brake fluid
Bremslicht nt brake light
Bremsseil brake cable (car)
Bremszug brake cable (bicycle)
brennen to burn
Brief m letter (message)
Briefkasten m letterbox ; postbox
Briefmarke(n) f stamp(s)
Briefpapier nt writing paper
Brieftasche f wallet
Briefträger(in) m/f postman/woman
Briefumschlag m envelope
Brille f glasses (spectacles)
Brillenetui nt glasses case
bringen to bring
britisch British
Brombeeren pl blackberries
Bronchitis f bronchitis
Bronze f bronze
Brosche f brooch
Broschüre f brochure
Brot nt bread ; loaf
Brötchen nt bread roll
Bruch m fracture
Brücke f bridge
Bruder(Brüder) m brother(s)
Brühe f stock (for soup, etc)
Brühwürfel pl stock cubes
Brunnen m well (for water) ; fountain
Brust f breast ; chest
Buch nt book
buchen to book
Buchhandlung f bookshop
Büchsen canned
Büchsenöffner m can-opener
Buchstabe m letter (of alphabet)
Bucht f bay (along coast)
Buchung f booking
Bügel m coat hanger
Bügel drücken! press down!

Bügelbrett nt ironing board
Bügeleisen nt iron (for clothes)
bügeln to iron
Bundes- federal
Bundesrepublik Deutschland f Federal Republic of Germany
Bungee-Springen nt bungee jumping
bunt coloured
Burg f castle ; fortress (medieval)
Bürger(in) m/f citizen
bürgerlich middle-class
Bürgermeister(in) m/f mayor(-ess)
Bürgersteig m pavement ; sidewalk
Büro nt agency ; office
Bürogebäude nt office block
Bürste f brush
Bus(se) m bus(es) ; coach(es)
Busbahnhof m bus/coach station
Busfahrschein m bus ticket
Busfahrt f bus tour
Bushaltestelle f bus stop
Buslinie f bus route
Busreise f coach trip
Busstisch m picnic table
Busverbindung f bus service
Büstenhalter m bra
Butangas nt Calor gas®
Butter f butter

C

campen to camp
Campingführer m camping guide(book)
Campingkocher m camping stove
Campingplatz m campsite
Campingtisch m picnic table
CD-ROM CD ROM
CD-Spieler m CD player
Cent m cent (euro)
Champignon(s) m mushroom(s)
Charterflug m charter flight
Chatroom chatroom (internet)
Check-in m check-in
Chef(in) m/f boss
chemische Toilette f chemical loo
Chili chilli
Chinarestaurant nt Chinese restaurant
Chips pl crisps ; chips (gambling)
Chor m choir
Cocktailbar cocktail bar
Cola f Coke®
Computer m computer
Computerprogramm nt computer program
Computerspiel nt computer game
Conditioner m conditioner (hair)

Cousin(e) m/f cousin
Creme f cream (lotion)
Creme(speise) f mousse

D

da there
    nicht da out (not at home)
Dach nt roof
Dachboden m attic
Dachgepäckträger m roof-rack
daheim at home
Damen ladies
Damenbinde(n) f sanitary towel(s)
Dampfer m steamer (boat)
danach after (afterwards)
Dänemark nt Denmark
danke thank you
danken to thank
Darmgrippe f gastric flu
das the ; that ; this ; which
Datei f file (computer)
Datum nt date (day)
Dauer f length ; duration
Dauerwelle f perm
Daumen m thumb
Debitkarte debit card
Decke f blanket ; ceiling
Deckel m top ; lid
dein your (singular familiar)
denken to think
Denkmal(-mäler) nt monument(s)
Deo nt deodorant
der the ; who(m) ; that ; this ; which
Desinfektionsmittel nt disinfectant
desinfizieren to disinfect
destilliertes Wasser nt distilled water
Details pl details
deutsch adj German
Deutsch nt German (language)
Deutsche(r) m/f German
Deutschland nt Germany
Devisen pl foreign currency
Dezember m December
Dia(s) nt slide(s)
Diabetes m diabetes
Diabetiker(in) m/f diabetic person
Diamant m diamond
Diät f diet (special)
dick fat
die the ; who(m) ; that ; this ; which
Dieb(in) m/f thief
Diebstahl m theft
Dienst m service
    im Dienst on duty

Dienstag m Tuesday
dienstbereit open (pharmacy) ; on duty (doctor)
Dienstreise f business trip
Dienstzeit f office hours
dies this
diese these
diese(r/s) this (one)
Diesel m diesel
Dieselöl nt diesel oil
Digitalkamera f digital camera
Digitalradio nt digital radio
Ding(e) nt thing(s)
Diplomat(in) m/f diplomat
direkt direct (route, train)
Direktflug m direct flight
Direktor(in) m/f managing director
Diskette f computer disk (floppy)
Disko f disco
Dokumente pl documents
Dollar m dollar
Dolmetscher(in) m/f interpreter
Dom m cathedral
Donner m thunder
Donnerstag m Thursday
Doppel- double
Doppelbett nt double bed
doppelt double
Doppelzimmer nt double room
Dorf(Dörfer) nt village(s)
Dorn m thorn
dort there (over there) ; that one
Dose f box ; tin ; can
Dosenöffner m tin-opener
Down-Syndrom Down's syndrome
  er/sie hat Down-Syndrom he/she has Down's syndrome
Dozent(in) m/f teacher (university)
Drachenfliegen nt hang gliding
Draht m wire
Drahtseilbahn f cable railway
draußen outdoors ; outside
drehen to turn ; to twist
Dreibettabteil nt three-berth compartment
Dreieck nt triangle
Dreikönigstag m Epiphany
dringend urgent
drinnen indoors
Droge f drug
Drogerie f chemist's (not for prescriptions)
drücken push
Druckschrift f block letters
du you (familiar form)
dumm stupid

dunkel dark
dunkelblau dark blue
dünn thin ; weak (tea)
dunstig misty
durch through ; well-done (steak)
Durchfahrt verboten no through traffic
Durchfall m diarrhoea
Durchgang m way ; passage
Durchgangsverkehr m through traffic
durchgehend direct (train, bus) ; 24 hour
Durchsage f announcement
durchwählen to dial direct
Durchzug m draught (of air)
dürfen to be allowed
Dürre f drought
Durst haben to be thirsty
durstig thirsty
Dusche f shower
Duschhaube f shower cap
Duschvorhang m shower curtain
Dutzend nt dozen
DVD f DVD
DVD-Spieler m DVD player

E

Ebbe f low tide
echt real ; genuine
Ecke f corner
Edelstein m jewel ; gem
ehemalig ex-
ehrlich honest
Ei(er) nt egg(s)
Eiche f oak
eifersüchtig jealous
Eigelb nt egg yolk
Eigentum nt property
Eigentümer(in) m/f owner
Eil- urgent
Eilbrief m express letter
Eilzustellung f special delivery
Eimer m bucket
ein (with 'das'/'der' words) a ; one
ein(geschaltet) on (machine)
Einbahnstraße f one-way street
Einbrecher(in) m/f burglar
einchecken to check in
eine (with 'die' words) a ; one
einfach simple ; single ticket ; plain (unflavoured)
Einfuhr f import
einführen to insert ; to import
Eingang m entrance
Eingangstür f front door
eingeschlossen included (in price)

eingeschneit snowed up
Eingeweidebruch m hernia
eingießen to pour
einige(r/s) some ; a few
einkaufen to shop
Einkaufswagen m shopping trolley
Einkaufszentrum nt shopping centre
einladen to invite
Einladung f invitation
Einlass ab 18 no entry for under 18s
einlaufen to shrink
einlösen to cash (cheque)
einmal once
einnehmen to take (medicine)
einordnen to get in lane
Einrichtungen pl facilities
eins one
einschalten to switch on (light, TV)
einschieben to insert
einschließlich including
Einschreiben nt registered letter
  per Einschreiben by recorded delivery
einsteigen to get in(to) (bus, etc)
einstellen to adjust ; to appoint ; to stop
Einstellplatz car port
Eintopfgericht nt stew
eintreten to enter
Eintritt m entry ; admission (fee)
Eintritt frei free entry
Eintrittskarte(n) f ticket(s)
Eintrittspreis m admission charge/fee
einwerfen to post ; to insert
einwickeln to wrap up (parcel)
Einwurf m slot ; slit
  Einwurf 2 Euro insert 2 euros
Einzahlung f deposit
Einzel- (not double)
Einzelbett nt single bed
Einzelfahrschein m single ticket
einzeln single ; individual
Einzelzimmer nt single room
Eis nt ice cream ; ice
Eisbahn f skating rink
Eisbecher m knickerbocker glory
Eisdiele f ice-cream parlour
Eisen nt iron (metal)
Eisenbahn f railway
Eisenwarenhandlung f hardware shop
Eiskaffee m iced coffee
Eistee m iced tea
Eiswürfel pl ice cubes
Eiweiß nt egg white
Elastikbinde f elastic bandage
elastisch elastic

Elektriker(in) m/f electrician
elektrisch electric(al)
elektrischer Schlag m electric shock
elektrische Zahnbürste electric toothbrush
Elektrizität f electricity
elektronisch electronic
elektronische Organizer electronic organizer
Elektrorasierer m electric razor
Ellbogen m elbow
Eltern pl parents
E-Mail f e-mail
E-Mail-Adresse f e-mail address
Empfang m reception
empfangen to receive (guest) ; to greet
Empfangschef m receptionist
Empfangsdame f receptionist
Empfangsschein m receipt
empfehlen to recommend
Ende nt end ; bottom (of page, etc)
Endstand m final score (of match)
Endstation f terminal
Endsumme f total (amount)
eng narrow ; tight (clothes)
England nt England
Engländer(in) m/f Englishman/woman
Englisch nt English (language)
Enkel m grandson
Enkelin f granddaughter
entdecken to discover
Ente f duck
enteisen to de-ice
entfernt distant
  2 Kilometer entfernt 2 km away
Entfernung f distance
entfrosten to defrost
Enthaarungscreme f depilatory cream
enthalten to hold (to contain)
entkoffeinierter Kaffee m decaffeinated coffee
entkommen to escape
entrahmte Milch f skimmed milk
entschädigen to reimburse
Entschuldigung f pardon ; excuse me
entweder ... oder either ... or
entwickeln to develop (photos)
Entzündung f inflammation
Epileptiker(in) m/f epileptic
epileptischer Anfall m epileptic fit
er he ; it
erbrechen to vomit
Erbsen pl peas
Erdbeben nt earthquake
Erdbeeren pl strawberries

Erde f earth
Erdgeschoss nt ground floor
Erdnuss(-nüsse) f peanut(s)
Erdrutsch m landslide
erfreut pleased
Erfrischungen pl refreshments
erhalten to obtain ; to receive
erhältlich available
Erkältung f cold (illness)
erkennen to realize ; to recognize
erklären to explain
Erklärung f explanation
erlauben to permit (something) ; to allow
Ermäßigung f reduction
Ernte f harvest
Ersatz m substitute ; replacement
Ersatzrad nt spare wheel
Ersatzteile pl car parts
erste(r/s) first
   erste Hilfe first aid
   erste Klasse first class
ertrinken to drown
Erwachsene(r) m/f adult
erzählen to tell
es it
essbar edible
essen to eat
Essen nt food ; meal
Essen zum Mitnehmen take-away food
Essig m vinegar
Esslöffel m tablespoon
Esszimmer nt dining room
Etage f floor ; storey
Etagenbetten pl bunk beds
etwas something
Eule f owl
Euro m Euro (currency)
Eurocent m euro cent
Europa nt Europe
europäisch European
Europäische Union (EU) f European Union (EU)
Euroscheck m Eurocheque
Exemplar nt copy
Experte (Expertin) m/f expert
exportieren to export

F

Fabrik f works ; factory
Facharzt (Fachärztin) m/f specialist (medical)
Fächer m fan (hand-held)
Faden m thread
Fahne f flag

Fahrbahn f carriageway
Fähre f ferry
fahren to drive ; to go
Fahrer(in) m/f driver (of car)
Fahrgast m passenger
Fahrkarte f ticket (train, bus, etc)
Fahrkartenschalter m ticket office
Fahrplan m timetable (trains, etc)
Fahrplanhinweise pl travel information
Fahrpreis(e) m fare(s)
Fahrrad(-räder) nt bicycle(s)
Fahrradflickzeug nt bicycle repair kit
Fahrradschloss nt bicycle lock
Fahrradvermietung f bike hire
Fahrschein(e) m ticket(s)
Fahrscheinentwerter m ticket stamping machine
Fahrscheinheft nt book of tickets
Fahrspur(en) f lane(s)
Fahrstuhl m lift ; elevator
Fahrt f journey ; drive ; ride (in vehicle)
   gute Fahrt! safe journey!
Fahrzeug nt vehicle
Fall m instance
   im Falle von in case of
fallen to fall
fällig due (owing)
falsch false (name, etc) ; wrong
Falten pl wrinkles
Familie f family
Familienname m surname
Familienstand m marital status
Familienzimmer nt family room
Fan m fan (football)
Farbe f colour ; paint ; suit (cards)
färben dye
farbenblind colour-blind
Farbfilm m colour film
farbig coloured
Farbstoff m dye
Fasching m carnival
Fass nt barrel
   vom Fass on tap ; on draught
Fassbier nt draught beer
Fastnachtsdienstag m Shrove Tuesday
faul lazy
Fax nt fax
faxen to fax
Faxnummer f fax number
Februar m February
Feder f spring (coil) ; feather
Federball m badminton
Federung f suspension (in car)
fehlen to be missing

Fehler m fault ; mistake
Fehlgeburt f miscarriage
feiern to celebrate
Feiertag m holiday
Feige f fig
Feile f file (nail)
Feinkostgeschäft nt delicatessen
Feld nt field
Felsen m cliff (in mountains)
Fenster nt window
Fensterladen m shutter (on window)
Fensterplatz m window seat
Ferien pl holiday(s)
Ferienhaus nt chalet (holiday)
Ferienwohnung f holiday flat
Fern- long-distance
Fernbedienung f remote control
Ferngespräch nt long-distance call
Fernglas nt binoculars
Fernlicht nt full beam (headlights)
Fernsehen nt television
Fernseher m TV set
Fernsprecher m public phone
fertig ready ; finished
Fest nt celebration ; party ; festival
Festplatte f hard disk
Fett nt fat ; grease
fettarm low-fat
fettarme Milch f low-fat milk
fettig greasy
feucht damp
Feuchtigkeitscreme f moisturizer
Feuer nt fire
feuerfeste Form f ovenproof dish
feuergefährlich inflammable
Feuerlöscher m fire extinguisher
Feuermelder m fire/smoke alarm
Feuertreppe f fire escape
Feuerwehr f fire brigade
Feuerwehrauto nt fire engine
Feuerwerk nt fireworks
Feuerzeug nt cigarette lighter
Fieber nt fever
   Fieber haben to have temperature
Filet nt sirloin ; fillet (of meat, fish)
Filiale f branch (of store, bank, etc)
Film m film (at cinema, for camera)
filmen to film
Filter m filter
Filzstift m felt-tip pen
finden to find
Finger m finger
Fingernagel m fingernail
Firma f company (firm)

Fisch m fish
Fischladen m fishmonger's
FKK-Strand m nudist beach
flach flat (level) ; shallow (water)
Flamme f flame
Flasche f bottle
Flaschenbier nt bottled beer
Flaschenöffner m bottle opener
Fleck m mark (stain)
Fleckenmittel nt stain-remover
Fleisch nt meat ; flesh
Fleischerei f butcher's
Flickzeug nt puncture repair kit
Fliege f bow tie ; fly
fliegen to fly
Flitterwochen pl honeymoon
Flöhe pl fleas
Flohmarkt m flea market
Flug(Flüge) m flight(s)
Fluggast m passenger
Fluggesellschaft f airline
Flughafen m airport
Flughafenbus m airport bus
Flugplan m flight schedule
Flugauskunft f flight information
Flugschein(e) m plane ticket(s)
Flugsteig m gate
Flugstrecke f route ; flying distance
Flugticket(s) nt plane ticket(s)
Flugzeug nt plane, aircraft
Flur m corridor
Fluss(Flüsse) m river(s)
Flussfahrt f river trip
Flüssigkeit f liquid
Flut f flood ; high tide
Föhn m hairdryer
föhnen to blow-dry
folgen to follow
Forelle f trout
Form f shape ; form
Formular nt form (document)
Fortsetzung f sequel (book, film)
Foto nt photo
Fotoapparat m camera
Fotogeschäft nt photo shop
Fotografie f photography
fotografieren to take a photo
Foto-Handy camera phone
Fotokopie f photocopy
fotokopieren to photocopy
Fracht f cargo ; freight
Frage f question
fragen to ask
frankieren to stamp (letter)

Frankreich nt France
Franzose (Französin) m/f Frenchman/woman
französisch adj French
Frau f wife ; Mrs ; Ms ; woman
Frauenarzt (Frauenärztin) gynaecologist
Fräulein nt Miss
frei free / vacant
  im Freien outdoor
Freibad nt open-air pool
freiberuflich freelance ; self-employed
Freigepäck nt baggage allowance
Freiland- free-range
  Eier aus Freilandhaltung free-range eggs
freimachen to stamp
Freisprecheinrichtung hands-free kit (for phone)
Freitag m Friday
Freizeichen nt ringing tone
Freizeit f spare time ; leisure
Freizeitzentrum nt leisure centre
fremd foreign ; strange (unknown)
Fremde(r) m/f stranger
Fremdenführer(in) m/f tourist guide
Fremdenverkehrsbüro nt tourist office
Freude f joy
Freund m friend ; boyfriend
Freundin f friend ; girlfriend
freundlich friendly
Frieden m peace
Friedhof m cemetery
frisch fresh ; wet (paint)
Frischhaltefolie f cling film
Frischkäse m cream cheese
Friseur (Friseuse) m/f hairdresser
Frosch m frog
Frost m frost
Frostschutzmittel nt antifreeze
Früchte pl fruit
Früchtetee m fruit tea
Fruchtsaft m fruit juice
früh early
früher earlier
Frühling m spring (season)
Frühstück nt breakfast
Fuchs m fox
fühlen to feel
führen to lead
Führer(in) m/f guide
Führerschein m driving licence
Führung(en) f guided tour(s)
füllen to fill
Füller m pen
Fundbüro nt lost property office

Fundsachen pl lost property
funktionieren to work (machine)
für for
  Benzin für 30 Euro 30 euros worth of petrol
  für immer forever
Fuß(Füße) m foot(feet)
  zu Fuß gehen to walk
Fußball m football ; soccer
Fußballer(in) m/f football player
Fußballplatz m football pitch
Fußballspiel nt football match
Fußgänger(in) m/f pedestrian
Fußgängerüberweg m pedestrian crossing
Fußgängerzone f pedestrian precinct
Fußpfleger(in) chiropodist
Fußweg m footpath
füttern to feed

G

Gabel f fork (for eating)
Gabelung f fork (in road)
Galerie f gallery
Gang m course (of meal) ; aisle (theatre, plane)
Gangschaltung f gears
Gans f goose
ganz whole ; quite
ganztägig full-time
Garage f garage (private)
Garantie f guarantee ; warrant(y)
Garderobe f cloakroom
Garten m garden
Gartenlokal nt garden café
Gärtner(in) m/f gardener
Gas nt gas
Gasflasche f gas cylinder
Gasherd m gas cooker
Gaspedal nt accelerator
Gasse f alley ; lane (in town)
Gast m guest
  nur für Gäste patrons only
Gästezimmer nt guest-room
Gasthaus nt inn
Gasthof m inn ; guesthouse
Gastritis f gastritis
Gaststätte f restaurant
Gaststube f lounge ; restaurant
Gate nt gate (airport)
Gebäck nt pastry (cake)
gebacken baked
Gebäude nt building
gebeizt cured ; marinated
geben to give

Gebiet *nt* region ; area
Gebiss *nt* dentures
geboren born
  geborene Schnorr née Schnorr
gebraten fried
gebrauchen to use
Gebraucht- used *(car, etc)*
gebrochen broken
Gebühr *f* fee
gebührenpflichtig subject to fee
Geburt *f* birth
Geburtsdatum *nt* date of birth
Geburtsort *m* place of birth
Geburtstag *m* birthday
Geburtstagsgeschenk *nt* birthday
  present
Geburtstagskarte *f* birthday card
Geburtsurkunde *f* birth certificate
Gedeckkosten *pl* cover charge *(in
  restaurant)*
gedünstet steamed
Gefahr *f* danger
gefährlich dangerous
Gefälle *nt* gradient
Gefängnis *nt* prison
Geflügel *nt* poultry ; fowl
gefroren frozen *(food)*
gefüllt stuffed
gegen versus ; against ; toward(s)
Gegend *f* district ; region
gegenüber opposite ; facing
Gegenverkehr *m* two-way traffic
gegrillt grilled
Geheimzahl *f* PIN number
gehen to go ; to walk
  wie geht es Ihnen? how are you?
Gehirnerschütterung *f* concussion
gehören to belong to
gekocht boiled ; cooked
gelb yellow ; amber *(traffic lights)*
Gelbe Seiten *pl* Yellow Pages
Gelbsucht *f* jaundice
Geld *nt* money
  Geld abheben withdraw cash
  Geld einwerfen insert money
Geldautomat *m* cash dispenser ; atm
Geldbeutel *m* purse
Geldrückgabe *f* coin return
Geldschein *m* banknote
Geldstrafe *f* fine *(to be paid)*
Geldstück *nt* coin
gelegentlich occasionally
Gelenk *nt* joint *(of body)*
Geltungsdauer *f* period of validity
gemischt mixed ; assorted

Gemüse *nt* vegetables
Gemüseladen *m* greengrocer's
genau accurate ; precise ; exact
Genehmigung *f* approval ; permit
genfrei GM-free
genmanipuliert Genetically modified
genug enough
Genuss *m* enjoyment
geöffnet open
Gepäck *nt* luggage
Gepäckablage *f* luggage rack
Gepäckaufbewahrung *f* left-luggage office
Gepäckausgabe *f* baggage reclaim
Gepäckermittlung *f* luggage desk
  (for queries)
Gepäcknetz *nt* luggage rack *(in train)*
Gepäckschließfach *nt* left-luggage locker
Gepäckträger *m* luggage rack
  (on car) ; porter
Gepäckversicherung *f* luggage insurance
Gepäckwagen *m* luggage trolley
gerade even *(number)*
geradeaus straight ahead
Gerät *nt* appliance ; gadget
geräuchert smoked *(food)*
Gericht *nt* court *(law)* ; dish *(food)*
gerieben grated *(cheese)*
geröstet sauté ; fried ; toasted
Geruch *m* smell
Gesamtsumme *f* total amount
Geschäft(e) *nt* business ; shop(s)
Geschäftsadresse *f* business address
Geschäftsführer(in) *m/f* manager
Geschäftspartner(in) *m/f* partner *(business)*
Geschäftsstunden *pl* business hours
Geschäftszentrum business centre
geschehen to happen
Geschenk(e) *nt* gift(s)
Geschenkeladen *m* gift shop
Geschenkpapier *nt* wrapping paper
Geschichte *f* history
geschieden divorced
Geschirrspülmaschine *f* dishwasher
Geschirrspülmittel *nt* washing-up liquid
Geschirrtuch *nt* tea/dish towel
Geschlecht *nt* gender ; sex
Geschlechtskrankheit *f* venereal disease
geschlossen closed/shut
Geschmack *m* taste ; flavour
geschmort braised
geschnittenes Brot *nt* sliced bread
Geschoss *nt* storey
geschützt sheltered
Geschwindigkeit *f* speed

geschwollen swollen
Geschwür nt ulcer
Gesellschaft f company
Gesetz nt law
gesetzlicher Feiertag m public holiday
Gesicht nt face
Gesichtswasser f cleanser (for face)
Gesichtspflege f facial (beauty treatment)
gesperrt closed
Gespräch nt talk ; phone call
Gesprächsguthaben credit (on mobile phone)
Gestank m smell (unpleasant)
gestattet permitted
gestern yesterday
gestochen stung ; bitten (by insect)
gestreift striped
gesund healthy
Gesundheit f health ; bless you!
Getränk(e) nt drink(s)
Getränkekarte f list of beverages
getrennt separated (couple)
  getrennt bezahlen to pay separately
Getriebe nt gearbox ; gears
Gewehr nt gun
Gewicht nt weight
gewinnen to win
Gewitter nt thunderstorm
gewöhnlich usual(ly)
Gewürz nt spice ; seasoning
Gezeiten pl tide
gibt es...? is/are there...?
Gift nt poison
giftig poisonous
Gipfel m summit ; mountain top
Gips m plaster (for broken limb)
Gitarre f guitar
Glas nt glass ; jar
Glatteis nt black ice
Glatteisgefahr f danger – black ice
glatzköpfig bald (person)
glauben to believe ; to think (be of opinion)
gleich same
Gleise pl platforms ; tracks
Gletscher m glacier
Glocke f bell
Glück nt happiness ; luck
glücklich happy ; lucky
Glühbirne f light bulb
gluten gluten
  glutenfrei gluten-free
Gold nt gold
Golf nt golf
Golfplatz m golf course

Golfschläger m golf club
gotisch Gothic
Gott m God
Gottesdienst m church service
GPS GPS (global positioning system)
Grad m degree (of heat, cold)
Gramm nt gram(me)
Grapefruit f grapefruit
Gras nt grass
Gräte f fish bone
grau grey
Grenze f frontier ; border (of country)
Grenzpolizei f border police
Griff m handle ; knob
Grill m barbecue ; grill
grillen to grill
Grillstube f steak house ; grillroom
Grillteller m mixed grill
Grippe f flu
groß tall ; great ; big ; high (number, speed)
Großbritannien nt Great Britain
Großbuchstabe m capital letter
Größe f size (of clothes, shoes) ; height
Großeltern pl grandparents
Großmutter f grandmother
Großraumwagen m (in train) open plan carriage
Großvater m grandfather
großzügig generous
grün green ; fresh (fish)
Grünanlage f park
Grundstücksmakler m estate agent's
grüne Versicherungskarte f green card (car insurance)
grüner Salat m green salad
Gruppe f group
Gruß m greeting
Grußkarte f greetings card
Guave guava
Gulasch nt goulash
gültig valid
Gummi m rubber ; elastic
Gummiband nt rubber band
Gummihandschuhe pl rubber gloves
Gummistiefel pl wellington boots
günstig convenient ; cheap
Gurke(n) f cucumber(s) ; gherkin(s)
Gürtel m belt
Gürtelrose f shingles
Gürteltasche f bumbag ; moneybelt
gut good ; well ; all right (yes)
  alles Gute all the best ; with best wishes
guten Abend good evening
guten Appetit enjoy your meal

guten Morgen good morning
gute Nacht good night
guten Tag hello ; good day/afternoon
Güter *pl* goods
Guthabenkarte charge card *(for mobile phone)*
Gutschein *m* voucher ; coupon
Gynäkologe (Gynäkologin) gynaecologist

H

H-Milch *f* long-life milk
Haar *nt* hair
Haarbürste *f* hairbrush
Haare *pl* hair
Haargel *nt* hair gel
Haarklemme *f* hairgrip
Haarschnitt *m* haircut
Haarspray *nt* hair spray
haben to have
Hackfleisch *nt* mince meat
Hacksteak *nt* hamburger *(usually without the bread)*
Hafen *m* harbour ; port
Hafer *m* oats
Haftung *f* liability
Hagel *m* hail
Hahn *m* tap *(for water)* ; cockerel
Hähnchen *nt* chicken
halb half
   zum halben Preis half-price
halb durch medium rare *(meat)*
halber Fahrpreis *m* half fare
Halbfettmilch *f* semi-skimmed milk
Halbinsel *f* peninsula
Halbpension *f* half board
Hälfte *f* half
hallo hello
Hals *m* neck ; throat
Halskette *f* necklace
Halspastillen *pl* throat lozenges
Halsschmerzen *pl* sore throat
Halstuch *nt* scarf *(round neck)*
Halt *m* stop
Haltbarkeitsdatum *nt* sell-by date
Haltebucht *f* layby
halten to hold ; to stop
Halten verboten no stopping
Haltestelle *f* bus stop
Hammer *m* hammer
Hämorrhoiden *pl* haemorrhoids
Hand *f* hand
Handbremse *f* handbrake *(car)*
Handel *m* trade ; commerce

Handgelenk *nt* wrist
handgemacht handmade
Handgepäck *nt* hand-luggage
Handschuhe *pl* gloves
Handtasche *f* handbag
Handtuch *nt* towel
Handwerker(in) *m/f* craftsperson
Handy mobile *(phone)*
Handynummer *f* mobile number
Harke *f* rake
hart hard *(not soft)*
hart gekochtes Ei *nt* hard-boiled egg
Hase *m* hare
Haselnuss(-nüsse) *f* hazelnut(s)
hässlich ugly
häufig frequent ; common
Haupt- major ; main
Hauptbahnhof *m* main station
Hauptgericht *nt* main course
Hauptstadt *f* capital *(city)*
Hauptstraße *f* major road
Hauptverkehrszeit *f* peak hours
Haus *nt* house ; home
   zu Hause at home
Hausarbeit *f* housework
Hausbrauerei micro-brewery
Hausfrau (Hausmann) *f/m* housewife/househusband
Haushaltswaren *pl* household goods
Hausschuhe *pl* slippers
Haustier *nt* pet
Hauswein *m* house wine
Haut *f* hide *(leather)* ; skin
Hecht *m* pike
Hefe *f* yeast
Heft *nt* exercise book
Hefter *m* stapler
Heftklammern *pl* staples
Heftpflaster *nt* sticking plaster
Heidelbeeren *pl* blueberries
heilig holy
Heiligabend *m* Christmas Eve
Heim *nt* home *(institution)* ; hostel
Heimweh haben to be homesick
heiraten to marry
heiß hot
   heiße Schokolade *f* hot chocolate
heißen to be called
   wie heißen Sie? what's your name?
Heißwassergerät *nt* water heater
Heizgerät *nt* heater
Heizkörper *m* radiator
Heizung *f* heating
helfen to help

Helikopter *m* helicopter
hell light *(pale)* ; bright
hellblau light blue
helles Bier *nt* lager
helles Fleisch *nt* white meat
Helm *m* helmet
Hemd(en) *nt* shirt(s)
Hepatitis *f* hepatitis
Herbst *m* autumn
Herd *m* cooker ; oven
herein in ; come in
hereinkommen to come in
Hering *m* herring ; tent peg
Herr *m* gentleman ; Mr
Herren gents *(toilet)*
heruntergehen to go down
Herz *nt* heart
Herzanfall *m* heart attack
herzliche Glückwünsche!
  congratulations!
Herzschrittmacher *m* pacemaker
Heuschnupfen *m* hay fever
heute today
heute Abend tonight
hier here
hiesig local *(wine, speciality)*
Hilfe *f* help
Himbeeren *pl* raspberries
Himmel *m* heaven ; sky
hin there
Hin- und Rückfahrt *f* round trip
hineingehen to go in
hinten behind
hinten einsteigen enter at rear
hinter behind
Hinweis *m* notice ; information
Hirnhautentzündung *f* meningitis
historisch historic
hoch high
Hochsaison *f* high season
Höchstgeschwindigkeit *f* maximum
  speed
Höchsttarif *m* peak rate
Hochzeit *f* wedding
Hochzeitsgeschenk *nt* wedding present
Hochzeitskleid *nt* wedding dress
Hochzeitstag *m* wedding anniversary
Hochzeitstorte *f* wedding cake
Hoden *pl* testicles
Hof *m* court
hoffen to hope
höflich polite
Höhe *f* altitude ; height
hoher Blutdruck *m* high blood pressure

höher higher
  höher stellen to turn up *(heat, volume)*
Höhle *f* cave
holen to fetch
holländisch Dutch
Holz *nt* wood *(material)*
Holzkohle *f* charcoal
Homepage *f* homepage
Homöopathie *f* homeopathy
homöopathisch homeopathic *(remedy, etc)*
homosexuell homosexual
Honig *m* honey
hören to hear
Hörer *m* receiver *(phone)*
Hörgerät *nt* hearing aid
Hörnchen *nt* croissant
Hose *f* trousers
Hotel *nt* hotel
Hotel garni *nt* bed and breakfast hotel
hübsch pretty
Hubschrauber *m* helicopter
Hüfte *f* hip
Hügel *m* hill
Huhn *nt* hen
Hühnchen *nt* chicken
Hummer *m* lobster
Hund *m* dog
Hundeleine *f* dog lead
hundert hundred
Hunger haben to be hungry
Hupe *f* horn *(of car)*
husten to cough
Husten *m* cough
Hustenbonbons *pl* cough sweets
Hustensaft *m* cough mixture
Hut *m* hat
Hütte *f* mountain hut

I

ich I
Idiotenhügel *m* nursery slope
ihm him
ihnen them
ihr(e) her ; their
Imbiss *m* snack
Imbissstube *f* snack bar
immer always
Immunisierung *f* immunisation
Impfung *f* vaccination
in in *(place, position)* ; inside ; into
  in Ordnung all right *(agreed)*
Infektion *f* infection
Informationsbüro *nt* information office
Ingenieur(in) *m/f* engineer

Inhalationsapparat *m* inhaler *(medication)*
Inhalt *m.* contents
inklusive inclusive
Inland *nt* domestic *(flight, etc)*
Inlandsgespräch(e) *nt* national call(s)
innen inside
Innenkabine *f (on ship/ferry)* inside cabin
Innenstadt *f* city centre
innerlich for internal use *(medicine)*
Insekt *nt* insect
Insektenschutzmittel *nt* insect repellent
Insel *f* island
Insulin *nt* insulin
intelligent intelligent
interessant interesting
Internet *nt* internet
   haben Sie Internet-Anschluss? do you
   have internet access?
Internet-Café *nt* internet café
Internet-Seite *f* website
Internetadresse *f* website addres
Intrauterinpessar coil *(IUD)*
iPOD iPOD®
Ire (Irin) *m/f* Irishman/woman
irgendjemand someone
irgendwo somewhere
irisch *adj* Irish
Irland *nt* Ireland
Irrtum *m* mistake
Isomatte *f* camping mat
Italien *nt* Italy
Italiener(in) *m/f* Italian
italienisch *adj* Italian

J

ja yes
Jacht *f* yacht
Jachthafen *m* marina
Jacke *f* jacket ; cardigan
Jagderlaubnis *f* hunting permit
jagen to hunt
Jahr *nt* year
Jahrestag *m* anniversary
Jahreszeit *f* season
Jahrgang *m* vintage
Jahrhundert *nt* century
jährlich annual ; yearly
Jahrmarkt *m (fun)* fair
Januar *m* January
jeder everyone
Jeans *pl* jeans
jede(r/s) each
jemand somebody ; someone
jene those

jetzt now
Jod *nt* iodine
joggen to jog
Jogginganzug *m* tracksuit
Joghurt *m* yoghurt
Johannisbeere(n) *f* currant(s)
Journalist(in) *m/f* journalist
jucken to itch
Jude/Jüdin *m/f* Jew
Jugendherberge *f* youth hostel
Jugendliche(r) *m/f* teenager
Juli *m* July
jung young
Junge *m* boy
Junggeselle *m* bachelor
Juni *m* June
Juwelier *m* jeweller's

K

Kabel *nt* cable ; lead *(electrical)*
Kabelfernsehen *nt* cable TV
kabellose Internet-Verbindung wireless
   internet
Kabine *f* cabin ; berth *(train, ship)*
Kaffee *m* coffee
Kaffeehaus *nt* café
Kaffeemaschine *f* percolator
Kai *m* quayside
Kakao *m* cocoa
Kakerlake *f* cockroach
Kalb *nt* calf *(young cow)*
Kalbfleisch *nt* veal
kalt cold
Kamera *f* camera
Kameratasche *f* camera case
Kamillentee *m* camomile tea
Kamin *m* fireplace
Kamm *m* comb ; ridge
kämpfen to fight
Kanada *nt* Canada
Kanadier(in) *m/f* Canadian
kanadisch *adj* Canadian
Kanal *m* canal ; *(English)* Channel
kandiert glacé
Kaninchen *nt* rabbit
Kanister *m (petrol)* can
Kanu *nt* canoe
Kapelle *f* chapel ; orchestra
kaputt broken ; out of order
kaputtmachen to break *(object)*
Kapuze *f* hood *(of jacket)*
Karaffe *f* decanter ; carafe
Karfreitag *m* Good Friday
Karotten *pl* carrots

Karte f card ; ticket ; map ; menu
Kartentelefon nt cardphone
Kartoffel(n) f potato(es)
Kartoffelpüree nt mashed potato
Kartoffelsalat m potato salad
Karton m box (cardboard) ; carton
Käse m cheese
Kasino nt casino
Kasse f cash desk
Kasserolle f casserole
Kassette f cassette ; cartridge ; tape
Kassettenrekorder m cassette player ;
  tape recorder
Kassierer(in) m/f cashier
Kastanie f chestnut
Katalog m catalogue
Katalysator m catalytic convertor (car)
Kater m hangover ; tomcat
katholisch Catholic
Katze f cat
kaufen to buy
Kaufhaus nt department store
Kaugummi m chewing gum
Kaution f deposit
Kehle f throat
Keilriemen m fan belt
kein... no...
keine(r/s) no ; none
Keks(e) m biscuit(s) (sweet)
Keller m cellar
Kellner(in) m/f waiter/waitress
kennen to be acquainted with
Keramik f pottery
Kern m pip
Kerze f candle
Kette f chain
Kfz-Versicherung f car insurance
Kiefer f pine
Kiefer m jaw
Kilo(gramm) nt kilo(gram)
Kilometer m kilometre
Kind(er) nt child(ren)
Kinderbett nt cot
Kindermädchen nt nanny
Kindersitz m child seat (car)
Kinderstuhl m high chair
Kinderteller m child's helping
Kinderwagen m pram
Kinn nt chin
Kino nt cinema
Kiosk m kiosk
Kirche f church
Kirmes f funfair
Kirsche(n) f cherry (cherries)

Kissen nt cushion ; pillow
Kiste f box (wooden)
Kiwi kiwi fruit
Klage f complaint
klar clear
Klarer m schnapps
Klärgrube f septic tank
Klasse f class ; grade
Klavier nt piano
Klebeband nt adhesive tape
kleben to stick (with glue)
Klebstoff m glue
Kleid nt dress
Kleider pl clothes
Kleiderbügel m coat hanger
Kleiderschrank m wardrobe
klein little (small) ; short
Kleingeld nt change (money)
Klempner(in) m/f plumber
Klettband nt Velcro®
klettern to climb (mountains)
Klimaanlage f air-conditioning unit
klimatisiert air-conditioned
Klingel f doorbell
klingeln to ring (bell, phone)
Klinik f clinic
Klippe f cliff (along coast)
klopfen to knock (on door)
Kloß m dumpling
Kloster nt monastery ; convent
Kneipe f pub
Knie nt knee
Kniestrümpfe pl pop socks
Knoblauch m garlic
Knöchel m ankle
Knochen m bone
Knödel m dumpling
Knopf m button ; knob (radio, etc)
Knoten m knot
Koch m chef
kochen to boil ; to cook
Kocher m cooker ; stove
Köchin f cook
Kochschinken m cooked ham
Kochtopf m saucepan
Kode m code
Köder m bait (for fishing)
koffeinfreier Kaffee m decaffeinated
  coffee
Koffer m suitcase ; trunk
Kofferanhänger m luggage tag
Kofferraum m carboot
Kognak m brandy
Kohl m cabbage

Kohle f coal
Kohlrübe f swede
Koje f berth (in ship) ; bunk
Kollege (Kollegin) m/f colleague
Köln Cologne
Kölnischwasser nt eau de cologne
komisch funny (amusing)
kommen to come
Kommode f chest of drawers
Komödie f comedy
Kompass m compass
Komponist(in) m/f composer
Kondensmilch f condensed milk
Konditorei f cake shop ; café
Kondom nt condom
Konfektions- ready-made (clothes)
Konferenz f conference
Konfitüre f jam
König m king
Königin f queen
königlich royal
können to be able to ; to know how to
Konsulat nt consulate
Kontaktlinsen pl contact lenses
Kontaktlinsenreiniger m contact lens cleaner
Konto nt bank account
Kontrolle f check ; control
kontrollieren to check (passports, tickets)
Konzert nt concert
Konzertsaal m concert hall
Kopf m head
Kopfhörer pl headphones
Kopfkissen nt pillow
Kopfsalat m lettuce
Kopfschmerzen pl headache
Kopftuch nt scarf (headscarf)
Kopie f copy (duplicate)
kopieren to copy
Kopiergerät photocopier
Korb m basket
Korinthe f currant
Korken m cork (of bottle)
Korkenzieher m corkscrew
Körper m body
Körperpuder m talc
Kortison nt cortisone
Kosmetiksalon m beauty salon
Kosmetiktücher pl paper tissues
kosten to cost
Kosten pl cost (price)
kostenlos free of charge
köstlich delicious
Kostüm nt suit (woman's)

Krabbe f crab
Kräcker m cracker
Kraftstoff m fuel
Kragen m collar
Krämpfe pl cramps
krank ill ; sick
Krankenhaus nt hospital
Krankenkasse f medical insurance
Krankenwagen m ambulance
Krankheit f disease
Kräuter pl herbs
Kräutertee m herbal tea
Krawatte f tie
Krebs m crab (animal) ; cancer (illness)
Kreditkarte f credit card
Kreisverkehr m roundabout
Kreuz nt cross (also crucifix)
Kreuzfahrt f cruise
Kreuzschlitzschraubenzieher m Phillips screwdriver®
Kreuzung f junction ; crossroads
Kreuzworträtsel nt crossword
Krieg m war
Kristall nt crystal
Krone f crown
Krücken pl crutches
Krug m jug
Küche f kitchen ; cuisine
Kuchen m flan ; cake
Küchenbrett nt chopping board
Küchenpapier nt kitchen paper
Kugel f ball ; scoop (of ice cream)
Kugelschreiber m pen ; biro
Kuh f cow
kühl cool
Kühlbox f cool-box (for picnic)
kühlen to chill (wine, food)
Kühler m radiator (of car)
Kühlschrank m fridge
Kümmel m caraway seed ; cumin ; schnapps
Kunde (Kundin) m/f client ; customer
Kundenkarte store card
Kunst f art
Kunstfaser f man-made fibre
Kunstgewerbearbeiten pl crafts
Kunsthalle f art gallery
Kunsthandwerksmarkt craft fair
Künstler(in) m/f artist
künstlich artificial ; man-made
künstliche Hüfte f hip replacement
Kupfer nt copper
Kupplung f clutch (of car)
Kurierdienst m courier service

Kurort m spa
Kurs m course ; exchange rate
Kurve f curve ; corner ; bend
kurz short ; brief
Kurz(zeit)parkplatz m short-stay car park
kurzsichtig short-sighted
Kurzwarengeschäft nt haberdasher's
Kuss m kiss
küssen to kiss
Küste f coast ; seaside
Küstenwache f coastguard

L

lächeln to smile
Lächeln nt smile
lachen to laugh
Lachs m salmon
Lack m varnish
Laden m shop ; store
Lagerhalle f warehouse
Lakritze f liquorice
Lamm nt lamb
Lampe f lamp
Land nt country (Italy, France, etc) ; land
landen to land
Landkarte f map (of country)
Landschaft f countryside
Landung f landing (of plane)
Landwein m table wine
lang long
Länge f length
Langlauf m cross-country skiing
langsam slow(ly)
langsamer werden to slow down
langweilig boring
Langzeitparkplatz m long-stay car park
Lappen m cloth (rag)
Laptop m laptop
Laptop-Tasche laptop bag
Lärm m noise
lassen to let (allow)
Last f load
Laster m truck
Lastwagen m truck ; lorry
Lätzchen nt bib (baby's)
Lauch m leek
laufen to run
Laugenbrezel f soft pretzel
laut noisy ; loud(ly) ; aloud
läuten to ring (doorbell)
Lautsprecher m loudspeaker
Lautstärke f volume (of sound)
Lawine f avalanche
Lawinengefahr f danger of avalanches

leben to live (exist)
Lebensgefahr f danger to life
Lebensmittel pl groceries
Lebensmittelvergiftung f food poisoning
Lebensversicherung f life insurance
Leber f liver
Lebkuchen m gingerbread
Leck nt leak (of gas, liquid)
Lederwaren pl leather goods
ledig single (not married)
leer empty ; flat (battery) ; blank (disk/tape)
Leerlauf m neutral (gear)
legen to lay
Lehrer(in) m/f teacher (school) ; instructor
leicht light (not heavy) ; easy
Leid nt grief
  es tut mir Leid (I'm) sorry
leider unfortunately
leihen to rent (car) ; to lend
Leihgebühr f rental (fee)
Leinen nt linen (cloth)
leise quietly ; soft ; faint
  leiser stellen to turn down (volume)
Leiter f ladder
Leitung f telephone line
Lenker m handlebars
Lenkrad nt steering wheel
lernen to learn
  er/sie hat eine Lernschwäche he/she has a learning disability
lesbisch lesbian
lesen to read
letzte(r/s) last ; final
Leuchtturm m lighthouse
Leute pl people
Licht nt light
  das Licht anschalten to switch on lights
Lichtmaschine f alternator
Lichtschalter m light switch
Lichtschutz-Faktor factor (sunblock)
  Lichtschutz-Faktor 25 factor 25
Lidschatten m eye shadow
liebe(r) dear (in letter)
Liebe f love
lieben to love
liebenswürdig kind
lieber rather
Lieblings- favourite
Lied nt song
Lieferwagen m van
Liegestuhl m deckchair
Liegewagen m couchette
Lift m elevator ; lift
Liftpass m lift pass (on ski slopes)

Likör m liqueur
Limonade f lemonade
Limone f lime *(fruit)*
Lineal nt ruler
Linie f line *(row, of railway)*
Linienflug m scheduled flight
linke(r/s) left(-hand)
links to the left ; on the left
Linkshänder(in) m/f left-handed person
Linse f lens
Linsen pl lentils
Lippen pl lips
Lippenpflegestift m lip salve
Lippenstift m lipstick
Liste f list
Liter m litre
Loch nt hole
lochen to punch *(ticket, etc)*
locker loose *(screw, tooth)*
Löffel m spoon
Loge f box *(in theatre)*
Lohn m wage
Loipe f cross-country ski run
Lokal nt pub
Lorbeerblatt nt bayleaf
los loose
  das ist los? what's wrong?
Los nt lot *(at auction)* ; ticket *(lottery)*
lösen to buy *(ticket)*
löslich soluble
Lounge f lounge
Löwe m lion
LSF or **(SF)** SPF *(sun protection factor)*
  LSF or (SF) 30 SPF 30
Luft f air
Luftfilter m air filter
Luftfracht f air freight
Luftkissenboot nt hovercraft
Luftmatratze f air bed/mattress
Luftpost f air mail
Luftpumpe f pump *(bike/airmattress)*
Lüge f lie *(untruth)*
Lunge f lung
Lupe f magnifying glass
Lutscher m lollipop
Luxus m luxury

M

machen to make ; to do
  das macht nichts that doesn't matter
Mädchen nt girl
Mädchenname m maiden name
Made f maggot
Magen m stomach

Magenschmerzen pl stomachache
Magentabletten pl indigestion tablets
Magenverstimmung f indigestion
Magermilch f skimmed milk
Magnet m magnet
Magnetkarte swipecard
Mai m May
Mais m sweetcorn
Make-up nt make-up
malen to paint
Malzbier nt malt beer
man one
managen to manage *(be in charge)*
manchmal sometimes
Mandarine f tangerine
Mandel f almond ; tonsil
Mandelentzündung f tonsillitis
Mangel m flaw
Mango mango
Maniküre manicure
Mann m man ; husband
Männer pl men
männlich masculine ; male
Manschettenknöpfe pl cufflinks
Mantel m coat
Margarine f margarine
marineblau navy blue
mariniert marinated
Marke f brand *(of product)* ; token
  (for phone)
Markise f awning *(on house)*
Markt m market
Marktplatz m market place
Marmelade f jam
Marmor m marble
März m March
Maschine f machine
Maschine schreiben to type
Masern pl measles
Maßband nt tape measure
Maße pl measurements
Massage massage
Mast m mast
Material nt material
Matratze f mattress
Mauer f wall
Maus f mouse *(animal/computer)*
Maut f toll *(motorway)*
Mayonnaise f mayonnaise
MB Mb *(megabyte)*
Mechaniker(in) m/f mechanic
Medikament nt drug ; medicine
Medizin f medicine
Meer nt sea

Meeresfrüchte *pl* seafood
Mehl *nt* flour
Megabyte *nt* megabyte
  128 Megabyte 128 megabytes
mehr more
Mehrwegflasche *f* returnable bottle
  (usually with a deposit)
Mehrwertsteuer (MWST) *f* value-added
  tax (VAT)
meiden to avoid (person)
Meile *f* mile
mein my
meiste(n) most
Meisterwerk *nt* masterpiece
melden to report (tell about)
Melone *f* melon ; bowler hat
Memorystick *m* memory stick (for camera,
  etc)
Menge *f* crowd
Messe *f* fair (commercial) ; mass (church)
Messegelände *nt* exhibition centre
messen to measure
Messer *nt* knife
Messing *nt* brass
Metall *nt* metal
Meter *m* metre
Metro *f* metro (underground)
Metzgerei *f* butcher's
mich me (direct object)
Mikrophon microphone
Mietauto *nt* hire car
Miete *f* rent
mieten to hire ; to rent (house, etc)
Mietgebühr *f* rental charge
Mietvertrag *m* lease (rental)
Migräne *f* migraine
Mikrowelle *f* microwave oven
Milch *f* milk
Milchprodukte *pl* dairy produce
Milchpulver *nt* powdered milk
Millimeter *m* millimetre
Million *f* million
minderwertig low-quality
Mindest- minimum
Mineralwasser *nt* mineral water
Minidisk minidisk
Minimum *nt* minimum
Minister(in) *m/f* minister (politics)
Minute(n) *f* minute(s)
Minze *f* mint (herb)
mir me (indirect object)
mischen to mix
Missverständnis *nt* misunderstanding
mit with

Mitfahrgelegenheit *f* lift (in car)
Mitglied *nt* member (of club, etc)
mitnehmen to give a lift to
  zum Mitnehmen take-away (food)
Mittag *m* midday
Mittagessen *nt* lunch
Mitte *f* middle
Mitteilung *f* message
Mittel *nt* means
  ein Mittel gegen a remedy for
mittelalterlich medieval
Mittelmeer- Mediterranean
Mitternacht *f* midnight
Mittwoch *m* Wednesday
Mixer *m* blender ; mixer
Möbel *pl* furniture
Möbelpolitur *f* furniture polish
Mobiltelefon *nt* mobile phone
möbliert furnished
Modem *nt* modem
modern fashionable ; modern
mögen to enjoy (to like)
möglich possible
Mohn *m* poppy
Möhre(n) *f* carrot(s)
Mole *f* jetty
Monat *m* month
monatlich monthly
Mond *m* moon
Montag *m* Monday
Moped *nt* moped
Morgen *m* morning
morgen tomorrow
Morgendämmerung *f* dawn
Morgenmantel *m* dressing gown
Moschee *f* mosque
Moskitonetz *nt* mosquito net
Motor *m* motor ; engine
Motorboot *nt* motor boat
Motorhaube *f* bonnet (car)
Motorrad *nt* motorbike
Motte *f* moth (clothes)
Mountainbike *nt* mountain bike
MP3-Spieler *m* MP3 player
Mücke *f* midge
müde tired
Müll *m* rubbish
Müllbeutel *m* bin liner
Mülleimer *m* bin (dustbin)
Mülltrennung *f* waste separation
  (for recycling)
Mumps *m* mumps
München Munich
Mund *m* mouth

Mundwasser *nt* mouthwash
Münster *nt* cathedral
Münze(n) *f* coin(s)
Münzfernsprecher *m* payphone
Münztelefon *nt* payphone *(with coins)*
Muscheln *pl* mussels
Museum *nt* museum
Musik *f* music
Muskat *m* nutmeg
Muskel *m* muscle
müssen to have to ; to must
mutig brave
Mutter *f* mother
Mütze *f* cap *(hat)*
MWST *f* VAT

N

nach after ; according to ; to *(with names of places)*
Nachbar(in) *m/f* neighbour
Nachmittag *m* afternoon
nachmittags pm ; in the afternoon
Nachname *m* surname
Nachricht *f* note *(letter)* ; message
Nachrichten *pl* news
Nachspeise *f* dessert ; pudding
nächste(r/s) next
Nacht *f* night
  über Nacht overnight
Nachtdienst *m* night duty *(chemist)*
Nachthemd *nt* nightdress
Nachtisch *m* dessert
Nachtklub *m* night club
nachzahlen to pay extra
nackt nude ; naked ; bare
Nadel *f* needle
Nagel *m* nail *(metal)*
Nagelbürste *f* nailbrush
Nagelfeile *f* nail file
Nagellack *m* nail polish/varnish
Nagellackentferner *m* nail polish remover
Nagelschere *f* nail scissors
Nähe *f* proximity
  in der Nähe nearby
nähen to sew
Name *m* name ; surname
Narkose *f* anaesthetic
Nase *f* nose
nass wet
national national
Nationalität *f* nationality
Natur- natural
Naturlehrpfad *m* nature trail

Naturschutzgebiet *nt* nature reserve
Nebel *m* mist ; fog
neben by *(next to)* ; beside
Nebenstraße *f* minor road
Nebensaison *f* low season
neblig foggy
Neffe *m* nephew
Negativ *nt* negative *(photo)*
nehmen to catch *(bus, train)* ; to take *(remove)*
nein no
Nektarine *f* nectarine
Nelke *f* carnation
nennen to quote *(price)*
Nervenzusammenbruch *m* nervous breakdown
Nest *nt* nest
nett nice *(person)* ; kind
Netto- net *(income, price)*
Netz *nt* net ; network
neu new
neueste(r/s) newest ; latest
Neujahr(stag) *m* New Year's Day
Neuseeland *nt* New Zealand
nicht not ; non-
Nichte *f* niece
Nichtraucher *m* non-smoker
nichts nothing
nie never
Niederlande *pl* Netherlands
Niedersachsen *nt* Lower Saxony
niedrig low
Niedrigwasser *nt* low tide
niemand no one ; nobody
Niere(n) *f* kidney(s)
niesen to sneeze
nirgends nowhere
noch still *(up to this time)* ; yet
noch ein(e) extra *(more)* ; another
Norden *m* north
Nordirland *nt* Northern Ireland
nördlich north ; northern
Nordsee *f* North Sea
Normal(benzin) *nt* regular *(petrol)*
normal standard *(size)*
Notarzt *m* emergency doctor
Notaufnahme *f* accident & emergency
Notausgang *m* emergency exit
Notdienstapotheke *f* on-duty chemist
Notfall *m* emergency
nötig necessary
Notizblock *m* note pad
Notruf *m* emergency number
Notrufsäule *f* emergency phone *(on motorway)*

Notsignal nt distress signal
notwendig essential ; necessary
November m November
nüchtern sober
Nudeln pl pasta ; noodles
Null f nil ; zero ; nought
numerieren to number
Nummer f number ; act
Nummernschild nt numberplate
nur only
Nürnberg Nuremberg
Nuss (Nüsse) f nut(s)
nützlich useful

O

oben upstairs ; above ; this side up
oben auf on top of...
Oberschenkel m thigh
obligatorisch compulsory
Obst nt fruit
Obstkuchen m fruit tart
oder or
offen open
  offene Weine pl wine served by the glass
öffentlich public
öffnen to open ; to undo
Öffnungszeiten pl business hours
oft often
ohne without
ohnmächtig fainted
ohnmächtig werden to faint
Ohr(en) nt ear(s)
Ohrenschmerzen pl earache
Ohrringe pl earrings
okay OK
ökologisch ecological
ökonomisch economic
Ökotourismus eco-tourism
Oktober m October
Öl nt oil
Ölfilter m oil filter
Olive f olive
Olivenöl nt olive oil
Ölstandsanzeiger m oil gauge
Ölwechsel m oil change
Omelett nt omelette
Onkel m uncle
Oper f opera
Operation f operation (surgical)
Optiker m optician's
orange orange (colour)
Orange f orange (fruit)
Orangensaft m orange juice
Orchester nt orchestra

Ordner m file (for papers)
Oregano m oregano
organisch organic
organisieren to organize
Organspenderausweis m donor card
Ort m place
  an Ort und Stelle on the spot
örtlich local
örtliche Betäubung f local anaesthetic
Ortschaft f village ; town
Ortsgespräch nt local call
Ortszeit f local time
Osten m east
Osterei nt Easter egg
Ostermontag m Easter Monday
Ostern nt Easter
Österreich nt Austria
Österreicher(in) m/f Austrian
österreichisch adj Austrian
Ostersonntag m Easter Sunday
östlich eastern
Ozean m ocean

P

Paar nt pair ; couple
  ein paar a couple of
packen to pack (luggage)
Paket nt parcel ; packet
Palast m palace
Palmtop m palmtop computer
Pampelmuse(n) f grapefruit(s)
Panne f breakdown (of car)
Papier(e) nt paper(s)
Papiertaschentücher pl tissues
Pappe f cardboard
Paprikaschote f pepper (vegetable)
Parfüm nt perfume
Parfümerie f perfumery
Park m park
parken to park
  Parken verboten no parking
Parkett nt stalls (in theatre)
Parkhaus nt multi-storey car park
Parkkralle f wheel clamp
Parkplatz m car park
Parkscheibe f parking disk
Parkschein m parking ticket (to display)
Parkuhr f parking meter
Parkverbot nt no parking zone
Partei f political party
Partner(in) m/f partner (boy/girlfriend)
Party f party (celebration)
Pass m passport ; pass (in mountains)
  Pass geschlossen pass closed

Passagier m passenger
passen to fit
passieren to happen
Passionsfrucht passionfruit
Passkontrolle f passport control
Passnummer f passport number
Passwort nt password
Patient(in) m/f patient (in hospital)
Pauschalreise f package tour
Pauschaltarif m flat-rate tariff
Pause f pause ; interval
  keine Pausen no intervals
PDA (elektronische) Organizer m
  PDA (Personal Digital Assistant)
Pelz m fur
Pelzmantel m fur coat
Pendelverkehr m shuttle (service)
Penis m penis
Penizillin nt penicillin
Pension f boarding house
pensioniert retired
Peperoni chilli
per via ; by
  per Express by express mail
  per Post by post
perfekt perfect
Periode f period (menstruation)
Perlen pl pearls
perlend sparkling
Person f person
Personal nt staff
Personalausweis m identity card
Personalien pl particulars
persönlich personal(ly)
Perücke f wig
Pessar nt cap (diaphragm)
Petersilie f parsley
Pfalz f Palatinate
Pfand nt deposit
Pfandflasche f returnable bottle
  (with deposit)
Pfannkuchen m pancake
Pfarrer(in) m/f church minister
Pfeffer m pepper (spice)
Pfefferkuchen m gingerbread
Pfefferminzbonbon nt mint (sweet)
Pfefferminztee m mint tea
Pfeife f pipe (smoker's)
Pferd nt horse
Pferderennen nt horse-racing
Pfirsich(e) m peach(es)
Pflanze f plant (green)
Pflaster nt plaster (for cut)
Pflaume(n) f plum(s)
Pforte f gate

Pfund nt pound
Pfund Sterling nt sterling (pound)
Picknick nt picnic
Picknickdecke f picnic rug
Pier m jetty ; pier
pikant savoury
Pille f pill
Pilot(in) m/f pilot
Pils/Pilsner nt lager
Pilz(e) m mushroom(s)
Pilzkrankheit f thrush (candida)
Pinzette f tweezers
Pistazie f pistachio
Piste f runway ; ski run
Pizza f pizza
planmäßig scheduled
Planschbecken nt paddling pool
Plastik- plastic (made of)
Plastikbeutel m plastic bag
Platte f plate ; dish ; record
Platten blowout (bicycle)
Platz m seat ; space ; square (in town) ;
  court
Plätzchen nt biscuit(s)
Platzkarte f seat reservation (ticket)
Plombe f filling (in tooth)
plötzlich suddenly
pochiert poached (egg, fish)
Polen nt Poland
Polizei f police
Polizeirevier nt police station
Polizeiwache f police station
Polizist(in) m/f policeman/woman
Pommes frites pl chips (french fries)
Pony nt pony
Ponyreiten nt pony trekking
Porree m leek
Portier m porter (for door)
Portion f portion
Portrait nt portrait
Portugal nt Portugal
Portugiese/Portugiesin m/f Portuguese
portugiesisch adj Portuguese
Post f post ; post office
Post- postal
Postamt nt post office
Postanweisung f money order
Poster nt poster
Postkarte f postcard
postlagernd poste restante
Postleitzahl f postcode
praktisch handy ; practical
Pralinen pl chocolates
Präservativ nt condom

Praxis f doctor's surgery
Preis m prize ; price
Preiselbeersaft cranberry juice
Preisliste f price list
Priester m priest
Prinz m prince
Prinzessin f princess
privat private
Privatstrand m private beach
Privatweg m private road
pro per
  pro Stunde per hour
  pro Kopf per person
  pro Jahr per annum
probieren to taste ; to sample
Problem nt problem
Programm nt programme
Programmierer(in) m/f computer
  programmer
prost! cheers!
protestantisch Protestant
provisorisch temporary
Prozent nt per cent
prüfen to check (oil, water, etc)
Prüfung f exam (school, university)
Publikum nt audience
Puderzucker m icing sugar
Pullover m sweater ; jumper
Pulver nt powder
pulverförmig in powder form
Pulverkaffee m instant coffee
pünktlich on schedule ; punctual
Puppe f doll ; puppet
Puppenspiel nt puppet show
pur straight (drink)
Pute f turkey
Pyjama m pyjamas

Q

Qualität f quality
Qualitätswein m good quality wine
Qualle f jellyfish
Quantität f quantity
Quarantäne f quarantine
Quelle f spring (of water) ; source
quetschen to squeeze
Quetschung f bruise
Quittung f receipt
Quiz nt quiz show

R

Rabatt m discount
Rad nt wheel ; bicycle
Rad fahren to cycle

Radfahrer(in) m/f cyclist
Radiergummi m rubber (eraser)
Radieschen pl radishes
Radio nt radio
Radweg m cycle track
Rahmen m frame (picture)
Rand m verge ; border ; edge
Randstein m kerb
Rang m circle (in theatre) ; rank
Rasen m lawn
Rasierapparat m shaver ; razor
Rasiercreme f shaving cream
rasieren to shave
Rasierklinge f razor blade
Rasierschaum m shaving foam
Rasierwasser nt aftershave lotion
Rasthof m service area ; travel inn
Rastplatz m picnic area
Raststätte f service area
raten to advise
Rathaus nt town hall
rau rough
Rauch m smoke
rauchen to smoke
  Rauchen verboten no smoking
Raucher(in) m/f smoker
Raum m space (room)
rechnen to calculate
Rechnung f bill (account) ; invoice
rechte(r/s) right (not left)
rechts to the right ; on the right
Rechtsanwalt m lawyer ; solicitor
Rechtsanwältin f lawyer ; solicitor
reden to speak
reduzieren to reduce
reduziert reduced
Reformhaus nt health food shop
Regal nt shelf
Regen m rain
Regenmantel m raincoat
Regenschirm m umbrella
regnen to rain
Reibe f grater
reich rich (person)
Reich nt empire
reichhaltig rich (food)
reif ripe ; mature (cheese)
Reifen m tyre
Reifendruck m tyre pressure
Reifenpanne f blowout (tyre)
Reihe f row (line) ; tier
rein pure
reinigen to clean
Reinigung f dry-cleaner's

Reis m rice
Reise f trip (journey)
  gute Reise! have a good trip!
Reisebüro nt travel agency
Reiseführer m guidebook
Reiseführer(in) m/f tour guide
Reisegruppe f party (of tourists)
Reisekrankheit f travel sickness
reisen to travel
Reisepapiere pl travel documents
Reisepass m passport
Reisescheck m traveller's cheque
Reiseveranstalter m tour operator
Reiseziel nt destination
Reißverschluss m zip
reiten to ride (horse)
Reiten nt riding
Rennbahn f racecourse
rennen to run
Rennen nt race (sport)
Rentner(in) m/f pensioner ; senior citizen
Reparatur f repair
Reparaturwerkstatt f car repairs
reparieren to repair ; to mend
reservieren to book ; to reserve
reserviert reserved
Reservierung f booking (in hotel)
Reservierungen pl reservations
Restaurant nt restaurant
Restgeld nt change (money)
retten to rescue ; to save (person)
Rettungsboot nt lifeboat
Rettungshubschrauber air ambulance (helicopter)
Rettungsinsel f life raft
Rettungsring m lifebelt
Rettungsschwimmer(in) m/f lifeguard
Rezept nt prescription ; recipe
Rezeption f reception (front desk)
R-Gespräch nt reverse charge call
Rhein m Rhine
Rheinfahrten pl Rhine cruises
Rheumatismus m rheumatism
Richter(in) m/f judge
richtig correct ; right ; proper
Richtung f direction
riechen to smell
Rinderbraten m roast beef
Rindfleisch nt beef
Ring m ring
Ringstraße f ring road
Riss m tear (in material)
Rock m skirt
Roggenbrot nt rye bread

roh raw
Rohling blank (CD or DVD)
Rohr nt pipe (drain, etc)
Rollo nt blind (for window)
Rollschuhe pl roller skates
Rollstuhl m wheelchair
Rolltreppe f escalator
Roman m novel
romanisch Romanesque
Röntgenaufnahme f X-ray
rosa pink
Rose f rose (flower)
Rosenkohl m Brussels sprouts
Rosenmontag m carnival (Monday before Shrove Tuesday)
Roséwein m rosé wine
Rosine(n) f raisin(s)
Rost m rust ; grill
Rost- roast
Rostbraten m roast
rosten to rust
rostfreier Stahl m stainless steel
rostig rusty
Röstkartoffeln pl sautéed potatoes
rot red
Rote Bete f beetroot
Röteln pl German measles ; rubella
rote Johannisbeeren pl redcurrants
Rotwein m red wine
Rücken m back
Rückerstattung f refund
Rückfahrkarte f return ticket
Rückfahrt f return journey
Rückflugticket nt return airticket
Rückgrat nt spine
Rücklicht nt rear light
Rucksack m rucksack
Rückspiegel m rearview mirror
rückwärts backwards
rückwärts fahren to reverse (car)
Rückwärtsgang m reverse gear
Ruder nt rudder ; oar
Ruderboot nt rowing boat
rudern to row (boat)
rufen to shout
Rufnummer f telephone number
Ruhe f rest (repose) ; peace (calm)
  Ruhe! be quiet!
ruhen to rest
ruhig calm ; quiet(ly) ; peaceful
Rührei nt scrambled egg
Ruine f ruin (castle, etc)
rund round
Rundfahrt f tour ; round trip

Rundreise f round trip
Rundwanderweg m circular trail for ramblers
Rutschbahn f slide (chute)
rutschen to slip
rutschig slippery

S

Saal m hall (room)
Sache f thing
Sachen pl stuff (things) ; belongings
Sachsen nt Saxony
Sackgasse f cul-de-sac
Safe m safe (for valuables)
Saft m juice
sagen to say ; to tell (fact, news)
Sahne f cream (dairy)
  mit Sahne with whipped cream
Saison f season
Salat m salad
Salatsoße f salad dressing
Salbe f ointment
Salz nt salt
Salzkartoffeln pl boiled potatoes
Salzwasser nt salt water
Samstag m Saturday
Sand m sand
Sandalen pl sandals
Sandstrand m sandy beach
Sanitäter (Sanitäterin) m/f paramedic (in ambulance)
Satellitenfernsehen nt satellite TV
SatNav nt satnav (satellite navigation system, for car)
satt full
Sattel m saddle
Satteltaschen pl panniers (for bike)
Satz m set (collection) ; sentence
sauber clean
säubern to clean
sauer sour
Sauerkraut nt sauerkraut
Sauerstoff m oxygen
Sauger m teat (on bottle)
Säule f petrol pump
Saum m hem
Sauna f sauna
Säure f acid
saure Sahne f soured cream
S-Bahn f suburban railway
Schach nt chess
Schaden m damage
schädlich harmful
Schaf nt sheep

Schaffner(in) m/f conductor (bus, train) ; guard
Schale f shell (egg, nut) ; dish
schälen to peel (fruit)
Schallplatte f record (music)
Schalter m switch
Schaltgetriebe nt manual (gear change)
Schaltknüppel m gear lever ; gearshift
Schaltuhr f timer
Schaltzug gear cable (bike)
scharf hot (spicy) ; sharp
Schatten m shade
schätzen to value ; to estimate
Schauer m rain shower
Schaufel und Handfeger dustpan and brush
Schaufenster nt shop window
Schaukel f swing (for children)
Schaum m foam
Schaumbad nt bubble bath
Schaumfestiger m hair mousse
Schaumwein m sparkling wine
Schauspiel nt play
Schauspieler(in) m/f actor/actress
Scheck m cheque
Scheckbuch nt cheque book
Scheckkarte f cheque card
Scheibe f slice
Scheibenputzmittel nt screenwash
Scheibenwischer pl windscreen wipers
Schein(e) m banknote(s) ; certificate(s)
scheinen to shine (sun, etc) ; to seem
Scheinwerfer m headlight ; floodlight ; spotlight
  Scheinwerfer anschalten switch on headlights
Schere f scissors (pair of)
scherzen to joke
Scheuerlappen m floorcloth
Scheune f barn
Schi- see Ski-
schicken to send
schießen to shoot
Schiff nt ship
Schild nt sign ; label
Schinken m ham
Schirm m umbrella ; screen
Schlachterei f butcher's
schlafen to sleep
Schlafsack m sleeping bag
Schlaftablette f sleeping pill
Schlafwagen m sleeping car (on train)
Schlafzimmer nt bedroom
Schlag m shock (electric)
Schlaganfall m stroke (medical)

schlagen to hit
Schläger m racket (tennis, etc)
Schlagloch nt pothole
Schlagsahne f whipped cream
Schlange f queue ; snake
Schlangenbiss m snake bite
Schlauch m hosepipe ; inner tube
Schlauchboot nt dinghy (rubber)
schlecht bad ; badly
Schlepplift m ski tow
schließen to shut ; to close
Schließfach nt locker
schlimm serious
Schlitten m sleigh ; sledge
Schlittschuh laufen to ice skate
Schlittschuh(e) m ice skate(s)
Schlittschuhbahn f ice rink
Schloss nt castle ; lock (on door, etc)
Schluss m end
Schlüssel m key
Schlüsselbein nt collar bone
Schlüsselkarte f cardkey (for hotel)
Schlüsselring m keyring
Schlusslichter pl rear lights
Schlussverkauf m sale
schmecken to taste
schmelzen to melt
Schmerz m pain ; ache
schmerzhaft painful
Schmerzmittel nt painkiller
Schmerztablette f painkiller
Schmuck m jewellery ; decorations
schmutzig dirty
Schnäppchen nt bargain
Schnaps m schnapps ; spirit
schnarchen to snore
Schnee m snow
Schneebrille f snow goggles
Schneeketten pl snow chains
Schneepflug m snowplough
schneiden to cut
schnell fast ; quick
Schnellboot nt speedboat
Schnellimbiss m snack bar
Schnellzug m express train
Schnittbohnen pl green beans
Schnittlauch m chives
Schnittwunde f cut
Schnorchel m snorkel
Schnuller m dummy (for baby)
Schnur f string
schnurlose Telefon cordless phone
Schnurrbart m moustache
Schnürschuhe pl boots (ankle)

Schnürsenkel pl shoelaces
Schokolade f chocolate
schön lovely ; fine ; beautiful ; good (pleasant)
Schornstein m chimney
Schotte (Schottin) m/f Scot
schottisch Scottish
Schottland nt Scotland
Schrank m cupboard
Schraube f screw
Schraubenmutter f nut (for bolt)
Schraubenschlüssel m spanner
Schraubenzieher m screwdriver
schrecklich awful
schreiben to write
Schreibmaschine f typewriter
Schreibtisch m desk
Schreibwarenhandlung f stationer's
schriftlich in writing
Schritt m pace ; step
  Schritt fahren! dead slow
Schublade f drawer
Schuh(e) m shoe(s)
Schuhcreme f shoe polish
Schuhgeschäft nt shoe shop
Schuhputzmittel nt shoe polish
schulden to owe
Schulden pl debts
Schule f school
Schulter f shoulder
Schuppen pl scales (of fish) ; dandruff
Schürze f apron
Schüssel f bowl (for soup, etc)
Schuster m shoe mender's
Schutzhelm m helmet (for bike)
Schutzimpfung f vaccination
schwach weak
Schwager m brother-in-law
Schwägerin f sister-in-law
Schwamm m sponge
schwanger pregnant
schwarz black
Schwarzbrot nt brown bread
schwarze Johannisbeeren pl blackcurrants
Schwarzweißfilm m black and white film
Schwein nt pig
Schweinefleisch nt pork
Schweiß m sweat
Schweiz f Switzerland
Schweizer(in) m/f Swiss
schweizerisch adj Swiss
Schwellung f swelling
schwer heavy

Schwester f sister ; nurse ; nun
Schwiegermutter f mother-in-law
Schwiegersohn m son-in-law
Schwiegertochter f daughter-in-law
Schwiegervater m father-in-law
schwierig hard (difficult)
Schwimmbad nt swimming pool
schwimmen to swim
Schwimmflossen pl flippers
Schwimmweste f life jacket
schwindelig dizzy
schwitzen to sweat
See f sea
See m lake
seekrank seasick
Segel nt sail
Segelboot nt sailing boat
segeln to sail
sehen to see
Sehenswürdigkeit f sight
Sehne f tendon
sehr very
seicht shallow (water)
Seide f silk
Seife f soap
Seil nt rope
Seilbahn f cable railway ; funicular
sein(e) his
sein to be
seit since
Seite f page ; side
Seitenspiegel m wing mirror
Seitenstraße f side street
Seitenstreifen m hard shoulder
Sekretär(in) m/f secretary
Sekt m sparkling wine
Sekunde f second (time)
Selbstbedienung f self-service
Sellerie m celery
selten rare (unique)
seltsam strange (odd)
Senf m mustard
September m September
servieren to serve (food)
Serviette f napkin
Servolenkung f power steering
Sessel m armchair
Sessellift m chairlift
setzen to place ; to put
  sich setzen to sit down
  setzen Sie sich bitte please take a seat
Sex m sex (intercourse)
Shampoo nt shampoo
Shorts pl shorts

sicher sure ; safe ; definite
Sicherheit f safety
Sicherheitsgurt m seatbelt ; safety belt
Sicherheitskontrolle security check
Sicherheitsnadel f safety pin
Sicherung f fuse
Sicherungskasten m fuse box
sie she ; they
Sie you (polite singular and plural)
Sieb nt sieve ; colander
Silber nt silver
Silvester m New Year's Eve
SIM-Karte f SIM card
singen to sing
Sitz m seat
sitzen to sit
Ski(er) m ski(s)
  Ski fahren to ski
Skianzug m ski suit
Skihose f ski pants
Skijacke f ski jacket
Skilanglauf m cross-country skiing
Skilaufen nt skiing
Skilehrer(in) m/f ski instructor
Skilift m ski lift
Skipass m ski pass
Skipiste f ski run
Skistiefel pl ski boots
Skistock m ski stick/pole
Skiverleih m ski hire
Slip m knickers ; underpants
Slipeinlage f panty liner
SMS f text message
  eine SMS schreiben to text
  ich schreibe Ihnen/dir eine SMS I'll text you
Snack m snack
Snowboard nt snow board
Socken pl socks
Soda nt soda water
Sodbrennen nt heartburn
Sofa nt sofa
Sofabett nt sofa bed
sofort at once ; immediately
Software f computer software
Sohle f sole (of shoe)
Sohn m son
Sojabohnen pl soya beans
Sojamilch f soya milk
Sommer m summer
Sommerfahrplan m summer railway timetable
Sommerferien pl summer holidays
Sonder special
Sonderangebot nt special offer

sonn- und feiertags Sundays and public holidays
Sonnabend m Saturday
Sonne f sun
Sonnenaufgang m sunrise
sonnenbaden to sunbathe
Sonnenbrand m sunburn
Sonnenbräune f suntan
Sonnenbrille f sunglasses
Sonnencreme f suncream
Sonnendach nt sunroof
Sonnenöl nt suntan oil
Sonnenschirm m sun umbrella ; sunshade
Sonnenstich m sunstroke
Sonnenuntergang m sunset
sonnig sunny
Sonntag m Sunday
Sonntagsdienst m Sunday duty (chemist, doctor, etc)
sorgen für to look after ; to take care of
Soße f dressing ; sauce
Souterrain nt basement
Souvenir nt souvenir
Spam spam (email)
Spanien nt Spain
Spanier(in) m/f Spaniard
spanisch adj Spanish
Spannung f voltage
sparen to save (money)
Spargel m asparagus
Sparpreis m economy fare
Spaß m fun ; joke
spät late
Spaten m spade
Spätvorstellung f late show
Spaziergang m stroll ; walk
Speck m bacon
Speicherkarte f memory card
Speise f dish ; food
Speiseeis nt ice cream
Speisekarte f menu
Speisesaal m dining hall
Speisewagen m dining car
Spesen pl expenses
Spezialität f speciality
Spiegel m mirror
Spiegelei nt fried egg
Spiel nt game ; pack (of cards)
Spielbank f casino
spielen to gamble ; to play
Spielkarte f card (playing)
Spielplatz m playground
Spielzeug nt toy
Spielzeugladen m toy shop

Spielzimmer nt playroom
Spinat m spinach
Spirale f coil (IUD) ; spiral
Spirituosen pl spirits (alcohol)
Spitze f lace ; point (tip)
Splitter m splinter
Sportartikel pl sports equipment
Sportgeschäft nt sports shop
Sporttauchen nt scuba diving
Sprache f speech ; language
Sprachführer m phrase book
Sprachmitteilung voicemail
Spraydose f aerosol
sprechen to speak
  sprechen mit to talk to
Sprechstunde f surgery (hours of opening)
springen to jump
Spritze f injection ; hypodermic needle
sprudelnd fizzy
Sprudelwasser nt sparkling water
Sprungschanze f ski jump
Spucktüte f sick bag
Spülbecken nt sink (kitchen)
spülen to flush toilet ; to rinse
Spülkasten m cistern (of toilet)
Spülmittel nt washing-up liquid
Spur f lane (of motorway/main road)
Staatsangehörigkeit f nationality
Stachel m sting
Stadion nt stadium
Stadt f town ; city
Stadtführung f guided tour of the town
Stadtmitte f city centre
Stadtplan m map (of town)
Stadtzentrum nt town/city centre
Stahl m steel
Stand m stall ; taxi rank
ständig permanent(ly) ; continuous(ly)
Standlicht nt sidelight
stark strong
Starthilfekabel nt jump leads
Station f station ; stop ; hospital ward
statt instead of
stattfinden to take place
Statue f statue
Stau m traffic jam
Staub m dust
Staubsauger m vacuum cleaner
Staubtuch nt duster
stechen to bite (insect)
Stechmücke f mosquito ; gnat
Steckdose f socket (electrical)
Stecker m plug (electric)
Steckrübe f turnip

stehen to stand
stehlen to steal
steil steep
Stein m stone
Stelle f job ; place ; point (in space)
stellen to set (alarm) ; to put
Stellplatz pitch (for tent/caravan)
stempeln to stamp (visa)
Steppdecke f quilt
sterben to die
Stereoanlage f stereo
Stern m star
Steuer f tax
Steuerung f controls
Steward (Stewardess) m/f
  steward/stewardess
Stich m bite (by insect) ; stitch (sewing) ;
  sting
Stiefel pl boots (long)
Stiefmutter f stepmother
Stiefvater m stepfather
Stil m style
still still (motionless)
stilles Wasser nt still water
Stimme f voice
stimmt so! keep the change!
Stirn f forehead
Stock m cane (walking stick) ; stick ; floor
Stockwerk nt storey
Stoff m cloth (fabric)
Stoppschild nt stop (sign)
Stöpsel m plug (in sink)
stören to disturb (interrupt)
  bitte nicht stören do not disturb
stornieren to cancel
Stornierung f cancellation
Störung f hold-up ; fault ; medical
  disorder
Stoßdämpfer m shock absorber
stoßen to knock ; to push
Stoßstange f bumper (car)
Stoßzeit f rush hour
Strafe f punishment ; fine
Strafzettel m parking ticket (fine)
Strand m beach
Strandkorb m wicker beach chair with
  a hood ; beach hut
Straße f road ; street
  Straße gesperrt road closed
Straßenarbeiten pl roadworks
Straßenbahn f tram
Straßenkarte f road map
Streichhölzer pl matches
Streifenkarte f multiple journey travelcard
Streik m strike (industrial)

streiten to quarrel
Stress m stress
stricken to knit
Strickjacke f cardigan
Stricknadel f knitting needle
Strohhalm m straw (for drinking)
Strom m current ; electricity
Stromanschluss m electric point
Strömung f current (water)
Stromzähler m electricity meter
Strümpfe pl stockings
Strumpfhose f tights
Stück nt bit ; piece ; cut of meat ;
  play (theatre)
Student(in) m/f student
Studentenermäßigung f student
  discount
Stufe f step (stair)
Stuhl m chair
stumpf blunt (knife, blade)
Stunde f hour ; lesson
Sturm m storm
Sturzhelm m crash helmet
suchen to look for
Suchmaschine f search engine
Süden m south
südlich southern
Summe f sum (total amount)
Sumpf m marsh
Super(benzin) nt four-star petrol
Supermarkt m supermarket
Suppe f soup
Surfbrett nt surfboard
surfen to surf
süß sweet
Süßigkeiten pl sweets
Süßstoff m sweetener ; saccharin
Süßwaren pl confectionery
Synagoge f synagogue
Szene f scene

T

Tabak m tobacco
Tabakwarenhandlung f tobacconist's
Tablett nt tray
Tablette(n) f tablet(s) ; pill(s)
Tacho(meter) m speedometer
Tafel f table ; board ; bar of chocolate
Tafelwein m table wine
Tag m day
  jeden Tag every day
Tageskarte f day ticket ; menu of
  the day
Tagespauschale f daily unlimited rate
Tagessuppe f soup of the day

täglich daily
Taille f waist
Tal nt valley
Tampons pl tampons
Tank m fuel/petrol tank
Tankanzeige f fuel gauge
Tankdeckel m petrol cap
Tanksäule f petrol pump
Tankstelle f petrol station
Tanne f fir
Tante f aunt
Tanz m dance
tanzen to dance
Tarif m rate ; tariff
Tasche f pocket ; bag
Taschenbuch nt paperback
Taschendieb m pickpocket
Taschenlampe f torch ; flashlight
Taschenmesser nt penknife
Taschenrechner m calculator
Taschentuch nt handkerchief
Tasse f cup
Taste f button ; key (on keyboard)
  Taste drücken push button
taub deaf
Taube f pigeon
tauchen to dive
Tauchen nt diving
Taucheranzug m wetsuit
Taucherbrille f goggles (swimming)
tauschen to exchange
tausend thousand
Taxi nt taxi ; cab
Taxifahrer(in) m/f taxi driver
Taxistand m taxi rank
Tee m tea
Teebeutel m tea bag
Teekanne f teapot
Teelöffel m teaspoon
Teig m pastry
Teil nt part
teilen to divide ; to share
Teilkaskoversicherung f third party,
  fire and theft insurance
Telefon nt telephone
Telefonauskunft f directory enquiries
Telefonbuch nt phone directory
telefonieren to telephone
Telefonkarte f phonecard
Telefonnummer f phone number
Telefonzelle f phonebox
Telegramm nt telegram
Teller m plate
Tempel m temple

Temperatur f temperature
Tennis nt tennis
Tennisplatz m tennis court
Tennisschläger m tennis racket
Teppich m rug
Teppichboden m fitted carpet
Termin m date ; deadline ; appointment
Terminal m terminal (airport)
Terminkalender m diary ; Filofax®
Terminplaner Filofax®
Terrasse f patio ; terrace (of café)
Terrorist(in) m/f terrorist
Tesafilm® m Sellotape®
teuer dear (expensive)
Theater nt theatre
Theke f counter (in shop, bar, etc)
Thermometer nt thermometer
Thermosflasche f flask (thermos)
Thunfisch m tuna
Thüringen nt Thuringia
Thymian m thyme
tief deep ; low (in pitch)
Tiefkühltruhe f deep freeze ; freezer
Tier nt animal
Tierarzt (Tierärztin) m/f vet
Tinte f ink
Tintenfisch m octopus ; squid
Tisch m table
Tischdecke f tablecloth
Tischler(in) m/f carpenter
Tischtennis nt table tennis
Tischwein m table wine
Toastbrot nt sliced white bread for toasting
Tochter f daughter
Tochtergesellschaft f subsidiary
Toilette f toilet ; lavatory
Toilettenartikel pl toiletries
Toilettenbürste f toilet brush
Toilettenpapier nt toilet paper
Tollwut f rabies
Tomate f tomato
Tomatenpüree nt tomato purée
Tomatensaft m tomato juice
Tomatensoße f tomato sauce
Ton m sound ; tone ; clay
Tönung f hair dye
Töpferwaren pl pottery
Tor nt gate ; goal (sport)
Törtchen nt cake (small)
Torte f gâteau ; tart
tot dead
töten to kill
Tourist(in) m/f tourist
Touristeninformation f tourist information

Touristenkarte f tourist ticket
Touristenklasse f economy class
Touristenroute f tourist route
Touristenticket nt tourist ticket
tragbar portable
tragen to carry ; to wear
Tragflügelboot nt hydrofoil
Trainingsschuhe pl trainers
trampen to hitchhike
Trauben pl grapes
traurig sad
Treffen nt meeting
treffen to meet (by chance)
Treppe f stairs
Tresor m safe
Tretboot nt pedalo
trinken to drink
Trinkgeld nt tip (for waiter, etc)
Trinkwasser nt drinking water
trocken dry ; stale (bread)
Trockenmilch f powdered milk
Trockenobst nt dried fruit
trocknen to dry
Truthahn m turkey
Tschechien nt Czech Republic
tschüs cheerio ; bye
T-shirt nt T-shirt
Tuch nt cloth ; scarf ; towel ; shawl
tun to do ; to put
Tunfisch m tuna
Tunnel m tunnel
Tür f door
türkis turquoise (colour)
Turm m tower
Turnschuhe pl gym shoes
typisch typical

U

u.A.w.g. RSVP
U-Bahn f metro ; underground
übel sick (nauseous) ; bad
über over ; above ; about ; via
überall everywhere
überbuchen to overbook
Überfahrt f crossing (sea)
Überfall m mugging
überfällig overdue
überfüllt crowded (train, shop, etc)
übergeben to hand over ;
  to present (give)
  sich übergeben to vomit
Übergewicht nt excess baggage ;
  overweight
überhitzen to overheat

überholen to overtake
Überholverbot nt no overtaking
Übernachtung mit Frühstück bed and
  breakfast
überprüfen to check (to examine)
Überschwemmung f flash flood
übersetzen to translate
Übersetzung f translation
überweisen to transfer (money)
Überzelt nt fly sheet
Überzieher m overcoat
übrig left over ; extra (spare)
Ufer nt bank (of river) ; shore
Uhr f clock ; watch
Uhrarmband nt watch strap
Uhrmacher m watchmaker's
um around
  um 4 Uhr at 4 o'clock
umdrehen to turn around
umgeben von surrounded by
Umgehungsstraße f ring road ; bypass
  (road)
Umkleidekabine f changing room
  (at swimming pool, in shop)
Umleitung f diversion
Umschlag m envelope
umsonst free (costing nothing)
umsteigen to change
umstoßen to knock over (object)
Umweg m detour
Umwelt f environment
unbefugt unauthorized
  Unbefugten Zutritt verboten no entry
  to unauthorized persons
unbegrenzt unlimited
und and
Unfall m accident
Unfallstation f casualty department
ungefähr approximately
ungefährlich safe (not dangerous)
ungerade odd (number)
ungewöhnlich unusual
Unglück nt accident
ungültig invalid
ungültig werden to expire (ticket,
  passport)
Universität f university
unmöglich impossible ; unsafe
uns us
unser(e) our
unsicher uncertain (fact)
unten downstairs ; below
  nach unten downward(s) ; downstairs
unter under(neath)
unter Wasser underwater

unterbrechen to interrupt
Unterbrecher m circuit breaker
Unterbrecherkontakte pl points (in car)
untere(r/s) lower ; bottom
Unterführung f subway ; underpass (for pedestrians)
Unterhemd nt vest
Unterhose f underpants
Unterkunft f accommodation
unterrichten to teach
Unterrichtsstunde f lesson
unterschreiben to sign
Unterschrift f signature
Untersuchung f test ; medical examination
Untertasse f saucer
Untertitel pl subtitles
Unterwäsche f underwear ; lingerie
unwohl unwell
Urin m urine
Urlaub m leave ; holiday
  auf Urlaub on holiday ; on leave
Urlaubsgebiet nt resort (holiday)
Ursprungsland nt country of origin
USA pl USA

V

Vagina f vagina
Vanille f vanilla
Vanilleeis nt vanilla ice cream
Vanillesoße f custard
Vase f vase
Vater m father
Vegetarier(in) m/f vegetarian
vegetarisch vegetarian
Veilchen nt violet (flower)
Ventil nt valve
Ventilator m fan (electric) ; ventilator
Verband m bandage
Verbandskasten m first aid kit
verbinden to connect (join)
Verbindung f connection (train, etc) ; service (bus, etc) ; line (phone)
verbleit leaded
verboten forbidden
Verbrechen nt crime
verbrennen to burn
Verbrennung f burn
verbringen to spend (time)
verderben to go bad (food) ; to spoil
verdienen to deserve ; to earn
verdorben bad (fruit, vegetables)
Verein m society (club)
vereinbaren to agree upon ; to arrange

Vereinbarung f agreement
Vereinigtes Königreich nt United Kingdom
Vereinigte Staaten (von Amerika) pl United States (of America)
Verfallsdatum nt expiry date ; eat-by date
verfault rotten (fruit, etc)
Vergangenheit f past
Vergaser m carburettor
vergeben to forgive
vergessen to forget
vergewaltigen to rape
Vergewaltigung f rape
Vergnügen nt enjoyment ; pleasure
  viel Vergnügen! have a good time!
Vergnügungspark m amusement park
vergoldet gold-plated
Vergrößerung f enlargement
verhaften to arrest
verheiratet married
verhindern to prevent
Verhütungsmittel nt contraceptive
Verkauf m sale
verkaufen to sell
Verkäufer(in) m/f salesman/woman
Verkehr m traffic
Verkehrspolizist(in) m/f traffic warden
Verkehrszeichen nt road sign
verkehrt wrong
verkehrt herum upside down
verlängern extend (stay) ; renew (visa)
Verlängerungskabel nt extension cable
Verleih m rental company ; hire company
verletzen to injure
verletzt injured (person)
Verletzung f injury
verlieren to lose
verlobt engaged (to be married)
Verlobte(r) m/f fiancé(e)
verloren lost (object)
vermeiden to avoid
vermieten to rent ; to let (room, house)
Vermieter(in) m/f landlord/lady
Vermietung f hire
vermisst missing (person)
Vermittlung f telephone exchange ; operator
verpassen to miss (plane, train, etc)
Verrenkung f sprain
verschieben to postpone
verschieden different
verschiedene several ; different
verschlucken to swallow
  sich verschlucken to choke (on sth)
verschmutzt polluted

verschreiben to prescribe
verschwinden to disappear
verschwunden missing
versichern to insure
versichert sein to be insured
Versicherung f insurance
Versicherungsbescheinigung f insurance certificate
versilbert silver-plated
verspätet delayed
Verspätung f delay
versprechen to promise
Verstauchung f sprain
verstecken to hide
verstehen to understand
verstopft blocked (pipe) ; blocked (road) ; constipated
versuchen to try
Vertrag m contract
Vertreter(in) m/f sales rep
Verwandte(r) m/f relative
verwenden to use
verwirrt confused
Verzeihung! sorry ; excuse me
verzollen to declare goods (customs)
Video nt video
Videokamera f video camera
Videokassette f video cassette/tape
viel much
viele many
vielleicht perhaps
Viertel nt quarter
Viertelstunde f quarter of an hour
vierzehn Tage fortnight
Villa f villa
violett purple
Virus nt virus
Visitenkarte f business card
Visum nt visa
Vitamin nt vitamin
Vogel m bird
Voicemail voicemail
Volkslied nt folk song
Volkstanz m folk dance
voll full
Volleyball m volleyball
Vollkornbrot nt dark rye bread; wholemeal bread
Vollmilchschokolade f milk chocolate
Vollnarkose f general anaesthetic
Vollpension f full board
vollständig whole
voll tanken to fill tank (petrol)
von from ; of

vor before ; in front of
   vor 4 Jahren 4 years ago
voraus ahead
   im Voraus in advance
vorbei past
vorbereiten to prepare
Vorbestellung f reservation
Vorder- front
Vorderradantrieb m front-wheel drive
Vorfahrt f right of way (on road)
   Vorfahrt beachten give way
vorgekocht ready-cooked
Vorhang m curtain
Vorhängeschloss nt padlock
Vorname m first name
vorne einsteigen enter by front door
Vorschrift f regulation (rule)
Vorsicht f caution
Vorspeise f starter (in meal) ; hors d'œuvre
Vorstellung f performance
Vor- und Zuname m first name and surname
Vorverkauf m advance booking
Vorwahl(nummer) f dialling code
Vorzelt nt awning (caravan)
vorziehen to prefer
Vulkan m volcano

W

Waage f scales (weighing)
wach awake
Wache f security guard
Wachsbehandlung f waxing
Waffe f gun
Wagen m car ; carriage (railway)
Wagenheber m jack (for car)
Wahl f choice ; election
wählen to dial (number) ; to choose
Wählton m dialling tone
während while ; during
Währung f currency
Wald m wood ; forest
Waldlehrpfad m nature trail
Wales nt Wales
Waliser(in) m/f Welshman/woman
walisisch Welsh
Walnuss(-nüsse) f walnut(s)
wandern to hike
Wanderschuhe pl walking boots
Wanderstock m walking stick
Wanderung f hike
Wanderweg m trail for ramblers
Wange f cheek
wann? when?
Waren pl goods

warm warm
Wärmflasche f hot-water bottle
Warmwasser nt hot water
Warnblinkanlage f hazard warning lights
Warndreieck nt warning triangle
Warnung f warning
Wartehalle f lounge (at airport)
warten (auf) to wait (for)
Wartesaal m waiting room
warum? why?
was? what?
waschbar washable
Waschbecken nt washbasin
Wäsche f linen ; washing (clothes)
Wäscheklammer f clothes peg
Wäscheleine f clothes line
waschen to wash
Waschen und Föhnen wash and blow dry
Wäscheraum m laundry room
Wäscherei f laundry
Wäschereiservice m laundry service
Wäschetrockner m tumble dryer
Waschmaschine f washing machine
Waschmittel nt detergent
Waschpulver nt washing powder
Waschsalon m launderette
Wasser nt water
wasserdicht waterproof
Wasserfall m waterfall
Wasserhahn m tap
Wassermelone f water melon
Wassermotorrad nt jet ski
Wasserski fahren to water ski
Wassertreter m pedal boat/pedalo
Watte f cotton wool
Wattebausch m cotton bud
Website site (website)
Wechsel m change
Wechselgeld nt change (small coins)
Wechselkurs m exchange rate
wechseln to change (money) ; to give change
Wechselstube f bureau de change
Weckdienst m early morning call
Wecker m alarm clock
Weckruf m alarm call
weder ... noch neither ... nor
Weg m path ; way ; country lane
wegfahren to leave in vehicle
wegfahrsperre immobilizer (on car)
weggehen to leave on foot
Wegweiser m signpost
Wegwerfwindeln pl disposable nappies

weh tun to ache ; to hurt (be painful)
weiblich female ; feminine
weich soft
weich gekochtes Ei nt soft-boiled egg
Weihnachten nt Christmas
Weihnachtsgeschenk nt Christmas present
Weihnachtskarte f Christmas card
weil because
Wein m wine
Weinberg m vineyard
Weinbrand m brandy
weinen to cry (weep)
Weinhandlung f wine shop
Weinkarte f wine list
Weinkeller m wine cellar
Weinprobe f wine-tasting
Weinstube f wine bar
Weintrauben pl grapes
weiß white
Weißbrot nt white bread
Weißwein m white wine
weit far ; loose (clothing)
weiter farther ; further on
weitermachen to continue
weitsichtig long sighted
Weizen m wheat
welche(r/s) which ; what ; which one
Wellen pl waves (on sea)
Welt f world
Wende f U-turn (in car)
wenden to turn
wenig little
weniger less
wenn if ; when (with present tense)
wer? who?
Werbespot m advert (on TV)
werden to become
Werk nt plant (factory) ; work (of art)
Werkstatt f garage (for repairs)
Werktag m weekday
Werkzeug nt tool
Werkzeugkasten m toolkit
Wert m value
Wertbrief m registered letter
Wertsachen pl valuables
wertvoll valuable
wesentlich essential
Wespe f wasp
wessen? whose?
Weste f waistcoat
Westen m west
westlich western
Wetter nt weather
Wetterbericht m weather forecast

Wettervorhersage f weather forecast
Wettkampf m match (sport)
Whirlpool m jacuzzi
wichtig important
wie like ; how
  wie viel? how much?
  wie viele? how many?
wieder again
wiederaufladen to recharge (battery)
wiederholen to repeat
wiegen to weigh
Wien Vienna
Wiese f lawn ; meadow
Wild nt game (hunting, meat)
Wildleder nt suede
Wildschwein nt boar
willkommen welcome
Wimpern pl eyelashes
Wimperntusche f mascara
Wind m wind
Windeln pl nappies ; diapers
windig windy
Windmühle f windmill
Windpocken pl chickenpox
Windschutz m windbreak (camping)
Windschutzscheibe f windscreen
windstill calm (weather)
Winter m winter
Winterreifen pl snow tyres
wir we
wirksam effective (remedy, etc)
Wirt(in) m(f) landlord (landlady)
Wirtschaft f pub ; inn ; economy
wissen to know (facts)
Witwe(r) f(m) widow(er)
Witz m joke
wo? where?
Woche f week
Wochenende nt weekend
Wochenmarkt farmers' market
Wochentag m weekday
wöchentlich weekly
woher? where from?
wohin? where to?
Wohnadresse f home address
wohnen to stay ; to live (reside)
Wohnheim nt hostel
Wohnmobil nt dormobile
Wohnort m home address
Wohnung f flat (apartment)
Wohnwagen m caravan
Wohnzimmer nt living room ;
  lounge (in house)
wolkig cloudy

Woll- woollen
Wolldecke f blanket
Wolle f wool
wollen to want (wish for)
Wort nt word
  in Worten in words (on cheques)
Wörterbuch nt dictionary
Wunde f wound (injury)
Würfel m dice
Wurst f sausage
Würstchenbude f hot-dog stand
würzig spicy
Würzmischung f seasoning

Y
Yachthafen m marina

Z
zäh tough (meat)
Zahl f number (figure)
zahlen to pay
Zähler m meter
Zahn m tooth
Zahnarzt (Zahnärztin) m/f dentist
Zahnbürste f toothbrush
Zahncreme f toothpaste
Zähne pl teeth
Zahnpasta f toothpaste
Zahnschmerzen pl toothache
Zahnseide f dental floss
Zahnstocher m toothpick
Zange f pliers
Zäpfchen nt suppository
z.B. e.g.
Zebrastreifen m zebra crossing
Zehe f toe
Zeichentrickfilm m cartoon
Zeichnung f drawing
zeigen to show
Zeit f time (of day)
Zeitkarte f season ticket
Zeitschrift f magazine
Zeitung f newspaper
Zeitungskiosk m newsstand
Zelt nt tent
Zeltboden m groundsheet
zelten to camp
Zentimeter m centimetre
zentral central
Zentralheizung f central heating
Zentralverriegelung f central locking (car)
Zentrum nt centre
zerbrechlich fragile ; breakable
zerrissen torn

Ziege f goat
Ziegel m brick
ziehen pull
Ziel nt destination ; goal ; target
ziemlich quite (rather)
Zigarette(n) f cigarette(s)
Zigarettenpapier nt cigarette papers
Zigarre(n) f cigar(s)
Zimmer nt room (in house, hotel)
  Zimmer frei vacancies
Zimmermädchen nt chambermaid
Zimmernummer f room number
Zimmerservice m room service
Zirkus m circus
Zitrone f lemon
Zitronengras lemongrass
Zitronentee m lemon tea
ZOB m central bus station
Zoll m customs/toll
zollfrei duty-free
Zone f zone
Zoo m zoo
Zopf m plait
zornig angry
zu to ; off ; too ; at
  zu Hause at home
  zu mieten for hire
  zu verkaufen for sale
  zu viel too much
  zu viel berechnen to overcharge
zubereiten to prepare
Zucchini pl courgettes
Zucker m sugar
zuckerfrei sugar-free
Zuckerkrankheit f diabetes
zudrehen to turn off (tap)
Zug m train
Zuhause nt home
zuhören to listen

Zukunft f future
Zulassung f log book (vehicle registration document)
zum Beispiel f for example
Zuname m surname
Zündkerzen pl spark plugs
Zündschlüssel m ignition key
Zündung f ignition
Zunge f tongue
zurück back
zurückfahren to go back (by car)
zurückgeben to give back
zurückgehen to go back (on foot)
zurückkommen to come back
zurücklassen to leave behind
zusammen together
Zusammenstoß m crash (collision)
zusätzlich extra ; additional
zuschauen to watch
Zuschlag m surcharge ; supplement
zuschließen to lock
Zustellung f delivery (of mail)
Zutaten pl ingredients
Zutritt m entry ; admission
  Zutritt verboten no entry
zu viel too much
  zu viel berechnen to overcharge
zuzüglich extra
zwanglose Kleidung f informal dress
zwei two
Zweigstelle f branch (office)
zweimal twice
zweite(r/s) second
zweite Klasse f second class
Zwiebel f bulb ; onion
Zwillinge pl twins
zwischen between
Zwischenlandung f stopover (plane)
Zwischenstecker m adaptor
Zyste f cyst

How German Works

Nouns

> A **noun** is a word such as **car, horse** or **Mary** which is used to refer to a person or thing.

Unlike English, German nouns have a gender: they are either masculine (**der**), feminine (**die**) or neuter (**das**). Therefore words for *the* and *a(n)* must agree with the noun they accompany whether masculine, feminine, neuter or plural. Note that in German all nouns begin with a capital letter.

	masculine	*feminine*	*neuter*
the	der Mann	die Frau	das Licht
a, an	ein Mann	eine Frau	ein Licht

The plural forms vary from noun to noun – there is no universal plural as in English (cat – cats, dog – dogs):

singular	*plural*
Mann	**Männer**
Frau	**Frauen**
Tisch	**Tische**

The plural for **the** for all forms is **die**:

die Männer   **die Frauen**   **die Lichter**

There's no plural for the **ein** form. The plural noun is used on its own.

From the phrases in this book you'll see that the endings for the word for *the* vary according to what part the noun plays in the sentence: If the noun is the subject of the sentence, i.e. carrying out the action, then it is in the *nominative* case (the one found in dictionaries), e.g. **der Mann steht auf** (*the man stands up*). The subject **der Mann** comes before the verb.

If the noun is the direct object of the sentence, i.e. the action of the verb is being carried out on the noun, then the noun is in the *accusative* case, e.g. **ich sehe den Mann** (*I see the man*). Note how **der** has changed to **den**. The same applies to **ein**, e.g. **ich sehe einen Mann** (*I see a man*).

If you see in front of the English noun *of*, or *'s* or *s'* at the end of the noun, then the noun is in the *genitive* case (i.e. it belongs to someone or something), e.g. **das Haus der Frau** (*the woman's house*). Note how **die** has changed to **der**. The same applies to **ein**, e.g. **das Haus einer Frau** (*a woman's house*).

If you see *to the* or *to a* in front of the English noun, then the noun is in the *dative* case, e.g. **ich gebe es der Frau** (*I give it to the woman*). Note how **die** has changed to **der**. The same applies to **ein**, e.g. **ich gebe es einer Frau** (*I give it to a woman*).

Other words used before nouns have similar endings to **der** and **ein**. Those like **der** are:

dieser (*this*) ; **jener** (*that*) ; **jeder** (*each*) ; **welcher** (*which*)

Those like **ein** are:

mein (*my*) ; **dein** (*your* – familiar singular) ; **Ihr** (*your* – polite singular and plural) ; **sein** (*his*) ; **ihr** (*her*) ; **unser** (*our*) ; **euer** (*your* – familiar plural) ; **ihr** (*their*)

Below are the cases for **der**:

	masculine	*feminine*	*neuter*	*plural*
Nominative	**der Mann**	**die Frau**	**das Licht**	**die Frauen**
Accusative	**den Mann**	**die Frau**	**das Licht**	**die Frauen**
Genitive	**des Mannes**	**der Frau**	**des Lichtes**	**der Frauen**
Dative	**dem Mann**	**der Frau**	**dem Licht**	**den Frauen**

Here are the cases for **ein**:

	masculine	*feminine*	*neuter*
Nominative	**ein Mann**	**eine Frau**	**ein Licht**
Accusative	**einen Mann**	**eine Frau**	**ein Licht**
Genitive	**eines Mannes**	**einer Frau**	**eines Lichtes**
Dative	**einem Mann**	**einer Frau**	**einem Licht**

The word **kein** (*no, not any*) also has the same endings as for **ein**, except that it can be used in the plural:

Nominative	**keine Männer**	*Genitive*	**keiner Männer**
Accusative	**keine Männer**	*Dative*	**keinen Männern**

My, your, his, her, our, its, their

These words all take the same endings as for **ein** and agree with the noun they accompany, i.e. whether *masculine*, *feminine*, etc and according to the noun's function (*nominative*, *accusative*, etc):

mein Mann kommt (*my husband is coming*) (*nominative*)

ich liebe meinen Mann (*I love my husband*) (*accusative*)

das Auto meines Mannes (*my husband's car*) (*genitive*)

ich gebe es meinem Mann (*I give it to my husband*) (*dative*)

meine Kinder kommen (*my children are coming*) (*nominative plural*)

ich liebe meine Kinder (*I love my children*) (*accusative plural*)

die Spielsachen meiner Kinder (*my children's toys*) (*genitive plural*)
ich gebe es meinen Kindern (*I give it to my children*) (*dative plural*)

Other words which take these endings are:

dein (*your* – familiar singular) ; **sein** (*his*) ; **ihr** (*her*) ; **unser** (*our*) ;
euer (*your* – familiar plural) ; **Ihr** (*your* – polite singular and plural) ; **ihr** (*their*)

Adjectives

> An **adjective** *is a word such as* **small, pretty** *or* **practical** *that describes a person or thing, or gives extra information about them.*

When adjectives are used before a noun, their endings vary like the words for **der** and **ein**, depending on the gender (*masculine, feminine* or *neuter*) and whether the noun is plural, and how the noun is used in the sentence (whether it is the subject, object, etc). Here are examples using the adjective **klug** – clever:

	masculine	*feminine*
Nominative	**der kluge Mann**	**die kluge Frau**
	ein kluger Mann	**eine kluge Frau**
Accusative	**den klugen Mann**	**die kluge Frau**
	einen klugen Mann	**eine kluge Frau**
Genitive	**des klugen Mannes**	**der klugen Frau**
	eines klugen Mannes	**einer klugen Frau**
Dative	**dem klugen Mann**	**der klugen Frau**
	einem klugen Mann	**einer klugen Frau**

	neuter	*plural*
Nominative	**das kluge Kind**	**die klugen Männer**
	ein kluges Kind	**kluge Frauen**
Accusative	**das kluge Kind**	**die klugen Männer**
	ein kluges Kind	**kluge Frauen**
Genitive	**des klugen Kindes**	**der klugen Männer**
	eines klugen Kindes	**kluger Frauen**
Dative	**dem klugen Kind**	**den klugen Männern**
	einem klugen Kind	**klugen Frauen**

When the adjective follows the verb, then there is no agreement:

der Mann ist klug / die Frau ist klug / das Kind ist klug

Pronouns

> A **pronoun** is a word that you use to refer to someone or something when you do not need to use a noun, often because the person or thing has been mentioned earlier. Examples are **it**, **she**, **something** and **myself**.

subject		direct object	
I	**ich**	me	**mich**
you (familiar singular)	**du**	you (familiar singular)	**dich**
he/it (masculine)	**er**	him/it (masculine)	**ihn**
she/it (feminine)	**sie**	her/it (feminine)	**sie**
it (neuter)	**es**	it (neuter)	**es**
we	**wir**	us	**uns**
you (familiar plural)	**ihr**	you (familiar plural)	**euch**
you (polite singular & plural)	**Sie**	you (polite singular & plural)	**Sie**
they (all genders)	**sie**	them (all genders)	**sie**

Indirect object pronouns are:

mir (to me) ; **dir** (to you) (familiar singular) ; **ihm** (to him/it) ; **ihr** (to her/it) ; **ihm** (to it) (neuter) ; **uns** (to us) ; **euch** (to you) (familiar plural) ; **Ihnen** (to you) (polite singular and plural) ; **ihnen** (to them)

In German there are two ways of addressing people: the familiar form – **du** (when talking to just one person you know well), **ihr** (when talking to more than one person you know well), and the polite form – **Sie** (always written with a capital letter), which can be used for one or more people.

Verbs

> A **verb** is a word such as **sing**, **walk** or **cry** which is used with a subject to say what someone or something does or what happens to them. **Regular verbs** (weak verbs in German) follow the same pattern of endings. **Irregular verbs** (strong verbs in German) do not follow a regular pattern so you need to learn the different endings.

There are two main types of verb in German – **weak** verbs (which are regular) and **strong** verbs (which are irregular).

	weak	*strong*
	SPIELEN (TO PLAY)	HELFEN (TO HELP)
ich	spiele	helfe
du	spielst	hilfst
er/sie/es	spielt	hilft
wir	spielen	helfen
ihr	spielt	helft
Sie	spielen	helfen
sie	spielen	helfen

Other examples of **strong** verbs are:

	SEIN (TO BE)	HABEN (TO HAVE)
ich	bin	habe
du	bist	hast
er/sie/es	ist	hat
wir	sind	haben
ihr	seid	habt
Sie	sind	haben
sie	sind	haben

To make a verb negative, add **nicht**:

ich verstehe nicht	*I don't understand*
das funktioniert nicht	*it doesn't work*

Past Tense

Here are a number of useful past tenses:

ich war	*I was*
wir waren	*we were*
Sie waren	*you were (polite)*
ich hatte	*I had*
wir hatten	*we had*
Sie hatten	*you had (polite)*
ich/er/sie/es spielte	*I/he/she/it played*
Sie/wir/sie spielten	*you/we/they played*
ich/er/sie/es half	*I/he/she/it helped*
Sie/wir/sie halfen	*you/we/they helped*

Another past form corresponds to the English *have ...ed* and uses the verb **haben (to have)**:

ich habe gespielt	*I have played*
wir haben geholfen	*we have helped*

In German the present tense is very often used where we would use the future tense in English:

ich schicke ein Fax	*I will send a fax*
ich schreibe einen Brief	*I will write a letter*